HEIDEGGER AND PSYCHOLOGY

CONTENTS

This issue originally appeared as Volume 16, nos. 1, 2, & 3 (1978-79) of the *Review of Existential Psychology & Psychiatry,* guest edited by Keith Hoeller. Many thanks to Thomas Lynaugh who graciously served as General Editor of the *Review* at the time. For this special edition of *Heidegger and Psychology*, Professor Lapointe's useful Heidegger Bibliography has been greatly expanded and updated and Professor Richardson's classic essay, "The Place of the Unconscious in Heidegger," has been added as an appendix.

To order copies, or for more information, write:

Review of Existential Psychology & Psychiatry
P.O. Box 23220
Seattle, WA 98102

Introduction

With this special issue on *Heidegger and Psychology* the REVIEW OF EXISTENTIAL PSYCHOLOGY & PSYCHIATRY is proud to enter its sixteenth volume. With the sole exception of Medard Boss' article, which appears here in English translation for the first time, all of the essays in this volume have been written especially for this issue. *Heidegger and Psychology* thus constitutes a major new contribution to an understanding of the German philosopher's impact upon psychology, psychiatry, and psychotherapy.

I. *BEING AND TIME*

Martin Heidegger (1889-1976), long known throughout Germany as an excellent teacher, first gained his worldwide reputation with the publication of *Being and Time* in 1927. This work asked a seemingly esoteric question, "What is the meaning of Being?" However, it was Heidegger's intention to show that neither the question itself nor the answer were in fact esoteric, but concerned our own very Being. For in order to ask about the meaning of Being, we must first inquire into the nature of the particular being who is doing the questioning: man. Thus, the question of the meaning of Being is intimately related to the question of the meaning of man's, or as Heidegger puts it, *Dasein's* Being. Dasein in German means *existence*, and Dasein's essence lies in its existence. Heidegger therefore begins his work with a "Preparatory Fundamental Analysis of Dasein" and its existence.

The method Heidegger uses is the phenomenological one, which he borrows (though with several significant changes) from his teacher Edmund Husserl. Returning "to the things themselves," as Husserl urged him to do, Heidegger brilliantly described the everyday, average understanding we have of our existence. However, this basic understanding, which is handed down to us by society, is not the only one, and it was Heidegger's goal to show us that there are also other ways of Being which we can choose as our own, and thus pull ourselves out of the lostness in the crowd which characterizes so much of our lives. It is precisely *time* that reveals to us the freedom of our Being, and this knowledge comes to us in the temporal fact that we all must die. In facing our own deaths, in the mood of *Angst* (anxiety or dread), we can be freed into realizing that we are a Being-towards-death, and therefore have the freedom to choose an authentic existence that is our own. This authentic existence invites us to hear the call of our conscience, to return to ourselves and accept our own ontological guilt, and to understand this appeal of conscience as nothing less than the call of Care, the very center of our human Being.

3

II. AFTER *BEING AND TIME*:
THE LATER HEIDEGGER'S "TURNING"

Heidegger's own call did not fall on deaf ears and *Being and Time* was a success. Heidegger himself, however, did not regard it as a complete success and the concluding parts of it which he had promised remained unpublished throughout his lifetime. For him, it was the language itself which failed to express what he most deeply wanted to say: the meaning of Being. And while the preparatory analysis of Dasein's existence was a necessary first step, there still remained the task of refocusing once again on Being itself. This required a "turning" from Being and Time to Time and Being. For this shift of emphasis Heidegger turned to the great German poets like Hölderlin and Trakl, and to the Early Greek thinkers like Heraclitus and Parmenides. Language itself becomes more important and Heidegger's own language changes under the influence of poetry and the Early Greeks, and he even writes several pieces which are reminiscent of them.

But Heidegger's fundamental theme remains the same: Being. And the relation of man and Being also still remains at the center of his thought. The later Heidegger continues to speak in a way that addresses each of us personally. He speaks of the essence of the modern age, of subjectivism, of the essence of modern science and technology, and the danger that we may lose our very Being in the midst of the present domination of these forces. At the same time, however, he also continues to offer us the possibility of other ways of Being.

III. *HEIDEGGER AND PSYCHOLOGY*

With the exception of two still untranslated works written before *Being and Time*, his dissertation on *The Doctrine of Judgment in Psychologism* (1914) and a review of Jaspers *Psychology of World Views* (1919/21), Heidegger's works contain only passing references to psychology (and even these two works remain philosophical treatises). And in spite of the enormous relevance of *Being and Time* for psychology, Heidegger was careful to distinguish it from psychology and considered it to be a "fundamental ontology." However, this in no way diminished its impact upon numerous psychologists, and even spawned a new school of psychoanalysis called "Daseinsanalysis," whose foremost proponents are Ludwig Binswanger and Medard Boss.

Given this scarcity of works concerned with psychology, it is exciting to learn from Medard Boss' article, "Martin Heidegger's Zollikon Seminars," that for seventeen years Heidegger traveled to Switzerland to give seminars to Boss' medical students, professors, and therapists. The transcripts of these seminars, which presumably contain much bearing directly on psychology and psychiatry, will eventually be made public. In the meantime, we also learn of the close relationship and collaboration between Boss and Heidegger, even to the point of Heidegger having personally edited Boss' most recent application of Heidegger's thinking to the realm of medicine and psychology: *Existential Foundations of Medicine and Psychology*.

In his article, "Daseinsanalysis and Freud's Unconscious," Joseph Kockelmans examines the role of the unconscious in recent Daseinsanalysis and in Freud and asks whether or not, in light of Heidegger's fundamental ontology in *Being and Time*, the notion of the unconscious really refers to anything concrete and represents anything other than a superfluous hypothesis. He concludes that, in a fundamental ontology, there really is no room and no need for an "unconscious" and that Daseinsanalysis can effectively explain the relevant phenomena without recourse to such a construct.

Perhaps one of the major contributions that *Being and Time* makes to an understanding of human existence is its analysis of *Befindlichkeit*, commonly, but inappropriately, translated as "state of mind" or "mood." Eugene Gendlin's *"Befindlichkeit*: Heidegger and the Philosophy of Psychology" gives a detailed exposition and analysis of the role of *Befindlichkeit* in *Being and Time*, and then goes on to apply it to psychology and psychotherapy. Gendlin shows us how an adequate conception of Heidegger's understanding of *Befindlichkeit* calls for a new mode of conceptualization in the philosophy of psychology.

Due to the obvious psychological relevance of Heidegger's Daseinsanalysis in *Being and Time*, it is that work which has received the most attention from psychologists and psychotherapists. However, as we mentioned earlier, the later works are also rich with meaning for psychology, and it is one of the important contributions of the essays which follow that they make this relevance explicit. In her article, "Madness and the Poet," Jeffner Allen illuminates how Heidegger's later writings on poets and poetry can be an aid in understanding the unique madness of the poet, and can give us a model of madness that is much different from the usual conceptions.

In his "Psychotherapy: Being One and Being Many," Charles Scott gives us an example of a Heideggerian psychology in action, focusing on the identity and difference relation in psychotherapy. Returning to the Greeks, as the later Heidegger himself does, Scott begins with the understanding of the Greek experience of the one and the many and ends with a stirring phenomenological account entitled "When I Welcome the Eventfulness of My Being One and Many."

Following upon, and to a certain extent finding its point of departure in, Scott's essay, William Richardson's "The Mirror Inside: The Problem of the Self," discusses the notion of the self in both Lacan and Heidegger. Using as an example the case of a lonely young man who increasingly turns to alcohol and marijuana for comfort, Richardson concretizes the thought of these two significant thinkers.

David Levin's paper, "The Opening of Vision: Seeing Through the Veil of Tears," is concerned with the healing of our spirit through crying and the role that vision and the eyes play in our lives. Levin centers on the later Heidegger's notions of healing and seeing, in order to develop an original phenomenology of vision.

In his "Phenomenology, Psychology, and Science," Keith Hoeller turns to Heidegger's critique of science in order to raise anew the question of the compatibility of phenomenology and science, and asks whether or not a phenomenological psychology conceived as a human *science* is possible or desirable, or whether or not a phenomenological psychology must learn to understand itself in a different manner.

And finally, François Lapointe gives us an extremely useful "Bibliography on Martin Heidegger for the Behavioral Scientists," for those of us seeking additional material on the relation between Heidegger and Psychology.

For this special edition of *Heidegger and Psychology* Professor Richardson's classic essay, "The Place of the Unconscious in Heidegger," has been added as an appendix. In addition, Professor Lapointe's bibliography has been expanded and updated. [KH, Ed.]

Martin Heidegger's Zollikon Seminars*

MEDARD BOSS

Translated by Brian Kenny

The range of influence of Martin Heidegger's philosophical discoveries cannot yet be evaluated. Certainly, though, it extends far beyond the works of those who knowingly or unknowingly try to comprehend and emulate his thinking. Even more surely, it includes and encompasses the thinking of those who set themselves against a phenomenological fundamental ontology such as Heidegger's!

At best, I personally may call to memory only a quite small sector of the domain in which this phenomenology is at work. Thanks to the wonder that Martin Heidegger—who received yearly hundreds of letters from different parts of the world and answered scarcely a one of them—found my very first written communication worthy of an extremely warm response. That was 1946. It was only many years later, long after an intense philosophical teacher-pupil relationship, and far beyond that, the closeness of a life-long friendship, had developed, that I learned from him what had motivated him to this unusual step. He confided that he had hoped that through me—a physician and psychotherapist—his thinking would escape the confines of the philosopher's study and become of benefit to wider circles, in particular to a large number of suffering human beings. It had made a considerable impression that in my first letter to him I had expressly signalled out page 122 of his book *Sein und Zeit* (*Being and Time*), and drawn his attention to the fact that under the title of "vorspringende Fürsorge," he had described the ideal relationship between the psychoanalyst and his patient.[1] More than this: Heidegger's distinguishing this caring—"vorspringende Fürsorge"—which alone respects and preserves the dignity of the human being, from that other form of caring— "einspringende Fürsorge"—which constantly and necessarily violates the

*This article is a translation of Medard Boss' "Zollikoner Seminare," which appeared in *Erinnerung an Martin Heidegger* [*Recollection of Martin Heidegger*], edited by Günther Neske, Pfullingen: Neske, 1977, pp. 31-45. This book, containing forty articles by close friends of Martin Heidegger, was meant as a memory of the first anniversary of Heidegger's death.

In an agreement between Boss and Heidegger, nothing else of the Zollikon Seminars will be published until after their deaths. At that time, the protocols of the Zollikon Seminars will go to the Heidegger Archives in Marbach, West Germany.

We would like to express our gratitude to several people whose help has allowed us to include this article in the present volume: We wish to thank Professor Herbert Spiegelberg for suggesting the "Zollikon Seminars" to us. We also wish to thank Günther Neske, publisher, Pfullingen, West Germany, for kindly granting us permission to publish the English translation. We are also grateful to Dr. Brian Kenny, Physician-in-Chief of the "Bellevue" sanatorium in Kreuzlingen, Switzerland, and the successor to Ludwig Binswanger there, for the excellent translation. Finally, we would like to express our deepest appreciation to Dr. Medard Boss and the Medard Boss Foundation for the helpful cooperation and support we received in bringing this publication to fruition (*Eds.*).

7

other, enables the analytical therapist to distinguish explicitly his particular therapeutic procedure in its originality and uniqueness from all the other, almost exclusively "einspringende," medical procedures and thereby set them their limits.[2]

Initially, this contact by letter was followed "only" by a first short personal encounter with Heidegger in his Black Forest mountain house. However, from the very first moment a mutual spontaneous liking developed. It was this that made tolerable the enormous difference and disproportion between Heidegger's capacity for fundamental thinking and the narrowness of my merely natural scientific capacity to calculate. It was as a direct consequence of this personal liking that that visit and return visits followed one another in ever shorter intervals. After only a few years of combined efforts, Heidegger's wife, Elfrida, and I succeeded in seducing him to leave his already long isolation and to undertake for the first time a common journey with us to Assissi.

However, a dark shadow fell over the first days of this trip. Each morning during our 10 o'clock walks, Heidegger would fall silent and be inaccessible to my desperate attempts to cheer him. I feared I had offended and wounded him in some undiscoverable way. In the meantime, I had become very aware of Heidegger's extreme sensitivity to the finest nuances of the atmosphere between people. After several repetitions of this apparently ill-humored behavior, I broke the silence to ask directly what I had done to incur his displeasure. Heidegger was highly astounded. "Absolutely nothing!" he replied. "Always at this time of day "das Denken" comes over me. Then, if I do not want to do myself painful violence, I have to surrender myself to it."[3]

A few years later, it took much less trouble to induce Heidegger to spend holidays with us in Taormina in Sicily. In 1965, it was Heidegger's own initiative that led us to undertake a cruise on the Aegean Sea to Troy, Ephesus, Pergamos and Istanbul. During this third overseas journey, a new "shadow phenomenon" appeared. As long as we cruised in the vicinity of Greece and Greek Antiquity, Heidegger was always in the best of spirits. Ever cheerful and tireless, he was inspired by these old centers of culture to a thousand ideas. We had scarcely left Pergamos and sailed northeast towards Istanbul, when Heidegger became increasingly physically and psychically "vexed." From a distance, one could see his ill humor. He scarcely regarded the few places of interest which we could induce him to visit. He seemed rather revolted by them.

On the way back to Athens, however, Heidegger's mood changed as soon as our ship entered Greek waters again. He was once more the old, familiar, spontaneous travelling companion whose eyes and ears were wide-open for all the beauties of nature and of what had been formed by the human hand. Our intimacy was such that I could ask him directly what his recalcitrant behavior in Istanbul had meant. He replied, "The Islamic air simply does not suit me. The stark ornamentation on and in the Mohammedan mosques lets one feel the absence of any reference to the human being or to anything in nature. Such extreme reduction and abstraction in artistic creativity freezes my soul." What I had learned much earlier from a Mohammedan friend had evidently escaped Heidegger's attention: namely, the abstention of the Mohammedan artist from any representation of a living creature does not arise out of his being far removed from his god, but rather from the deepest reverence for him. It is of such depth that it forbids the counterfeiting of what has been created by the hand of God. It was a sign of Heidegger's readiness to accept criticism that he spontaneously assured me that he would in the future see Mohammedan art with different eyes.

From the beginning, Heidegger's holidays in my mountain house on the 1500 meter high Lenzerheide were unproblematic. During the winter, though, it was occasionally difficult and time consuming to pilot him, who was accustomed only to skiing on the modest heights of the Black Forest, down from one or another of the high alpine peaks. But Heidegger loved this little corner of the earth. Its quiet, calm heights obviously lent wings to his thinking.

Besides these week long holidays together, there developed from 1958 on an additional teaching rhythm. Up to three times each semester Heidegger spent two weeks as my house guest in Zollikon. For years he conducted during each visit four evening seminars, each of three hours duration, for a chosen group of fifty to seventy medical students and assistants of the Psychiatric University Clinic in Zürich. He desisted only when his great age forbade him the stress of this undertaking. Here he endeavoured to introduce his listeners to a phenomenonological way of seeing the things which most urgently concerned them in their therapeutic and diagnostic caring for their patients. However, it required no little preliminary work on my part before Heidegger was willing to engage in such teaching activity. Even before our first encounter, I had heard of Heidegger's abysmal aversion to all modern scientific psychology. To me, too, he made no secret of his opposition to it. His repugnance mounted considerably after I had induced him with much guile and cunning to delve directly for the first time into Freud's own writings. During his perusal of the theoretical, "meta-psychological" works, Heidegger never ceased shaking his head. He simply did not want to have to accept that such a highly intelligent and gifted man as Freud could produce such artificial, inhuman, indeed absurd and purely fictitious constructions about homo sapiens. This reading made him literally feel ill. Freud's "Papers on Technique," in which he gives advice on the practical conduct of the therapeutic analysis of the neurotic patient, made Heidegger more conciliatory. He immediately discovered the crass mutual contradiction of these writings: namely, the unbridgeable gulf between the absolute, natural scientific determinism of his theories and the repeated emphasis of the freeing of the patient through psychoanalytic practice.

We appreciated it then all the more that Heidegger, despite his contempt for the psychological and psychopathological theories that filled our heads, accepted to work within the framework of the "Zollikon Seminars" for the duration of the next seventeen years and to undertake the Sisyphian task of mediating to my friends, colleagues and pupils an adequate and appropriate intellectual foundation for our activities as medical practitioners. In the tireless, never flagging patience and forbearance with which Heidegger endured and fulfilled this undertaking, even unto the limits of his physical possibilities, is to be found the unshakeable evidence of the greatness of his own humanity. With this conduct towards our Zollikon circle, he demonstrated unequivocally that he not only knew how to write and speak of that highest form of humanness in the relation to others, namely, of that selfless, loving, "vorspringende" caring which frees the other to his own selfhood, but that he also knew how to live it in an exemplary way.

Only the participants of those first seminars are able to estimate what endless effort it cost until his medical listeners, trained solely in natural science, began to even suspect what Heidegger was trying to say. These seminars led often to the fantasy that a Mars man had encountered a group of Earth dwellers for the first time and was trying to communicate with them. To illustrate vividly how the mounting embarrassment in these seminars occasionally reached a painful degree, a short excerpt of the literal protocol of the seminar of the twenty sixth of January, 1961, is cited:

Heidegger: "How does Dr. R. relate to the table before him?"
Listener A: "He is sitting behind it and looking at it."
Heidegger: "At one with this, the 'nature' of Dr. R.'s Da-sein also reveals itself—but as what?"
Five minutes of silence . . . .
Heidegger: "I remain silent because it is senseless to want to lecture you about Dr. R.'s existing. Everything depends on your learning to *see* the matter for yourselves, that you are patiently attentive to the matter, so that it may reveal itself to you in the totality of its own proper meaningfulness."
Listener C: "Dr. R. is separated from the table by an interval of space."
Heidegger: "What, then, is space?"
Listener D: "The distance between Dr. R. and the table."
Heidegger: "What is distance?"
Listener E: "A definition of space."

MARTIN HEIDEGGER'S ZOLLIKON SEMINARS

Heidegger:	"What then is space as such?"
	Ten long minutes of silence. . . .
Listener F:	"We have never heard such questions and do not know what you regard as important, what you want to hear, what you want to say."
Heidegger:	"I am only concerned that you open your eyes and do not immediately dim and distort your vision once more with artificial suppositions or theoretical explanations. How is it, then, with this matter that you have called an interval of space?"
	Seven minutes of silence. . . .
Heidegger:	"Must not that which is spatial between Dr. R. and the table be penetrable so that the table can appear at all to Dr. R.? This spatiality consists then of penetrability, of openness, of freedom. Can one then say that openness, freedom—that which is cleared—is itself spatial?"
Listener A:	"Now I really understand nothing."
	Five minutes of silence!!!!
Heidegger:	"Perhaps the wisdom of the German language can help you. You know not only the substantive "Raum" (space), but also the verb "Räumen." This verb "Räumen" means nothing other than a making-free, making-open. A forest clearing: this is a place which has been cleared, i.e., a place where the Earth has been laid free of tree trunks, cleared ("geräumt") of them. So it is that spatiality as such is rooted by its very nature in freedom, openness and clearedness, and not the reverse."

In the face of such enormous difficulties in understanding one another, perhaps the most singular facet of the Zollikon Seminars might well be the strange fact that they never became too disagreeable for either Heidegger or the participants in the seminars. With obstinate persistence through the years the teacher and the medical students of these first lessons worked their way towards one another.

At times, though, it was quite different, as the case of a man from Australia illustrates in typical fashion. He was a highly gifted, and medically, an unusually well-trained specialist in the two fields of internal medicine and psychiatry. For considerable time, he had sought my consent to conduct his training in Daseinsanalytical therapy. I had just let him come and allowed him to take part in the next seminar with Heidegger. He was deeply inspired by the extraordinarily liberating effect of Heidegger's radically new insights into human existence, into the basic nature of his world and the relation of the one to the other. Later he confided to me,

"Just after the first hour, I thought, 'So! This is Europe whose intellectual heights and tradition so surpass the miserable pragmatism of my own land.' It was only much later that I realized that even in Europe these Heidegger seminars were a unique bright spot."

A no less convincing evidence for the earnestness of Heidegger's own lived "vorspringende" caring for his fellow humans is to be seen in his equally patient and painstaking care for my personal scientific works. In particular, Heidegger watched attentively over my *Grundriss der Medizin und Psychologie* (appearing in English under the title, *Existential Foundations of Medicine and Psychology*, Aronson, 1979) during the whole eight years of its development. The magnitude of his care for the work is vividly illustrated by the facsimile of a page of the manuscript which Heidegger corrected in his own hand. Here his supplementary comments are of general interest in that they deal not only with a phenomenon that is of specially central concern to modern people, namely, the phenomenon of "stress," but they refer also to two world renowned authors: the brilliant and open-minded physician, Plügge, and Heidegger's own teacher, Husserl. (see pages 14-19.)

As the band of medical practitioners and psychologists trained in Daseinsanalytic oriented therapy had reached considerable proportions, they petitioned that a proper institute be organized for such training. For a long time, I refused the fulfilment of their wish. I felt too strongly that what Heidegger had taught me did not consist of a framework of special knowledge which could serve as a basis for yet another "school" of psychotherapy. Had not Heidegger "merely" helped me expand my field of vision, in that he lanced that cataract which eliminated all seeing except that in terms of the pre-scientific, philosophical presuppositions concerning the fundamental nature of beings as such? As the insistence became ever more vehement, I sought Heidegger's advice. He pondered long over every aspect of the matter. At last, he came to the conclusion that I would do better to give up my resistance to an institutionalization. He considered the danger great that if there were no such institute, the Daseinsanalytic foothold already won in medical circles in Zürich would rapidly be lost after my demise. I yielded. In due course, the first "Daseinsanalytic Institute for Psychotherapy and Psychosomatic Medicine" was founded in Zürich in 1971. Today, it is evident how Heidegger, through this institute, initiated a humanizing not only of psychotherapy, but of medicine as a whole. The undiminished power of his spirit is to be seen perhaps not least in that branches of our institute have already begun to appear overseas.

In conclusion, I wish to return to what was most intimately and specifically his own in Heidegger's make-up. His dream life gives me the occasion to do this. Heidegger was a "bad" dreamer, because, then, of a lack of adequate personal experience, he did not adduce the human being's

12

ability to dream in *Sein und Zeit* (*Being and Time*), although it too is to be recognized as an "Existential" on its own account, as one particular, fundamental characteristic of human being, just as its mood-attunement and its bodyhood are.

As far as he knew, Heidegger's whole dream life consisted of a single dream happening. To be sure, since his student days, he dreamed these events repeatedly at longer or shorter intervals. This too disappeared, but only after he had deepened and broadened the traditional interpretation of Antiquity of "Sein" ("Being") as "Anwesen" ("presence") to the discernment of the "Ereignis"[4] which allows "Sein" ("Being") and "Menschenwesen" ("human being as presence") to be seen as belonging together in an indivisible identity, as "vereignet" ("ordered") "zugeeignet" ("assigned"), "übereignet" ("appropriated") to one another.[5]

Previously, he had dreamed repeatedly he was in the situation of his matriculation examination at the Constance high school. All the professors who had examined him at that time sat once more physically present before him and harassed him with relentless questions.

To understand such dreaming in the context of a life history and in a way appropriate to human nature, it is first necessary to dispose of all the current "depth psychology" theories of dreaming as undemonstrable, and as arbitrary instructions leading solely to distorting interpretations of the dream phenomena. In their place, we have to practice a phenomenological approach as was taught by Heidegger himself. Then, what is characteristic of our dreaming as a whole, as well as this single specific dreaming of Heidegger, appears effortlessly of itself. It is specific of our dreaming state that the meaningfulness that appears to us addresses us mostly only from sensorily perceptible present beings, which, moreover, do not belong to our own existing. For example, in Heidegger's dreaming, he is addressed primarily by his matriculation examiners. In the following, more clear-sighted waking state, we may be addressed by the same "fulfilled meanings," but from more characteristic, much more central facts, or better, "givens," of our existing. So Heidegger's waking perception, too, expanded and focused to an ever clearer awareness of the meaningfulness of being examined, but in an incomparably more comprehensive way than previously in high school. He came to see how he had long been examined out of the center of his being, which consisted primarily of a fundamental ability to think ("des Denkenkönnens"). It brought him suffering enough, that in his waking state he was exposed to the never slackening demand emanating from this center of his being that he endure and pass the maturity examination of his philosophizing. However, his dreaming vision was so highly constricted that of all possible examinations of maturity only that of his high school matriculation examination could occur to him. His own proper and fundamental self-realization was evidently reached with his waking discernment of that state of affairs which revealed itself to him

(con't. on page 20)

13

wie Stress? Es gehört zum Menschsein. Hetto handeln wir zuerst von Stress und dann von der Wissenschaft. Die Vieldeutigkeit des

Namens Stress deutet auf die Vielfältigkeit der Sache hin, sodass wir die Vieldeutigkeit wenn wir sachgemäss

bleiben wollen. Worte und Begriffe haben einen anderen Charakter als diejenigen, die in der exakten Wissenschaft gebraucht

werden.

Stress meint Beanspruchung. Damit ist gesagt, dass Stress in den Bereich von Beanspruchung und Entsprechung gehört. Wenn wir statt von Stress von Beanspruchung sprechen, so ist das nicht nur ein anderer Titel, sondern das Wort Beanspruchung bringt die Sache sofort in den Bereich des ekstatischen Menschseins, d.h.

in den Bereich, wo von ~~primär~~ gesagt werden kann, dass es so und so

sei. Etwas als etwas so und so sagen, ist ~~von~~ der Sache ein

Apophainesthai, ein Sich-zum-zeigen-bringen. Das eigentliche Wesen

der Sprache ist solches Sagen oder Zeigen.

[β →]

~~Husserl~~ nahm als das dem Bewusstsein primär Gegebene die

sog. hyletischen Daten an, d.h. die reinen Sinnesempfindungen.

Hyle heisst griechisch der Stoff, die Materie, ~~auch~~ das Holz.

Plügge spricht auf S.238,2.Spalte, von "objektiven Sachverhalten",

diese kann es nur da geben, wo vergegenständlicht wird, dort wo

ich den akustischen Reiz als Phon messen kann. Dies ~~braucht~~ ein

Apparat, der die Schallwellen misst, er kann jedoch nicht das

Geräusch des Pressluftbohres hören. Ist das Wahrnehmen eines lärmen-

15

den Motorrades zunächst ein Hören von Phone und nachträglich ein

Hinaufügen der Bedeutung eines Motorrades [?] Die Auffassung von

Flügge geht auf die Position Husserls zurück, bei der die Dinge

Gegenstände sind. Dabei wären als hyletischen Daten das Primäre auf einen Gefühl

und hiernach würden diese durch die Noesis eine Bedeutung bekommen.

Das ist eine reine Konstruktion. Zu jeder Wahrnehmung gehört ein

bedeutunggebender ... ist dieselbe Position wie bei Kant

Phonstärke ... nicht wahrgenommen, ...

... mit einer Maschine zu messen. ... Welche Struktur hat die Wahrnehmung ? Sie hat mit meinem Umweltverhältnis zu tun. Worauf bin

ich bezogen bei der Wahrnehmung : auf eine bedeutungsbehaftete

Empfindung oder auf die Kinder und die Zementmischmaschine (Beispiel

v.Plügge) ? Plügge hört die lärmenden Kinder, sie stören ihn nicht,

weil er sie Kinder sein lässt, weil er mit ihnen

Dieses Phänomen gehört zum Sein-lassen zum Mit-Sein Wahrnehmung

kann man nicht isolieren, sonst bekommt man ihre Struktur nie zu

Gesicht. Sie hängt mit der Frage nach der Erkenntnis zusammen.

Words in brackets are Heidegger's. Notes on opposite page indicate what Heidegger wished to replace in the lines he crossed out in the text.

In what context does something such as stress belong?[1] ~~It belongs to human being. Today we will concern ourselves with stress and then with science.~~ The multiplicity of meanings of the term stress is an indication of the manifoldness of the matter at hand. This multiplicity is then necessary if we are to do justice to the matter. In this connexion, words and concepts have [*within the realm we have to deal with now*] a character different from that which they have when used in the exact sciences.

Stress signifies "laying claim to" [*and at first an excessive one*]— "Beanspruchung"—"a stress*ing*."[2] ~~This statement shows that stress belongs in the realm of "Beanspruchung"—"laying claim to" or "stressing"—and "Entsprechung"—"corresponding responsivity."~~ If we speak of stressing instead of stress, we have not simply given the phenomenon in question a new name, but the word stressing—"Beanspruchung"—brings the matter immediately into the realm of ek-static human being, i.e., into that realm where it can be said of [*that which addresses itself to us*] that it is so and so. But to say of a matter that it is, as such, so and so is ~~in itself~~ an Apophainesthai, a bringing to light [*in itself*]. The basic character of language is exactly such saying or showing.

~~Husserl assumed the so-called hyletic data as the primary "given" for the consciousness.~~[3] Hyle means in Greek material or stuff, matter, as well as [*primordially*] wood or timber. On page 238, column 2, Plügge speaks of an "objective state of affairs." This can only be present where reification occurs, i.e., there where I can measure an acoustic stimulus in phons. ~~For~~ this [*is done by*] an apparatus ~~is necessary~~ which measures the intensity of sound waves. It cannot, though, hear the sound of a pneumatic drill. Is the perception of a noisy motorbike first a hearing of phons and subsequently the addition of the meaningfulness "motorbike"?[4] Plügge's interpretation is based on the position of Husserl for whom things are constellated as objects.[5] ~~Thereby the hyletic data are primary and only secondarily do they receive meaning from the "Noesis." This is a pure artificiality and corresponds exactly to Kant's position that a meaning-giving act belongs necessarily to every perception.~~ [*However,*] the intensity of ~~sound is not~~ [*phons cannot be immediately*] perceived ~~as phons~~. This is physical quantity that can be measured by an appropriate machine. What structure does perception have?[6] It has to do with my relation to the world. To what am I related when I perceive? Am I related to a sensation loaded with meaning, or am I related to the children and to the cement mixer (See the example cited by Plügge)? Plügge hears the children making noise. They do not irritate him because he lets them be [*his*] children, because he is ~~in a common world~~ with them [*as with his own ones,*].[7] ~~This phenomenon belongs to a "letting be"—"Sein-Lassen," to a "being with"—"Mit-Sein." Perception cannot be isolated. If it were, one could never focus on its structure. The question of perception is necessarily linked with that of knowledge.~~

1 We answer: Stress belongs to the state of human existing as defined by its thrownness, by understanding, and by language.

2 In general, stressing requires some sort of corresponding responsivity, to which unresponsiveness, as well as an inability to respond, belong as its privative form.

3 Here we have above all to consider and more thoroughly think through what it is that primarily addresses the existing human being; namely, the world in which he exists day by day.

If, however, the human being is posited in Descarte's sense as "ego cogito," as consciousness, and one then asks in accord with this positing, what is then the "primäre Gegebenheit" ("primary given (given as substantive)") for consciousness, then according to the teachings of English empiricism—which dominated still in the nineteenth century and was long determining for Husserl's thinking—one must answer, sensation! Husserl defined this "Gegebenheit" ("given") more precisely as "the hyletic data," (cf. Husserl, *Ideas*).

4 Is it not rather the reverse? Primarily and in the everyday, I hear the motorbike, the call of a bird, the church bell. It requires a highly artificial viewpoint to distill a pure sensation out of the things heard.

5 . . . on the basis of the hyletic data, in that these data receive meaning through an act of consciousness.

6 This question can only unfold and be answered when we seek out perception there where it belongs, namely, in the everyday involvement with things.

7 On the other hand, the neighbor's "brats" disturb him because he does not concede them their noisy game. If he let these "brats" be playing children, they could not disturb or irritate him. Because he does not respond to them in accord with the nature of their being as children, he is distressed by them. Here it becomes clear that this "Beanspruchung" ("stressing") (i.e., correctly understood "Stress" ("stress") has to be measured with quite other standards of measurement (not with phons), namely, in accord with our already innate response to something stressing and our ability to respond to such, i.e., in accord with our existing relation to world, to our fellows and to ourselves. The physico-physiological reduction of stress to measurable stimulation of the sense organs seems on the surface to be a scientific investigation of stress, but is in truth an arbitrary and violent abstraction which totally loses sight of the existing human being as such. In passing, Husserl abandoned to a *certain* degree his Cartesian position after the publication of my *Sein and Zeit* (1927). Since 1930, the title "Lebenswelt" ("lifeworld") appears in his manuscripts.

as "das Ereignis." It was this that allowed him to make the audacious leap from the ground of Parmenides' ancient saying, which he then knew how to say in German as, "Das Selbe nämlich ist Vernehmen (Denken) sowohl als auch Sein" ("Perceiving (thinking) and being: the same."). If this lightning like revelation of the "Ereignis" had not corresponded to the true completion of his selfhood, how could it be at all comprehensible that Heidegger forthwith not only never again dreamt of having to stand the scrutiny of his examining high school professors, but, now waking, found his way out of the earlier constant pressure to think, and into a wise, serene composure in the depths of his heart.

TRANSLATOR'S NOTES

1 To translate "vorspringende Fürsorge" literally would not illuminate what is meant. It describes that selfless caring for the other in which one goes before him in an existential sense, thereby opening to him the possibility of his perceiving more of his own innate potentiality for existing, but leaving him free in the face of this potentiality to fulfil it, or not to fulfil it.

2 In an "einspringende Fürsorge," one does not go before the other—"ihm vorspringen"—existentially, opening the world to him, but rather steps into his place—"einspringen"—and thinks and acts for him, thereby hindering him in his attaining a self-reliant, independent selfhood.

3 In this context, it would be directly misleading to translate "Denken" simply as "thinking." It has rather to be understood in the same sense in which it appears in the statement, "Das Selbe nämlich ist Vernehmen (Denken) sowohl als auch Sein."—"Perceiving (thinking) and being: the same."

4 The usual English translation of this word is "event" or "happening," which is here totally inadequate as a translation of Heidegger's use of the word "Ereignis."

5 To translate this last sentence even more or less adequately into English would require volumes.

Daseinsanalysis and Freud's Unconscious

JOSEPH J. KOCKELMANS

I. INTRODUCTION

In this essay I wish to reflect on Freud's theory of the unconscious in light of contemporary Daseinsanalysis. First I shall try to give a brief description of Freud's conception of the unconscious. Then I shall attempt to deal with the question of whether or not the unconscious can be maintained within the framework of a Daseinsanalysis which takes its point of departure in the fundamental ontology developed by Heidegger in *Being and Time*. Since the question has been answered by different authors in different ways, I shall briefly report on the most important views proposed thus far, in order then to formulate my own answer to the question.

Before turning to these issues I wish to make a few observations on the meaning of *Being and Time* for psychiatry as an empirical science and on the meaning and function of Daseinsanalysis with respect to Freud's psychoanalytic theory. For many people tend to bring together under one general heading whatever has been written on psychiatry from a philosophical perspective other than the positivist perspective from which Freud himself developed his psychoanalytic theory. Yet in so doing they fail to distinguish between work influenced by Jaspers, work inspired by Husserl's phenomenology, work developed on the basis of ideas first proposed by Sartre and Merleau-Ponty, and work which was effectively inspired by Heidegger's analytic of Dasein. In the pages to come I shall not be concerned with phenomenological psychiatry, but exclusively with the Daseinsanalytic trend in contemporary psychiatry which had its origin in Binswanger and was developed further by Medard Boss. Finally, in view of the fact that in my opinion Boss' interpretation of Heidegger's analytic of Dasein is more faithful to Heidegger's original ideas than that proposed by Binswanger, I shall focus predominantly on Boss' conception of Daseinsanalysis. Yet for issues on which Binswanger and Boss are in full agreement, I shall obviously make use of Binswanger's works, too.

II. SOME GENERAL OBSERVATIONS ON THE RELEVANCE OF HEIDEGGER'S FUNDAMENTAL ONTOLOGY FOR CONTEMPORARY PSYCHIATRY[1]

The influence of Heidegger's fundamental ontology on contemporary psychopathological research and contemporary psychiatry can be shown in two different but closely related ways. First of all, one can show that those inspired by Heidegger's *Being and Time* have learned to conceive of the nature and function of psychiatry in a manner which is notably different from the conception proposed by those who take their point of departure exclusively in Freud. Secondly, one can show that those inspired by Heidegger have learned to formulate an overall theoretical framework, an encompassing a priori synthesis, from which they can state problems and try to find answers for them, and which is yet totally different from the framework implicit in Freud's psychoanalytic theory.

As far as the first issue is concerned, I assume that every empirical science is autonomous in its own domain; yet I assume at the same time that no empirical science understands itself fully merely by having a clear awareness of the subject matter to be investigated, the basic concepts to be employed, and the research methods by means of which it conducts its investigations. Thus, although each individual empirical science is autonomous in its own domain, it nonetheless can be subjected to logical, methodological, epistemological, and ontological analyses. Each kind of analysis describes certain minimal conditions which every empirical science must fulfill. Most philosophers of science limit themselves to logical and epistemological reflections. Heidegger does not deny the validity and importance of these investigations, but argues that typically ontological analyses are to be added to the former, if one is to come to a proper understanding of the *possibilities* and *limitations* inherent in every empirical science. The latter analyses focus primarily on the following issues and questions: What is empirical research? How is empirical research to be distinguished from and related to other forms of theoretical reflection? How is the theoretical attitude itself to be distinguished from and related to man's primordial form of understanding? How does each empirical science delineate its own realm of investigation, and how does it project the ontological, a priori framework of meaning from which all entities to be studied by the science in question are to be understood? What are the implications of the basic 'thematization' for the selection of basic concepts and methods? To what degree does every form of scientific thematization imply objectivation, abstraction, idealization, and formalization? How does one relate the insights of two different disciplines concerned with the same realm of phenomena?

Whereas most empirical disciplines rest upon their own particular kind of thematization, psychiatry appears to imply two different types of thematization and thus two different ontological frameworks of meaning, and two types of scientific understanding. In a clinical context psychiatry treats mentally ill human beings from the perspective of a biological horizon of understanding; thus the psychiatrist is here concerned with a

22

sick organism. On the other hand, in *psychotherapy*, the psychiatrist views the mentally ill human being precisely as a *human being* and thus within the perspective of an 'anthropological' horizon of meaning; the psychiatrist is here concerned with the mentally ill fellowman. These two conceptual horizons (the biological and the anthropological) are incompatible and their incompatability cannot be resolved within the domain of psychiatry itself. Many psychiatrists who were unable to understand the necessity of both of these conceptual frameworks, have tried in theory at least to reduce the anthropological to the biological. In *actual practice* the two conceptual orientations are usually found together in that a clinician usually also relates to his patient as a human being, whereas the medical psychotherapist will also view his patient from a medico-biological point of view. Other psychiatrists have tried to justify the dual theoretical framework by appealing to a dualist conception of man. Yet these people failed to realize that the so-called body-mind-problem is not an ontological problem at all, but merely a theoretical one which results from the fact that two different scientific conceptions of man were to be developed on the basis of two different research interests. The body-mind-problem can be solved only if one, as it were, goes behind both scientific, conceptual horizons to a horizon in which one does not yet objectify a fellow man or subjectify an organism and, thus, to a horizon in which nature and culture are not yet separated and opposed to one another. This horizon is provided for by Heidegger's analytic of Dasein.[2]

Psychiatry finds itself in a period of crisis today. Freud's original conception of psychiatry has been changed from the inside by three different efforts: by psychoanalysis' deepened understanding of its own theoretical foundations, by an ever increasing insight into psychosomatics, and by the investigations of those psychiatrists who, rejecting the original positivist interpretation of psychiatry's foundational framework, have attempted to develop a broader and more adequate interpretation of that framework.

Heidegger's analytic of Dasein is important to psychiatry in all of these efforts, even though it cannot take credit for all aspects of this development. We have just seen that the analytic of Dasein is capable of clarifying the ontological dimension of psychiatry as a science. Secondly, the analytic of Dasein does not inquire into particular regions of phenomena to be found in human beings, but rather inquires into the very Being of man as a whole. The conception of man as a physical-psychological-spiritual unity is inadequate; the very Being of man cannot be ascertained by the summative enumeration of the ontologically ambiguous modes of body, mind, and soul. What is needed is a return to man's primordial understanding of himself as Being-in-the-world, transcendence, and freedom. From this conception of man which from the start stresses unity and totality, it can be shown on the one hand how

23

certain scientific thematizations of man led to different conceptions of man (body, organism, mind, subjective spirit), and on the other hand that none of these dimensions and reductive conceptions are neglected or denied in the encompassing conception. The analytic of Dasein offers the possibility of understanding man both as a part of nature, and as a part of culture with its tradition and heritage; yet it offers equally the possibility of understanding him as transcendence. In this way the *separation* of body, mind, soul, and spirit can be obviated, without having to declare their *distinction* to be meaningless.[3]

As for the third effort mentioned, Binswanger and Boss have developed a Daseinsanalysis founded upon Heidegger's fundamental ontology articulated in *Being and Time*. Yet Daseinsanalysis, taken in the sense of Binswanger and Boss, is not a philosophical anthropology, nor is it an empirical discipline. Formulated in the language adopted by both Husserl and Heidegger, Daseinsanalysis could be called a regional ontology of the human reality as such. Regional ontologies use descriptive and interpretative methods. Their task is to mediate between a given empirical discipline concerned with a certain region of phenomena and the corresponding philosophical reflection concerned with the same phenomena.

As a regional ontology, Daseinsanalysis takes its point of departure in Heidegger's fundamental ontological conception of man. Man is understood there as Dasein, Being-in-the-world, transcendence. Man's mode of Being, i.e., his transcendence, is to be articulated by the ek-sistentials described in *Being and Time*.[4] The term transcendence is taken here in a literal sense and means surpassing. Yet taken as a basic constitutive and characteristic of Dasein, transcendence should not be understood in a spatial sense, although Dasein can among other things spatially surpass a spatial boundary or gap. Transcendence should not be understood in terms of a subject-object-opposition either. As transcending, Dasein neither surpasses a boundary which lies before a subject and forces it to remain within its own immanence, nor a gap which separates it from an object. What is surpassed in transcendence are the beings or things, i.e., every being which can become unconcealed to Dasein as well as the very being as which Dasein itself ek-sists. In surpassing, thus, Dasein first attains to the very being that it is; what it so attains to is its own self. Thus transcendence constitutes selfhood. Only insofar as Dasein ek-sists as a self can it relate itself to other beings which it equally transcends. That toward which Dasein transcends and surpasses all beings is called the world. Thus we can now define transcendence as Being-in-the-world.[5]

To prevent misunderstanding it is perhaps of some importance to spell out more carefully the meaning of Daseinsanalysis for psychology and psychiatry. Taken as a regional ontology, Daseinsanalysis is not a substitute for psychiatry or psychology, nor is it some kind of psychotherapeutic praxis or method. The expression refers to a new methodical approach to the human reality which is neither philosophical nor empirical in the strict sense of the term. Its function in regard to psychiatry and psychology is threefold: 1) to clarify the genuine meaning of the ontological frameworks from which these sciences thematize their respective subject matters, 2) to examine the presuppositions and basic conceptions of both psychiatry and psychology with respect to their adequacy in regard to the essence of man, and 3) to provide psychiatry and psychology with new impulses for research and confront them with problems which hitherto remained hidden. It attempts to achieve these goals by foregoing all traditional theoretical abstractions and constructions and instead focusing directly on the phenomena themselves which can be experienced immediately.

Those concerned with Daseinsanalysis are of the opinion that both psychology and psychiatry work with models which are inadequate to characterize the human reality. These models were taken from the natural sciences: physics, chemistry, and biology. These models are often atomistic, mechanistic, deterministic, and give the impression that a human being really is something which has a great similarity to a machine or computer. Even those who explicitly rejected an atomistic and mechanistic conception still maintained the idea that a human being is some object or thing, which is to be characterized by its typical dynamics, expediency, and productivity. The classical psychoanalytic school (Freud) as well as certain schools in psychology may have tried to overcome a too one-sided physical and technical conception of man, but they, too, continued to speak of forces, tensions, functions, psychisms, energy sources, drives, needs, etc.

The psychopathology and the psychiatry which were developed on the basis of one of these technological psychologies, tried to explain psychical and mental illnesses by referring to disturbances of individual functions of the psychic system. Textbooks of general psychiatry often still begin with a careful description of the disturbances of drives, emotions, feelings, perceptions, memories, or thoughts and, then, try to develop descriptions of the typical kinds of diseases on the basis of these 'symptoms'. If certain disturbances in perception, manner of thinking, emotions, or feelings can be established in a patient, one may then conclude that the patient is a schizophrenic, manic, or hysteric. Finally, one tries to relate the symptoms to some kind of malfunctioning of the human body, the brain, the nervous system, certain glands, etc. Yet it will be obvious that such an 'explanation', however important within certain limits, is totally irrelevant to the question of precisely how certain emotions and feelings, ideas, illusions, hallucinations, etc., are to be related to these alleged organic disturbances. Furthermore, it is certain also that there are some mental disturbances which are not to be related to any organic malfunctioning.

Joseph J. Kockelmans

Daseinsanalysis does not question the relevance and validity of research in biology, physiology, and neurology for psychiatry. It merely claims that the human reality cannot be *understood* in this manner and that for that reason psychic and mental illnesses cannot be *understood* merely from the viewpoint of disturbances in man's functions. By conceiving of man in terms of transcendence, Daseinsanalysis is capable of explaining all symptoms of psychic and mental illnesses as flowing from the typical manner in which each patient relates to his world.

It should be noted here that *many* psychologists and psychiatrists have tried to overcome the one-sided mechanistic and technological conception of man in psychiatry. In this connection one could mention the work of Jung, Bleuler, Gebsattel, E. Minkowski, E. Straus, and Zutt. Yet those who concern themselves with Daseinsanalysis firmly believe that these efforts began to bear real fruit only after Binswanger and others began to re-interpret Heidegger's ontological analytic of Dasein systematically.

Daseinsanalysis, thus, attempts to provide psychiatry and psychology with a theoretical framework which does not make a machine out of a human being, but lets man show himself as human. As such it has very little similarity to the psychotherapeutic praxis. Psychiatrists will have to treat their patients with all the reasonable means available to them as suggested by contemporary medicine, psychoanalysis, and empirical psychology. Yet those who concern themselves with Daseinsanalysis are convinced that the latter provides them with an overall framework from which the therapeutic praxis becomes humanly meaningful in that it can establish the link between the scientific objectivations and the genuinely human in the patient. Furthermore, Daseinsanalysis has been able to develop a therapy of its own which can be employed with people who could not be helped otherwise; in this case Daseinsanalysis is no longer part of a therapeutic process, but rather becomes a necessary condition for any therapeutic procedure to be effective. Finally, Daseinsanalysis appeared to be meaningful also in those cases where no therapy could be helpful. In these cases it facilitates a meaningful contact between doctor and patient, even though this contact will not lead to recovery.[6]

From the preceding it will be clear that in Daseinsanalysis the concept of world occupies a privileged position and will be used as a methodical clue. The typical conception of world always gives information about the manner in which a human being is as Being-in-the-world and, thus, as a self. World should not be taken here in the sense of von Uexküll's, von Weizsäcker's, or Goldstein's biological worlds, although it is true that the latter conceptions are of great importance for biology and physiology, and in each case have at least something in common with the conception of world as interpretatively described by Daseinsanalysis. Daseinsanalysis is not concerned with living organisms, but with beings who can speak up for themselves. The latter explains why the phenomena to be explained in

DASEINSANALYSIS AND FREUD'S UNCONSCIOUS

Daseinsanalysis are to a large extent language phenomena. In order to gain access to the particular structure of ek-sistence in the exploration of a psychosis, for instance, the psychiatrist must take his clue from the typical conception of world that is implied therein, i.e., the typical form of temporalization, spatialization, concern, etc., in regard to the world toward which the given type of ek-sistence casts itself as transcendence. Employing this clue systematically, Daseinsanalysis has been able to describe and interpret the worlds of the manic, the hysteric, the schizophrenic, etc. To explore and ascertain the world of these patients means to explore and ascertain in what way everything that is, is accessible to these modes of ek-sistence.[7]

As for the possibility of exploring language phenomena, Daseinsanalysis does not, as psychoanalysis usually does, focus merely on the historical context, on references to a certain pattern of the inner life history; nor does it only watch the content of speech for possible references to facts pertaining to certain functions or desires, as the psychopathologist does. Daseinsanalysis is concerned primarily with the linguistic expressions and manifestations insofar as they point to a certain conception of world in which the speaker lives or has lived, as well as to the way in which this particular type of ek-sistence surpasses what is, toward that world.

In some cases one has an abundance of 'spontaneous' and immediately comprehensible verbal manifestations available in the form of self-descriptions, dream accounts, diary entries, poems, letters, paintings, autobiographical drafts, etc. In other cases one must carefully collect all the necessary data over a long period of time. Only when all the necessary information has thus been collected, can one attempt to discern the 'world' or 'worlds' in which the patient lives. This is a very difficult task; but only when all the available data can be 'fitted' into an overall conception of world, can one understand the mode of the patient's ek-sistence in the sense of what we call neuroses and psychoses. A certain concern with the patient's life history plays an important part here also; yet whereas for psychoanalysis the connections of the life history are the goal of the investigation, for Daseinsanalysis they merely provide material for that investigation.

Yet it should be stressed once more that Daseinsanalysis is not a substitute for scientific investigation and research; nor is it a substitute for psychopathology and psychotherapy. The results of the Daseinsanalysis should be recast by psychopathology and psychotherapy into forms which are peculiar to them and which equally reflect the insights gained by empirical investigation. However, psychopathology and psychotherapy would be digging their own graves, if they were to refuse to test their concepts of functions and symptoms against the phenomenal content to which these concepts are to be applied.[8]

27

III. ON THE MEANING AND FUNCTION OF THE
UNCONSCIOUS IN FREUD'S PSYCHOANALYSIS[9]

Freud's psychoanalytic theory as a whole consists of two apparently contradictory parts, an energetics which is concerned with conflicting forces and a doctrine of interpretation concerned with meanings and relations of meaning. The basic difficulty of any attempt to comprehend psychoanalysis consists in finding a possible solution to the problem of how Freud tried to overcome the gap between these two orders of discourse: how can the economic, physiological explanation be related to a doctrine of interpretation dealing with meaning.[10]

Originally, Freud strongly stressed the physiological approach to psychic phenomena. In "Projects for a Scientific Psychology" (1895) he wrote: "The intention of this project is to furnish us with a psychology which shall be a natural science: its aim, that is, is to represent psychical processes as quantitatively determined states of specifiable material particles [neurons] and so to make them plain and void of contradictions."[11] Thus at that time Freud believed that in principle it would be possible to adequately explain all pyschic phenomena by means of physiological processes which are governed by the same principles and laws as all other natural phenomena, and which in principle can be located somewhere in the human brain. In his view, psychoanalysis was to be conceived of as a "speculative superstructure" and a "rational foundation for . . . medical efforts." Psychoanalytic theory developed gradually and Freud himself was convinced that any part of it could eventually "be abandoned or changed without loss or regret, the moment its inadequacies have been proved"; it is an "artificial structure of hypotheses" which perhaps one day will be "blown away" in its entirety by the progress of scientific research.[12]

According to the original psychoanalytic theory, all so-called mental phenomena are products or results of the working of an entity called the *psyche*. The psyche itself is conceived of in terms of a complex apparatus which is capable of picturing things extraneous to itself within itself; thus it functions like a reflex mechanism.[13] In view of the fact that the psyche is an apparatus, it needs energy to perform its function. This energy is called *libido*. The energy is derived from the excitations of certain organs of the body and the first *psychic* manifestations of these excitations have the character of *wishes*.[14] In addition to the stimuli which the psyche receives from inside itself, there are other stimuli which originate from things of the outside world. These latter stimuli are transmitted to the psyche through the sense organs in the form of energy.[15]

Both types of stimuli are transformed in various ways while being cathected with libido. By means of *cathexis* the psyche then produces *perceptions* of the world as well as *ideas*; in so doing the psyche uses material which consists of the stimuli, memory traces, and unconscious, preconscious, and conscious strivings. The production of perceptions and ideas takes place in *causal processes*. The purpose of these processes of the psyche is a *motor discharge of energy* into the world in order that the apparatus may maintain itself without an excess of excitation. For, accumulation of excitation is felt as *unpleasure*, diminution of excitation as *pleasure*.[16] The working of the apparatus results in two different forms of *'thinking'*. The primary process thinking refers to *unconscious* processes and is to be characterized as incorrect and irrational. Secondary process thinking corresponds to the 'real' world and is to be characterized as rational, logical, and consistent, while maintaining harmony with the conditions of time and space.[17]

In 1900, in *The Interpretation of Dreams*, it appeared however that Freud had given up all attempts to combine the 'psychical apparatus' with certain anatomically localizable processes of the brain. Freud refers to 'dream thoughts' which are the accomplishments of desires or wishes; dreams are of a psychical nature; they can be interpreted and, thus, they have meaning. "The aim which I have set before myself is to show that dreams are capable of being interpreted. . . . 'interpreting' a dream implies assigning a meaning to it—that is, replacing it by something which fits into the chain of our mental acts as a link having a validity and importance equal to the rest."[18]

For Freud dreams have meaning and, thus, they are not a kind of waste product of a man's mental life; secondly, because dreams are meaning phenomena a purely organic explanation of dreams becomes very unlikely. By claiming that dreams are the expression of desires, Freud locates them at the intersection of meaning and physical force. "To say that a dream is the *fulfillment* of a *repressed* wish is to put together two notions which belong to different orders": the 'discourse of meaning' and the 'discourse of force'.[19] Freud continues to describe the 'psychical apparatus' as having a spatial and temporal dimension in addition to being subject to forces and conflicts.[20] He also uses the expression 'psychical locality', which is to be understood psychologically, not anatomically; it is then said that the psychical apparatus functions *like* a photographic apparatus or *like* some other mechanical apparatus.[21] Yet it seems that Freud was unable to free his theory completely from the connotations of an apparatus or a locality which are to be understood both as being somehow spatial and mechanical.[22] Also, his attempts to translate the topographical way of representing things into a dynamic one[23] and the use of expressions such as "processes of excitation" and "modes of discharge" do not change the basic framework substantially. Consciousness is still described as "a sense organ for the perception of psychical qualities."[24] Ricoeur concludes that in *The Interpretation of Dreams* "the language of meaning implied by the work of interpretation, and the quasi-physical language implied by the language of the topography, are not yet perfectly coordinated."[25]

In developing his theory of the *unconscious*, Freud was guided by his aim to demonstrate the thorough-going meaningfulness of all mental phenomena. By the meaning of a mental phenomenon Freud understood "the intention which it serves . . ., its place in the mental sequence . . ., its tendency," its whence, its whither, and its why.[26] Thus the meaningfulness of a phenomenon signifies that it has a definite position and function in the process of the unfolding and maturing of a person's life. Freud thus maintained a teleological orientation in a man's psychic life; man is constantly on the way toward a goal, carrying out his life possibilities, guided by his strivings. The goal to be achieved in this way is freedom and 'full normality'. In order to relate this teleological conception with the mechanistic conception of the psyche, Freud had to assume that 'mind' and 'consciousness' cannot be identified and that, thus, a distinction is to be made within the realm of the mind between consciousness and the unconscious. Freud was inspired to this daring hypothesis by ideas proposed by Lipps and Prel.[27]

The concept of the unconscious soon became the most essential of all concepts introduced within Freud's psychoanalytic theory. He finally came to conceive of it as the "true psychical reality."[28] Developing Fechner's conception of psychic localities,[29] Freud began to consider the unconscious as a psychic system 'below' consciousness.[30] He was aware of the fact that in making this assumption he went far beyond the immediately observable phenomena; thus he called the idea of psychic localities a conjecture and regarded the doctrine of the unconscious as part of metapsychology.[31]

Yet he maintained that his theory of the unconscious was deduced from concrete observations. First there is the fact that ideas which are conscious now, are no longer conscious so a moment later. "What the idea was in the interval we do not know. We can say that it was *latent*."[32] Secondly, Bernheim's experiments with respect to posthypnotic suggestion showed that people can carry out tasks after awakening, without knowing the source of the suggestions. Thirdly, it seemed to Freud that dreams, neurotic symptoms, and parapraxes showed certain phenomena which cannot be explained except by assuming the existence of unconscious strivings and wishes in the relevant subjects. Once the existence of the unconscious was postulated, Freud made a distinction between that which is latently unconscious (preconscious) and that which is unconscious in the strict sense of the term.[33]

Originally, Freud had assumed that being unconscious of something is no more than an "enigmatic characteristic of a definite mental act."[34] Later, he substantially enlarged this first conception. The unconscious is much too important just to be conceived of as a property of certain acts. The unconscious then becomes a system with a distinct *locus* and a functioning according to laws of its own. "The *system* revealed by the sign that the single acts forming parts of it are unconscious we designate by the name 'the Unconscious'. . . ."[35] Thus, what originally had been considered to be a property of certain mental acts now becomes a psychic system, an independent entity that somehow can be 'localized' and functions according to principles and laws of its own.[36] In a subsequent essay, "The Unconscious," (1915) Freud maintained that the language of forces can never be overcome by the language of meaning; yet on the other hand no theory of physical forces can efface the fact that affects are the charge of ideas.[37] We have seen that Freud used the label of 'thinking as a primary process' for the mental activities which directly pertain to the unconscious, whereas the reality-oriented thinking of the waking adult is called 'thinking as a secondary process'.[38] Finally, in "The New Introductory Lectures," Freud attributed the basic characteristics formerly attributed to the unconscious to the *id*.[39]

In Freud's view, thus, the assumption of the unconscious is both necessary and legitimate. This assumption is necessary in that it is the only factor that can explain the numberless, large gaps in the data of consciousness. Many conscious acts "remain disconnected and unintelligible if we insist upon claiming that every mental act that occurs in us must also necessarily be experienced by us through consciousness; on the other hand, they fall into a demonstrable connection if we interpolate between them the unconscious acts which we have inferred. A gain in meaning is a perfectly justifiable ground for going beyond the limits of direct experience."[40] That the assumption is legitimate can in Freud's opinion be shown by the fact that both in everyday life and in science we appeal to assumptions which are not *directly* verifiable, when there are valid reasons for doing so. In the case of the unconscious these reasons are evident from the fact that successful practical therapeutic procedures can be developed on that basis.[41]

IV. DASEINSANALYSIS AND FREUD'S UNCONSCIOUS

The question to which I wish to turn now is one of whether or not the Freudian unconscious can be maintained within the perspective of Daseinsanalysis. The question is a very difficult one, partly in view of the fact that it appears to be possible to interpret the meaning of it in more than one way. The latter seems to be the reason why those who are convinced that one can employ ideas taken from Heidegger's analytic of Dasein to develop an 'anthropological' theory which can take the place of Freud's materialistic and mechanistic psychoanalytic theory, have tried to answer the question in different ways.

In "The Case of Ellen West. An Anthropological-Clinical Study,"[42] the originator of the Daseinsanalytic theory, Binswanger, writes that in his view it is indeed unacceptable to construe 'behind' the conscious personality an 'unconscious' second person. Yet one should realize that Freud himself did not at first speak of an 'ego' in this context, but merely of an 'id'. When Freud later used assertions to the effect that "parts of the ego and the superego," too, must be recognized as unconscious, he himself seems to have originated the popular conception of the unconscious as a second ego; but such a way of speaking obviously cannot be justified. Such an assumption would make the unconscious think. Yet in Freud's own view it is impossible to give the unconscious itself a consciousness; the unconscious is id and nothing but id.[43]

According to Binswanger, the unconscious in the strict sense (i.e., not the pre-conscious) points to a real dimension in man, but this dimension cannot be understood as implying a second subject. The id is a scientific construct which objectifies man's ek-sistence by conceiving of it in terms of a 'reservoir of instinctual energy'.[44] In *Vorträge*[45] Binswanger maintains the same view; what Freud calls the unconscious and from his own scientific frame of reference interprets mechanistically, does indeed refer to an important dimension in man and this dimension is to be articulated in Daseinsanalysis in a manner which avoids both materialism and mechanism. What psychoanalysis interprets from the perspective of consciousness, and thus calls the unconscious, must be interpreted by Daseinsanalysis ek-sistentially and temporally and, thus, related to what Heidegger calls thrownness and facticity. "We can say of the psyche as well as of the organism that they belong to the hidden, but as *hidden* 'disclosed' ontological character of the facticity of thrownness of the being we call man in his thereness (*Da*)."[46]

Richardson, too, is of the opinion that it is possible to discuss Freud's unconscious in terms of Heidegger's analytic of Dasein. Both Freud and Heidegger have made reference to the Oedipus myth and the self-revelation of Oedipus is taken by each author to be comparable to that process which is central to each one's basic enterprise, for Freud the process of psychoanalysis, for Heidegger the achievement of authenticity. Thus it may be expected that Heidegger's concern with authenticity can show us the place of the unconscious in his thought.[47]

At first sight one may be inclined to believe that he can locate Freud's unconscious within Heidegger's conception of phenomenology. As the science of phenomena, phenomenology must assume that in what shows itself first and foremost (phenomena), there is something that at first is still hidden, that this hidden meaning can be brought to light by phenomenological analysis and interpretation, and finally that what is so brought to light constitutes the 'truth' of what showed itself originally. Thus all conscious awareness implies a reference to something hidden, 'unconscious'. This is also true for the intentionality of consciousness itself. "For every explicit analysis of a given conscious intention presupposes that, before it can be taken as theme for explicitation, it must be a merely implicit intention of consciousness, i.e., it is wrapped up in a type of non-thematic, functional intentionality that is identical with the complex totality of lived experience as such. This non-thematic, functional lived intentionality may be called 'unconscious,' i.e., the intentionality of unconscious processes."[48]

One might obviously object here and say that these references are irrelevant to Freud's conception of the unconscious. For phenomenology attributes to the 'unconscious' the structure of consciousness itself, namely, intentionality, and thus reduces the unconscious to an inferior form of consciousness. Yet for Freud the unconscious is not a form of consciousness, but "a dynamic process which is the seat of all active, primitive, brutish, infantile, aggressive, and sexual drives, directed by the pleasure principle and ignoring time, death, logic, values, and morality. . . ."[49] A phenomenologist might answer this objection by pointing to the fact that the objection flows from an unfounded assumption, namely, that phenomenology a priori knows what consciousness is; but this is precisely what phenomenology is designed to examine. In its attempt to determine what consciousness is, phenomenology must take into consideration data of immediate consciousness as well as "the language of signs by which the unconscious reveals itself in consciousness" (dreams, parapraxes, symptomatic actions, etc.).[50]

Richardson is aware of the fact that the attempts made by Fink, De Waelhens, and Ricoeur to establish some relationship between phenomenology and psychoanalysis is to some degree problematic. He merely mentioned these reflections as a propadeutic to Heidegger. He concludes this part of his essay by stating that in his opinion psychoanalysis may profit from any attempt by phenomenologists to re-interpret Freud's own conception of the unconscious, which was couched in terms of the nineteenth century physical sciences, and according to which man is to be conceived of as an energized machine, into a conception which is part of an overall conception of man which is more human.[51]

Yet the idea that it is possible to locate Freud's unconscious within Heidegger's conception of phenomenology is, indeed, a fruitful one, provided one fully realizes that there is an enormous difference between Heidegger's hermeneutic phenomenology of Dasein and Husserl's transcendental phenomenology of the intentionality of consciousness. The intentionality of consciousness (whether this intentionality be explicitly thematized, or remains merely functional) is according to Husserl a relationship between two beings, the intending consciousness and the intended thing; from Heidegger's point of view the intentionality, as Husserl conceives of it, is a comportment on the ontic, existentiell level.

Furthermore, to conceive of man in Husserlian fashion as a being who is the subject of conscious (or unconscious) acts is to forget the true dimension of man's Being, his comprehension of Being. When Dasein enters into a comportment with other beings and becomes a conscious subject, it is this basic dimension, this ontological structure, which lets it be a subject and lets it be conscious. Yet taken as this structure, Dasein is not conscious at all. Dasein is a self, but as such not yet a conscious self or subject. Dasein is the pre-subjective, onto-conscious self. We may thus expect that the place where unconscious processes in the sense of Freud may be situated in Heidegger's thought seems to be in the existential-ontological dimension of the onto-conscious self.

Richardson admits that there is no textual foundation for the expression 'onto-conscious self'; he also points out why he wishes to avoid expressions such as non-subjective or pre-subjective. "We say 'onto-conscious' for want of something better, to suggest that the self in question is the ontological dimension of the conscious subject as conscious, the Being-dimension of Dasein by reason of which it is the There (*Da*) of Being among beings."[52] This dimension is not conscious; thus it may be called 'unconscious'. Thus Dasein is a self that is not yet a (conscious) subject; yet it is human and, therefore, belongs to someone who can say I. It is not a substance, but a process. In its normal everyday condition Dasein appears to itself as that which it really is not, namely, as a being in all respects like all other beings.

According to Medard Boss, Freud's unconscious cannot be maintained in a Daseinsanalysis. In making this claim, Boss was aware of the fact that other psychiatrists, who defend the possibility and necessity of developing a Daseinsanalysis in psychiatry, had made more moderate claims. Boss was aware also that he was not the first one to radically criticize Freud's theory of the unconscious. First of all, philosophers of science have pointed out that it is logically incorrect to conclude to the existence of the unconscious from the fact that its assumption can explain certain phenomena or lead to successful therapeutic procedures. For scientific explanations and successful techniques can and often have been derived from false hypotheses.

Secondly, in Boss' view any doctrine of the unconscious assumes that there is a universally accepted, clear, and 'true' conception of consciousness, even though no one has ever been able to state convincingly just what consciousness would have to be "if it is a primarily immanent, subjective thing and yet capable of receiving within itself external objects, of taking notice of them and their meaningful content." Boss implicitly refers here to Heidegger's criticism of a so-called closed consciousness, as found in Descartes' *res cogitans* and Kant's *Bewusstsein*, which flows from unacceptable assumptions and necessarily leads to ontological and epistemological quasi-problems.[53] Freud himself realized that the notion of the unconscious presupposes some definite conception of consciousness. On several occasions Freud explicitly tried to articulate such a conception of consciousness, but, in Boss' opinion, these attempts failed completely. For Freud, consciousness "is the *superficies* of the mental apparatus," which as such is part of the ego. The ego itself, in turn, is defined as the "coherent organization of mental processes."[54] The function of consciousness is "only that of a sense organ for the perception of psychical qualities. . . ."[55] In order that thought processes may become conscious, they must come into connection with the verbal images that correspond to them. The verbal images themselves are verbal memory-residues derived primarily from auditory perceptions.[56]

Freud was aware of the difficulties connected with his own theory of consciousness and admitted explicitly that his ideas about consciousness did not keep the promises which at first they had seemed to make.[57] He had to content himself with the observation that at least he had fully recognized the obscurity in regard to the entire problematic. In Boss' view it is simply impossible to try to understand consciousness as arising out of quality-less excitations, or as a property of the surface of an apparatus. It is equally impossible to understand it in connection with language in the manner in which Freud tried to do so. One cannot reduce language phenomena to residues and memories of sensory stimuli or auditory sensations. It is completely incomprehensible how consciousness can rise out of an enigmatic connection between unconscious thought processes and certain auditory stimuli.[58] The main reason why Freud failed in his theory of the unconscious consists in the fact that he attempted to account for phenomena of meaning in terms of causal processes and to explain human phenomena with the help of physical theories. "The assumption of an unconscious is necessary only if one accepts Freud's underlying philosophy as obviously true. Then, of course, the hypothesis of a psychic container, a psychic locality, or a psychic system is unavoidable. All the psychic transformation processes which Freud assumed behind the immediately given phenomena require such a psychic 'black box', since they admittedly can never be seen."[59] Anyone who rejects this basic philosophy does not further the genuine understanding of human forms of behavior by assuming an unconscious.

Obviously, one should not construe these critical remarks to imply a criticism of biology, physiology, and neurology, or even a criticism of the application of the insights gained in these sciences to a *scientific* study of man as a natural organism. Yet these remarks do imply that physiological processes in the sense organs and the brain can never directly contribute to an elucidation of human perception taken as an action concerned with meaning.[60]

In addition to these reasons for rejecting Freud's theory of the unconscious, reasons to which anyone can appeal, there are special reasons why people who employ the Daseinsanalysis feel that one should drop the assumption of the unconscious altogether. From a Daseinsanalytic point of view, the assumption of the unconscious is unacceptable, mainly because the existence of the unconscious is a superfluous hypothesis. All the phenomena which Freud employed to 'prove' the existence of the unconscious can, from a Daseinsanalytic point of view, be explained without an appeal to the unconscious.[61] One should realize that Freud's doctrine of the unconscious follows from his interpretation of the relevant phenomena *only on the assumption* that there are subjective images which mirror an independent, external reality, and that there are processes, occurring in some intrapsychic locality, which fabricate ideas and thoughts corresponding more or less to this external reality. If it is the essence of Dasein to light up, illuminate, and disclose things in the world, we shall always find man primordially *with* what he encounters. By using Heidegger's analysis of perception and knowledge, it can be shown that an explanation of the phenomena on which Freud based his theory by no means has to postulate the existence of an unconscious in Freud's sense. For according to that view "when Dasein directs itself toward something and grasps it, it does not somehow first get out of an inner sphere in which it has been proximally encapsulated, but its primary kind of Being is such that it is always 'outside' alongside entities which it encounters and which belong to a world already discovered. Nor is any inner sphere abandoned when Dasein dwells alongside the entity to be known, and determines its character. . . . And furthermore, the perceiving of what is known is not a process of returning with one's booty to the 'cabinet' of consciousness after one has gone out and grasped it; even in perceiving, retaining, and preserving, the Dasein which knows *remains outside.* . . ."[62]

Freud wondered how an idea could be present in consciousness at one moment and have disappeared in the next. In his view he had good reasons to ask what had become of it and to where it had disappeared. Yet Freud assumed here a conception of knowledge which is incorrect from a Daseinsanalytic point of view, in that it accepts the existence of a consciousness which somehow is to be conceived of as a kind of box in which ideas can be maintained without sufficient grounds. According to Boss, if one carefully examines all the phenomena on which Freud founded his conception of the unconscious, he finds time and again that Freud makes assumptions which are unjustifiable and that a legitimate explanation of these phenomena is possible without any appeal to the unconscious in the sense of Freud. Post-hypnotic suggestion, parapraxes, dreams, pathogenic factors in neuroses, etc., do not presuppose that there is an unconscious, but should be understood as being related to certain actual or possible modes of man's Being-in-the-world.[63]

DASEINSANALYSIS AND FREUD'S UNCONSCIOUS

V. CRITICAL REFLECTIONS

Before making an attempt to critically evaluate the suggestions made by the authors discussed in the preceding pages, I wish first to return to a remark made earlier in this paper. When we speak of Freud's psychoanalytic theory, we can interpret the meaning of this expression in at least two different ways. Originally, Freud's theory was merely a *scientific* theory, consisting of a number of interrelated scientific hypotheses, developed with the aim of explaining certain psychic phenomena and making possible a certain therapeutic praxis. At a later stage, this theory was 'expanded' into a philosophical anthropology and, ultimately, even into a universal *philosophy* of culture.[64]

If one now looks at Daseinsanalysis, one should realize that the latter expression, too, is to be interpreted in at least two different ways. Taken as an analytic of Dasein, the expression refers to Heidegger's *fundamental ontology* developed in *Being and Time* with the aim of finding a way to meaningfully approach the question concerning the meaning of Being. At a later stage, this fundamental ontology was re-interpreted by Binswanger, Boss, and others and changed into a *regional ontology* developed with the aim of explaining certain psychic phenomena and making a certain therapeutic praxis possible; this 'scientific theory' runs parallel to, and in many instances depends upon, Freud's psychoanalysis and psychotherapeutic theory.

If Daseinsanalysis is taken to refer to Heidegger's fundamental ontology and Freud's psychoanalysis as a philosophical theory, it can then be stated that these two theories are incompatible and that the one, viewed from the perspective of the other, is *totally* unacceptable. It seems to be meaningless to try to 'build' Freudian ideas into Heidegger's fundamental ontology or Heideggerian ideas into Freud's psychoanalysis. Personally, I reject Freud's philosophical ideas on the ground that they rest on assumptions which in my opinion cannot possibly be justified philosophically.

On the other hand, if both Daseinsanalysis and Freud's psychoanalysis are taken as 'scientific' theories, the question of how these two theories are to be related to one another is a meaningful one. It cannot be denied that the former perhaps never would have been developed, if Freud had not first developed his theory. Secondly, it cannot be denied either that many important elements of the Freudian theory are maintained in the Daseinsanalytic theory. Finally, as far as the application of the theories to therapeutic practices is concerned, the application of the former theory seems to presuppose the legitimacy of the application of Freud's theory at least in principle; furthermore, here, too, many elements of Freud's original conception are maintained.

Yet it is possible to ask the question of which of the two theories is the more reasonable theory both in light of the phenomena to be explained and the therapeutic praxis to be made possible. Since both theories claim to be able to explain the same phenomena, and since both theories have led to a successful therapeutic praxis, the question is one of logical consistency, epistemological acceptability, and ontological relevance in regard to the phenomena to be explained and the therapeutic praxis to be justified. Protagonists of the Daseinsanalytic theory claim unanimously that in their opinion Daseinsanalysis is by far preferable over the Freudian theory, simply because the former, contrary to the latter, does not presuppose entities which are really superflous and, furthermore, does not appeal to *ad hoc* hypotheses. In addition, the same authors claim that Daseinsanalysis is to be preferred over the Freudian psychoanalysis because the former theory is legitimately derived from human phenomena and not, as the Freudian theory is, simply superimposed upon these phenomena. Finally, Freud's theory is to be rejected because of its inherent dualism.

It should be noted here that from a fundamental ontological point of view there is nothing wrong with Freud's efforts in principle. The fundamental ontological doctrine of thematization leaves more than enough leeway for Freud's endeavors. Originally, Freud tried to explain scientifically certain (abnormal) phenomena which he had observed in his patients. In order to be able to deal with these phenomena he had to select an a priori synthesis upon which these phenomena could be projected. At first he selected this a priori framework from the biological sciences. When it later appeared that it is impossible to understand phenomena of meaning (such as dreams) in terms of brain processes, Freud turned to a broader a priori synthesis hoping that from this more encompassing framework both physiological processes and phenomena of meaning could be understood and brought into harmony with one another. Although fundamental ontology does not exclude the possibility of projecting a more encompassing framework for the phenomena with which Freud was concerned, it nonetheless seems, from that perspective, that in his actual efforts Freud made two important mistakes. First, Freud construed the entities projected by his own theory (such as organism, psyche, preconscious, unconscious, consciousness, etc.) as being ontic, real parts of the human reality. From the perspective of fundamental ontology these entities are not real things or real parts, but merely the hypostatization of the objectified entities created by Freud's scientific thematization. Secondly, Freud failed to show how the two elements of which his encompassing framework consists are to be combined with one another consistently. In other words, Freud never succeeded in resolving the 'tension' between the physiological part of his overall framework of meaning which speaks of forces, energies, drives, cathexis, etc., on the one hand, and the ontological part of the same framework which speaks about meaning, on the other. Daseinsanalysis provides us with a framework of meaning which is not affected by this unresolvable 'tension'. It obviously does not deny that a physiological framework can be applied to man, taken as an organism, but such a framework, developed by the biological sciences, *cannot be integrated* into the framework of meaning developed by Daseinsanalysis. A psychiatrist views his patients both as organisms which may be malfunctioning and as fellowmen for whom it has become impossible to live a meaningful life in the world in which they happen to find themselves. But one should realize here that the biological framework *need not be integrated* into the framework provided by Daseinsanalysis, in view of the fact that as far as man is concerned the *phenomena* explicitly thematized by the biological sciences are part and parcel of the subject matter of Daseinsanalysis, even though they are not thematized there in the same manner.

If we now return to the question concerning the legitimacy of Freud's conception of the unconscious, it will be clear at once that in a fundamental ontology there is no room and no need for an unconscious, just as little as such an ontology has room or need for a theory of consciousness, if the latter is understood in the sense of modern philosophy (Descartes, Kant). Thus, in my opinion, Richardson was wrong in trying to find a Daseinsanalytic parallel to Freud's unconscious within the perspective of fundamental ontology. Furthermore, for me it is difficult to understand how one could claim that Dasein, when it inauthentically conceives of itself as a 'being among beings', is not yet a conscious subject. Even in forgetting its ownmost authentic self, Dasein is still a *human* agent. As such it knows itself as being the agent of its own actions; thus it knows itself as a subject and as a self. It is precisely the tendency to conceive of its own self in terms of consciousness and subject which makes it difficult for Dasein to come to its authentic self, i.e., to conceive of itself as transcendence. In addition, Freud's unconscious was originally introduced as a scientific 'construct', postulated in order to be able to explain certain known phenomena. Freud never *described* the unconscious, nor did he ever *explain* its mode of Being; rather, it itself is a postulate on the basis of which certain phenomena can be described and explained.[65] Heidegger's conception of the inauthentic self, on the other hand, is not a scientific construct, nor is it itself ever used to explain certain phenomena; rather, its mode of Being is to be understood interpretatively in fundamental ontology.

On the other hand, if Daseinsanalysis is taken as a 'scientific' theory, then the question of whether or not an unconscious in the sense of Freud is to be introduced, may be asked legitimately. The answer to this question does not depend upon the philosophical a priori of the one who asks the question. Yet it seems to me that Boss' conviction that even then there is no room or need for a Freudian unconscious can be justified. If Daseinsanalysis as a 'scientific' theory indeed can explain all the phenomena for which Freud introduced the unconscious, then scientifically there is no longer any reason why one should maintain this hypothesis. One should note here first, that the claims made by Boss run parallel to similar claims made by Straus on grounds which are not at all related to Heidegger's fundamental ontology.[66] Secondly, it seems to me that Binswanger is correct where he states that Heidegger's conception of thrownness and facticity can be employed legitimately to explain some of the phenomena for which Freud introduced the unconscious. Finally, one should realize that, according to Boss, these reflections do not show that Daseinsanalysis is the only 'scientific' theory, nor that it is the 'true' psychological theory capable of explaining certain psychic phenomena and justifying a certain therapeutic praxis. Yet Boss does claim, and in my opinion correctly, that of the two theories discussed here the Daseinsanalytic theory is preferable over that originally proposed by Freud, even though without Freud's original ideas the Daseinsanalysis, taken as a 'scientific' theory, would perhaps never have been developed.

NOTES

1 Cf. Ludwig Binswanger, "Heidegger's Analytic of Existence and Its Meaning for Psychiatry," in J. Needleman, ed., *Being-in-the-World. Selected Papers of Ludwig Binswanger* (New York: Basic Books, 1963), pp. 206-221; "Über die daseinsanalytische Forschungsrichtung in der Psychiatrie," in *Ausgewählte Vorträge und Aufsätze*, 2 vols. (Bern: Francke Verlag, 1961), vol. I, pp. 190-217; "Daseinsanalyse, Daseinsanalytik und Psychiatrie," in *Ausgewählte Vorträge und Aufsätze*, vol. II, pp. 147-307; Medard Boss, "Die Bedeutung der Daseinsanalyse für die Psychologie und die Psychiatrie," in *Psyche* 6 (1952-53), 178-186; *Psychoanalyse und Daseinsanalytik* (Bern: Hans Huber, 1957); *Psychoanalysis and Daseinsanalysis* (New York: Basic Books, 1963); "Daseinsanalysis and Psychotherapy," in Hendrik Ruitenbeek, ed., *Psychoanalysis and Existential Philosophy* (New York: Basic Books, 1963). For a systematically developed Daseinsanalysis cf. L. Binswanger, *Grundformen und Erkenntnis menschlichen Daseins* (Zürich: Max Niehans, 1953); Medard Boss, *Psychoanalysis and Daseinsanalysis*, ch. 2, pp. 28-48, and passim.

2 L. Binswanger, "Heidegger's Analytic of Existence and Its Meaning for Psychiatry," pp. 208-210.

3 *Ibid.*, pp. 210-215.

4 L. Binswanger, "Über die daseinsanalytische Forschungsrichtung," pp. 190-194. For a brief summary of the most important themes of *Being and Time* relevant to psychiatry, cf. William J. Richardson, "The Place of the Unconscious in Heidegger," in *Review of Existential Psychology and Psychiatry*, 5 (1965), 265-290, pp. 285-287; cf. also: Medard Boss, *Psychoanalysis and Daseinsanalysis*, pp. 28-48.

5 Cf. William J. Richardson, *op. cit.*, pp. 274-279; Martin Heidegger, *Vom Wesen des Grundes* (Frankfurt: Klostermann, 1955), pp. 18-42.

6 Cf. Medard Boss, "Die Bedeutung der Daseinsanalyse für die Psychologie und die Psychiatrie," *loc. cit.*; L. Binswanger, "Heidegger's Analytic of Existence and Its Meaning for Psychiatry," *loc. cit.*, pp. 215-221.

7 Cf. Ludwig Binswanger, *Schizophrenie* (Pfullingen: Neske, 1957): *Drei Formen missglückten Daseins: Verstiegenheit, Verschrobenheit, Manieriertheit* (Tübingen: Niemeyer, 1956); Medard Boss, *Meaning and Form of Sexual Perversions* (New York: Grune and Stratton, 1949); *Der Traum und seine Auslegung* (Bern: Hans Huber, 1953); *The Analysis of Dreams* (New York: Philosophical Library, 1958); "Dreaming and the Dreamed in the Daseinsanalytic Way of Seeing," in *Soundings. An Interdisciplinary Journal*, 60 (1977), 236-263. Cf. also the publications listed in note I of this essay.

8 Ludwig Binswanger, "The Existential Analytic School of Thought," in R. May, E. Angel, H. F. Ellenberger, eds., *Existence. A New Dimension in Psychiatry and Psychology* (New York: Basic Books, 1960), 191-212, pp. 200ff.; *Ausgewählte Vorträge und Aufsätze*, vol. II, pp. 308-362.

9 Cf. Medard Boss, "Daseinsanalytic Re-evaluation of the Basic Conceptions of Psychoanalytic Theory," in *Psychoanalysis and Daseinsanalysis*, pp. 75-129; Ludwig Binswanger, "Freuds Auffassung des Menschen im Lichte der Anthropologie," in *Ausgewählte Vorträge und Aufsätze*, vol. I, pp. 159-189; Paul Ricoeur, *Freud and Philosophy. An Essay in Interpretation*, trans. D. Savage (New Haven: Yale University Press, 1970). pp. 59-167, and passim.

10 Paul Ricoeur, *op. cit.*, pp. 65-67.

11 S. Freud, *The Origins of Psychoanalysis*, trans. E. Mosbacher, J. Strachey (New York: Basic Books, 1954), 355-455, p. 355.

12 S. Freud, *These Eventful Years*, 2 vols. (London: Hogarth Press, 1924), vol. II, p. 515; *Autobiography* (New York: W.W. Norton, 1935), p. 61; "Beyond the Pleasure Principle," in *Standard Edition* (London: Hogarth Press, 1953ff.), vol. XVIII, p. 60; cf. Medard Boss, *op. cit.*, p. 75.

13 S. Freud, *The Interpretation of Dreams, Standard Edition*, vol. V, pp. 536-538.

14 *Ibid.*, p. 598.

15 *Ibid.*, p. 537.

16 *Ibid.*, pp. 598, 605.

17 *Ibid.*, pp. 596-597.

18 *Standard Edition*, vol. IV, p. 96.

19 Paul Ricoeur, *op. cit.*, p. 92.

20 S. Freud, *The Interpretation of Dreams, Standard Edition*, vol. V, pp. 536-549, 564-572, 598-608.

21 *Ibid.*, p. 537.

22 Paul Ricoeur, *op. cit.*, p. 107.

23 S. Freud. *op. cit.*, p. 610.

24 *Ibid.*, p. 602.

25 Paul Ricoeur, *op cit.*, p. 115.

26 S. Freud, *A General Introduction to Psychoanalysis* (Garden City: Doubleday, 1943), pp. 38, 251.

27 Medard Boss, *op. cit.*, pp. 85-86.

28 S. Freud, *The Interpretation of Dreams*, p. 613.

29 *Ibid.*, pp. 494-495.

30 *Ibid.*, pp. 536-537. Cf. Medard Boss, *op. cit.*, pp. 86-87.

31 Cf. S. Freud, "Papers on Metapsychology," *Standard Edition*, vol. XIV. Freud had originally planned to write a series of twelve papers to be published under the title *Preliminaries to a Metapsychology* (*SE*, vol. XIV, pp. 105-107). Vol. XIV of the *Standard Edition* contains 5 of these papers, including "The Unconscious," and "A Metapsychological Supplement to the Theory of Dreams."

32 S. Freud, *The Ego and the Id* (London: Hogarth Press, 1957), p. 10.

33 Medard Boss, *op. cit.*, p. 87; cf. S. Freud, *The Ego and the Id*, pp. 7-88.

34 S. Freud, "A Note on the Unconscious in Psychoanalysis," in *Standard Edition*, vol. XII, 250-266, p. 266.

35 *Ibid.*

36 Paul Ricoeur, *op. cit.*, pp. 117-119.

37 *Ibid.*, pp. 149-150.

38 Medard Boss, *op. cit.*, p. 88.

39 S. Freud, *New Introductory Lectures*, in *Standard Edition*, vol. XXII, p. 73; cf. Paul Ricoeur, *op. cit.*, pp. 443-444, 221.

40 S. Freud, "The Unconscious," *Standard Edition*, vol. XIV, pp. 166-167.

41 *Ibid.*, p. 167.

42 R. May, E. Angel, H. F. Ellenberger, eds., *Existence*, pp. 237-364, p. 326.

43 Paul Ricoeur, *op. cit.*, p. 438.

44 *Existence*, pp. 326-327.

45 Binswanger, *Ausgewählte Vorträge und Aufsätze*, vol. II, p. 299.

46 Cf. J. Needleman, *op. cit.*, p. 100.

47 William J. Richardson, *loc. cit.*

48 *Ibid.*, p. 273.

49 *Ibid.*, p. 273.

50 *Ibid.*, p. 274.

51 *Ibid.*, p. 274.

52 *Ibid.*, p. 280; cf. 279-280.

53 Medard Boss, *Psychoanalysis and Daseinsanalysis*, p. 89. Cf. Martin Heidegger, *Being and Time*, trans. J. Macquarrie and E. Robinson, (London: SCM Press, 1962), pp. 244-256, 86-90, and passim.

54 S. Freud, *The Ego and the Id*, pp. 19-20; cf. p. 15.

55 S. Freud, *The Interpretation of Dreams*, pp. 615-616.

56 S. Freud, *The Ego and the Id*, pp. 20ff.

57 S. Freud, "From the History of an Infantile Neurosis," in *Standard Edition*, vol. XVII, pp. 104-105; cf. *A General Introduction to Psychoanalysis*, p. 93.

58 Medard Boss, *op. cit.*, pp. 90-91.

59 *Ibid.*, p. 92.

60 *Ibid.*, p. 93.

61 *Ibid.*

62 Martin Heidegger, *op. cit.*, p. 89.

63 Medard Boss, *op. cit.*, pp. 93-101.

64 Paul Ricoeur, *op. cit.*, pp. 86, 155, 163, 312, and passim.

65 S. Freud, "The Unconscious," in *Standard Edition*, vol. XIV, p. 177; cf. Paul Ricoeur, *op. cit.*, pp. 430-439.

66 E. Straus, *Phenomenological Psychology. Selected Papers* (New York: Basic Books, 1966), Part II.

Befindlichkeit:[1] Heidegger and the Philosophy of Psychology

EUGENE T. GENDLIN

In this paper I will outline Heidegger's basic conception of the human feeling capacity and try to show the important implications of his conception. A new word is also needed because the usual way people think about "feeling" is greatly changed in Heidegger's way of thinking.

I will first offer a round delineation of Heidegger's concept in my own words, along with some discussion of the relation between philosophy and psychology. This will enable the reader to understand the relevance of what I will next present: an excerpt and some observations from psychotherapy, and why a new concept is needed in psychological theory. A few remarks that are again on the philosophical level will conclude my preliminaries.

I will then present Heidegger in his own words (Section II.).

In this way I will give its application to psychology before I present Heidegger's conception itself in detail. I would like the reader to see the lack of the needed concept, indeed, to become hungry for it, to see where it is needed and what its outlines have to be. Then, after I present Heidegger, I will go on to further application in the more usual order.

I. INTRODUCTION TO *BEFINDLICHKEIT*

Befindlichkeit is among the most frequently misunderstood concepts in Heidegger's work. Certainly it is the most important among those that are frequently misunderstood. *Befindlichkeit* is one of Heidegger's three basic parameters of human existence (*Existenziale*) which are involved in most of his other conceptions. The other two basic parameters are understanding and speech. The three are inherently interrelated so that one can only understand them together. In outlining them we will therefore go to the core of Heidegger's philosophy.

Heidegger says that *Befindlichkeit* refers to what is ordinarily called "being in a mood," and also what is called "feeling" and "affect." But Heidegger offers a radically different way of thinking about this ordinary experience. *Befindlichkeit* refers to the kind of beings that humans are, that aspect of these beings which makes for them having moods, feelings, or affects.

But Heidegger thinks about this human being in a very different way than most people do, and so he also thinks about mood and feeling very differently.

Let me give a rough initial impression of Heidegger's very different basic conception, *Befindlichkeit*.

43

Eugene T. Gendlin

In German a common way of asking "How are you?" is "Wie befinden Sie sich?" This literally says "How do you find yourself?" One can also say to a sick person "Wie ist Ihr Befinden?" ("How do you feel?") The same form can also be used to say that something or someone is situated somewhere, or in some way. For example, one can say, "The White House *finds itself* in Washington, D.C.," or "I find myself in Chicago," or "I find myself in happy circumstances."[2]

"Sich befinden" (finding oneself) thus has three allusions: The reflexivity of finding oneself; feeling; and being situated. All three are caught in the ordinary phrase, "How are you?" That refers to how you feel but also to how things are going for you and what sort of situation you find yourself in. To answer the question you must find yourself, find how you already are. And when you do, you find yourself amidst the circumstances of your living.

Heidegger coined a clumsy noun from the German colloquial forms. To translate it, let us not look for an existing noun in English, since he found none in German. His noun is like "how-are-you-ness" or perhaps "self-finding."

The reason for being careful about these allusions, and for keeping his sense of the word, is because *Befindlichkeit* is a new conception and cannot be rendered in old ones.

To view feelings, affects, and moods as *Befindlichkeit* differs from the usual view in the following ways:

1. Heidegger's concept denotes how *we sense ourselves in situations*. Whereas feeling is usually thought of as something inward, Heidegger's concept refers to something both inward and outward, but before a split between inside and outside has been made.

We are always situated, in situations, in the world, in a context, living in a certain way *with others*, trying to achieve this and avoid that.

A mood is not just internal, it is this living in the world. We sense how we find ourselves, and we find ourselves in situations.

Americans might say that "Befindlichkeit" is an "interactional" concept, rather than an "intrapsychic" one. But it is both and exists before the distinction is made. "Interaction" is also inaccurate for another reason. It assumes that first there are two, and only then is there a relation between them.

For Heidegger, humans *are* their living in the world with others. Humans are livings-in, and livings-with.

2. A second difference from the usual conception of "feeling" lies in this: *Befindlichkeit* always already has *its own understanding*. (Here is Heidegger's second basic parameter of human existence: "understanding.") We may not know what the mood is about, we may not even be specifically

44

aware of our mood, nevertheless there is an understanding of our living in that mood. It is no merely internal state or reaction, no mere coloring or accompaniment to what is happening. We have lived and acted in certain ways for certain purposes and strivings and all this is going well or badly, but certainly it is going in some intricate way. How we are faring in these intricacies is in our mood. We may not know that in a cognitive way at all; it is in the mood nevertheless, implicitly.

This understanding is active; it is not merely a perception or reception of what is happening to us. We don't come into situations as if they were mere facts, independent of us. We have had some part in getting ourselves into these situations, in making the efforts in response to which these are now the facts, the difficulties, the possibilities, and the mood has the implicit "understanding" of all that, because this understanding was inherent already in how we lived all that, in an active way.

3. This understanding is *implicit*, not cognitive in the usual sense. It differs from cognition in several ways: It is sensed or felt, rather than thought—and it may not even be sensed or felt directly with attention. It is not made of separable cognitive units or any definable units. When you are asked, "How are you?" you don't find only recognizables, but always also an implicit complexity. Certainly one can reflect and interpret, but that will be another, further step.

4. Heidegger says that speech is always already involved in any feeling or mood, indeed in any human experience. Speech is the articulation of understanding, but this articulation doesn't first happen when we try to say what we feel. Just as *Befindlichkeit* always already has its understanding, so also does it always already have its spoken articulation. This doesn't at all mean that there is always a way to say what one lives in words. But there are always speakings, with each other, and listening to each other, involved in any situation, and implicit in any living. Hearing each other, being open to each other's speech, is part of what we *are*, the living we *are*. And so it is always already involved in our living, whatever we may then actually say or not say.

So we see that, although Heidegger is talking about the ordinary experience of feelings, affects, or moods, he has given that experience a very different structure. We sense ourselves living in situations with others, with an implicit understanding of what we are doing and with communication between us always already involved. A feeling is all that. Our new conception of feeling has the structure I just outlined.

A Note on the Relation of Philosophy and Psychology

Certainly there is a difference between the theoretical structure of the concept of feeling, and a mere pointing to a feeling. *Befindlichkeit* names the structure, "feeling," "affect," or "mood," and these words can continue to name the ordinary event they always have. But the difference between philosophy and psychology is something else, not the difference between something and theory about it. After all, there is theory in psychology, too.

Philosophical discussion moves on a level from which all or many of the sciences are affected simultaneously. Philosophical discussion may, at some point, seem to be about people and sound like psychology, or about society and sound like sociology, or about matter and energy and sound like physics. But not only the science which seems to be the topic, rather also many others, will be altered by a philosophical discussion. I will illustrate this shortly, in order to be clear.

Philosophy moves on a different level than science. One can say that it is one level more abstract than science. I will say this first in terms of kinds of concepts, and then in terms of kinds of beings, as Heidegger does.

A philosophy examines and sometimes alters *basic* conceptions. That is why there is no way to explain a basic conception in terms of other, more familiar ones. One can grasp a basic conception only by grasping it. It is a new conceptual structure, a new pattern. What I mean here by "basic" gets at the difference between philosophy and any science, and also the usefulness of philosophy for science. Let me be more specific.

Most people, scientists and others, do not usually think about what *kind* of concept they are using. The most current *kind* is modeled on ordinary things like stones. A stone can be moved from one place to another without changing. It is still the same stone, now in a different spot. A thing like a stone may relate to other things, of course; for example, it may hit and break a porcelain pitcher. But these relations are external and additional to what the stone is. Whether it breaks a pitcher or not, even if it just sits in one spot, it is a stone. It would not be usual to say that a stone *is* pitcher-breaking, or window-smashing, or any such interaction.

Without being aware of it or capable of examining it (for then they would be engaged in philosophy), scientists currently tend to use this *kind* of concept.

An "electron," for example, is a thing-like concept of this kind. In one puzzling experiment, one electron seems to go through two different slits in two different locations. While an electron differs from a stone in many ways, of course, the same kind of concept is involved in how both are thought of. An electron must be in one place or another, not both. Similarly, there is a puzzle in biology why given well-defined molecules suddenly assume highly important additional powers when in the company of certain other molecules in a certain tissue. As a thing with its own traits, regardless of anything else (as this kind of concept renders everything), this is not understandable. The molecule cannot *be* its different interactions, it has to *be* with certain traits all its own, and only with these is it thought to interact.

HEIDEGGER & THE PHILOSOPHY OF PSYCHOLOGY

Psychologists, for example, use concepts like "self," "ego," "perception," "personal interaction," "feeling" or "affect," usually formulated in thing-like kinds of concepts. A self or an ego is like a thing in the person. A person is a larger thing in which the ego or self, as a smaller thing, resides like a stone in a box. Perception is a stimulus-thing making a representation-thing inside the box. Personal interaction is a relation between two such boxes, each separate before they interact, like a stone and a pitcher. Feelings or affects are little things inside the box, sometimes within the self and sometimes in the rest of the box. People supposedly feel these inside feeling things directly, but can feel other people only by imagining an analogy with their own feelings.

Heidegger brings us an entirely different *kind* of concept. Too roughly, I could say it is of a being that *is* its relating. But I say this roughly, and it is only for a simple contrast with the above caricature of the current kind. What I wish to convey is the level of discussion, not a discussion of this topic or that, but of *kinds* of concepts. I would like to bring home the importance of differences in kinds of concepts for all sciences.

Note that it must have implications for any science to develop a different kind of concept, for example, some of Heidegger's concepts such as *Befindlichkeit*. It eliminates certain ways of making distinctions, and replaces them with others. In my simple four point rendition of *Befindlichkeit*, we saw how the concept precedes and eliminates the distinction between *inside and outside*, as well as between *self and others*. Similarly, it alters *affective/cognitive*. Later I will show how it also alters the distinctions we are used to in space and time: here/there, and past/present/future. We will want to see exactly how Heidegger refashions all this, we will want to see a sharp and clear alternative structure to the one being eliminated, but it is certainly clear already that such basic changes in kind of concept must affect any science, not just psychology.

Let me now make the same point in a more Heideggerian way. (Of course, it is then not literally exactly the same point.)

Heidegger's philosophy is ontology. He is not directly concerned with kinds of concepts, but with kinds of being. (Of course, that leads to kinds of concepts, too.)

A tool, for example, *is* in a different way than a stone *is*; they are different kinds of being. Even if I use a stone as a tool; already it has a being like that of a tool; it *is* in a different way: Now it lies ready-to-hand in my tool chest, and it *is-for*. It is for the use, to which its shape and weight fit it, for me. Now it is in a way that involves me and my activity. It is no longer in that way in which all of its being was just there, by itself. A tool *is* contextually; that is a different way to be.

People *are* different than either stones or tools. They live-in and live-with. They live-in a world they themselves define with their living-in.

47

People, too, *are* not inside their skins, but *are* their living-in the world and their living-with others.

(In my terms, what kind of a concept is "living-in" and "living-with"? We will want to see that as a clear and sharp conceptual structure.)

Heidegger calls the human being "Dasein" (being-here.) This is again an ordinary colloquial German word. "Das menschliche Dasein" means something like "the human condition" or "being human." As with *Befindlichkeit*, Heidegger uses all the allusions of the colloquial form, both of "being" and of "here."

Humans are not at all some things among others, as dead bodies might be. Humans are being-here, they *are* in a self-locating sense. A stone can be here for me, but not for itself. This "here" is in the world, in situations, and situations are always with-others.

When Heidegger discusses *Dasein*, he is not discussing only humans, but also everything else that is-for humans, or is accessible to humans. It lies in the nature of the human way of being that other beings *are* in relation to it. The stone may lie on the table, but the stone's kind of being *is* not an openness to something it lies on. A human observer positions stone and table in relation to each other in space and dynamics, but their being doesn't do that.

Therefore, how anything is studied in any science depends first upon the nature of humans as open to access to . . . whatever is studied. Mathematics is not just there, its units and series have to be constituted by Dasein. Physics isn't just there, human observation and measurement are certain specific modes of how humans *are* as generating time and space and things. The basic ontological structure of Dasein therefore alters how we basically conceive of anything else, if we first consider that structure of Dasein.

If we speak of *Befindlichkeit* not merely as something about humans, but as basic to the way humans are open to anything, much more than psychology is affected. A basic method results, in which inquiry articulates what is at first only sensed, found implicitly. One must not forget that, as if to begin with sharp conceptions. The beginning is always how we sense ourselves, find ourselves already with . . . whatever we study, in an implicitly "understood" way, in our living.

Whatever conceptions are developed, in any science, they need to be related back to the implicit lived understanding we already have of the topic, and need to be viewed as articulations of that. Much changes if one employs such a method.

The structural parameters of this kind of concept ("Dasein," "Befindlichkeit"), too, as I have already said, will importantly alter any science.

Both method and structural parameters will of course have important implications for psychology, among other sciences. Let me at last go into that now. Even so, I must ask my reader to follow me on both levels, philosophically as well as in psychology. For philosophy my discussion will be an example, an instance. For psychology it will be directly pertinent. Philosophically, notice the kind of concept, and kind of being. For psychology notice our need for this specific concept (not only the kind). Of course we are talking about the same human being, and the same aspect of that human being, the structure of its "finding itself" in a mood, affect or feeling. Philosophically, that is basic to how we *are* and anything else *is*. Only one of the implications of that is the kind of concepts we use, and one instance of this being, and this kind of concept, is in psychology.

Some Observations of Psychotherapy

During a psychotherapy interview, the patient quite often says something, then stops, senses inwardly for half a minute or a minute, then says: "No, what I said isn't quite right. I can't say how it feels, yet, but it's different than I said."

At such times it is quite clear that more than just thoughts and words are being worked with. If the patient had only thoughts and words, there would be nothing to check against, nothing to indicate that a statement that seemed right and true is, after all, not right. The statement may still be true, may still describe events, behavior, but the patient has something else there which is felt directly, and that cannot yet be said. Although the patient does not know what that is, it is definite enough to indicate with certainty that it is not . . . what the patient had just said it was.

The experience is somewhat analogous to forgetting someone's name. We then still have "a feel for" that name, which is quite sufficient to enable us to reject any number of other names. We know it isn't Smith or Jamison or Rostenkowsy, and we can also sense the specificity of exactly the name we seek. This specificity is in some sense "in" the "feel" of the name, which we have.

If we, as it were, touch that "feel" of the name over and over, "touch" it with our attention, it may suddenly "open," so that the name appears. Then there is an unmistakable tension-release, a relief in the body, one exhales a long breath, whew. . . . There is no doubt, then, that this was indeed the name one had forgotten. There is an unmistakable continuity between the erstwhile "feel" and this name.

The metaphoric language I am using is troublesome: the name is "in" the "feel," there is "continuity" between them, the "feel" "opens"; none of this is theoretically satisfying.

49

With Heidegger we could say that the name is part of the "understanding" that the *Befindlichkeit* has, our feeling not just of the name, but of all our living with that person.

Let me continue the example. We could have saved ourselves the trouble of remembering, and have picked any name, or perhaps the best-sounding name we can find. We could have insisted that that's the name, all right. After all, it is the best-sounding and most desirable name. Or, perhaps we might have found the name by matching a name to the person's presumed ancestry, cultural group, or for some other intellectual reason. We don't do that, because we know that that is not authentic remembering.

Everyone also knows the case when we are close, but not quite right. "It must be ____," we say, expressing our dissatisfaction and unease in that very phrase: "It must be." Although it sounds like necessary concluding, we have not really remembered.

In the following excerpt from a psychotherapy interview, the patient at each step senses that what she just said isn't right, although she cannot yet say what would be right.

It must also be noticed how different this process is from reasoning ("It must be . . ."). Once she is able to articulate what she senses, at each step, it makes perfect sense and we can think about it logically in a rational way. But the steps she actually takes differ from rational ones, though they are certainly not irrational.

What does seem irrational is the way in which each new step begins by contradicting the previous one. Each step says, "It's not what I just said, but rather. . . ." Once we hear what it is, then that too makes sense. But the steps are not the reasonable chain that can be constructed in retrospect, after we have heard her. If we examine what we have at one step, we cannot, from that, get by reasoning or inference to the next step.

The sensing between each step and the next corrects her and changes the direction in a way that could not have been known in advance.

She says:

"I'm late. I knew I would be. I have this magic way of saying 'It will be all right,' when I don't have any idea how. When I make a schedule or a plan I put more things in it than I could possibly get done. But I can't choose among them. I'm afraid of making the wrong choice, I guess."

There is some silence. Then she says:

"It's not about making a wrong choice. I don't know what that is."

More silence. Then:

"There's something there, like 'I want it all!' That's really childish, like kids wanting everything they see."

More silence.

"It's not wanting it all. It's not wanting what I'm supposed to want. My sister was the one that did all the right things. I couldn't do what she did, always fit in. I became the one that had secrets, and did the things that were dangerous and not supposed to be done. I still like to endanger myself, go out with men where I can tell it won't be nice. It's an excitement, like violence, it takes over your whole mind. Living dangerously. That's what that wanting is."

More silence.

"Well, I don't really want that. When I think of them telling us how we're supposed to be, then I get this feeling of wanting that violence and excitement. But, if I just think, well, what would I like, then I don't want that stuff."

In this example one can see what I call "content mutation."[3] First, the content is why she is late and how unrealistic her scheduling is. It seems to be about a fear of making wrong choices. Then it isn't that at all, but a childish wanting everything. Then it isn't a childish wish for everything, but a wish for excitement and danger, violence. Finally, it is a reaction to authority beyond which a different wanting emerges.

In retrospect the steps can make a chain of thought, but moving forward each step comes by contradicting the previous one. What does this contradicting? It is the "sensing" that happens during the silences between. She has the "feel" of it, and this feel is each time different than what she has said.

This patient took only a few minutes for this process. The same kind of process, often more slowly, is found in any psychotherapy when it is effective at all. (I say this on the basis of research findings I shall cite shortly.)

Psychological Theory — Why a New Concept is Needed

Actually, the new kind of concept Heidegger makes possible is needed in many instances in psychology. I will pursue only the concept of "feeling" or "affect" and show how it needs to be restructured.

I will follow the same four points I presented before, now in relation to our psychotherapy excerpt.

1. She consults a feeling between her statements, yet this feeling is of how she has been planning, living, choosing men and getting into situations. Although the feeling seems "internal" as she sits there, silently, it is of her living in the situations in which she finds herself, and of course with other people. A feeling must be thought of both as sensed and as in the world.

2. She begins with a cognition ("I must be afraid of making wrong choices."), but the feeling has its own understanding. From the feeling

emerges something ("I want it all") which seems childish to her. The feeling again has its own understanding (desire to "live dangerously"). She now has the cognition that she wants danger. Again, the feeling has its own understanding (It's in relation to "them telling us how we're supposed to be."). A feeling must be thought of as containing its own understanding of how one is living.

3. A feeling's understanding or meaning is implicit, first in the sense that it may not yet be known at all. Secondly, the meaning is implicit in a more inherent respect, implicit in that it is never quite equal to any cognitive units. There is always more to go. Thirdly, it is a wholistic complexity: the feeling isn't just about being late, not just about scheduling, not just about choices, not just about men, nor these as separated things that happen to be together. Rather, there is a complex texture. Even in our short excerpt one can see how much was implicit in the feeling of—what seemed to be only—her chagrin at being late.

We also see (to be discussed later) the "lifting out" character of how cognitions are related to the feeling: at each step something is lifted out that is then both felt and cognized.

Furthermore, in the movement from implicit to being lifted out, the feeling itself changes. If it were not for this change, psychotherapy would not be effective. People would come to know much about themselves, but would not change. When psychotherapy is done by mere inferences, people indeed don't change. The felt understanding by which they live remains the same, and inarticulate. They seem to know why they act as they do, but not how to be different. In contrast, when feeling[4] (as complex texture) leads to this "lifting out," there is a directly felt changing of the feeling at each step. In our excerpt this is most visible at the last step, but that would not have been reached had the previous steps not each made its change in the feeling.

Thus feeling must be understood as *implicitly* meaningful, and as changing when there are steps of "lifting out," steps of explication or articulation. *To articulate is to live further.* To go *back* into how one *has been* living is a *forward-moving* step.

4. The feeling knows how to speak and demands just the right words. The feeling, more exactly, is sufficient to bring the words to the person's speech. We can see that, if we compare what her next steps are, with what they would have been, had she pursued the implications of what she first said. No logic could have led her as she did in fact proceed.

We don't want to think that the words were *in* the feeling in the sense that pebbles are *in* a box. How language relates to feeling and living needs re-thinking. But it is clear that just as in living she uses words as an inherent part of living, so also does the feeling-understanding already have the power to guide *speech*, even though, at first it is only felt.

A series of research studies[5] has shown that patients who engage in the kind of steps I described are successful in psychotherapy, while those who usually do not work in this way fail. Success is sometimes measured by patient and therapist judgment after the therapy is over, sometimes by psychometric tests given before and after therapy.

How was it possible to *measure* the degree to which patients engage in this process? It turns out to be quite measurable. Patients are highly consistent in how they approach psychotherapy. Two four minute segments from a tape-recorded interview are sufficient to give the same result as an analysis of whole hours. It is possible to pick out phrasings such as "I don't know what *that* is," as in our excerpt, statements that refer to something directly sensed but not known in a sharp cognitive way. It is noticeable that this kind of phrasing occurs between two quite different versions of content. There are also other signs, such as metaphoric language, often very original, that would have no meaning at all if it did not refer to what is sensed but not yet capable of being thought in usual terms. Raters of such tape-recorded segments arrive at reliable agreements. These scores correlate with the patient's, the therapist's, and the test's evaluation of outcome.

The older theories are remarkably poor for thinking about this observed behavior in psychotherapy. They are theories of what, rather than how—theories of what is supposedly *in* people, not theories about how the process I have described leads to change.

It is known that there is more *knowledge* in the person, somehow, than the person consciously possesses, but this is viewed as the "unconscious," a puzzling realm of internal entities. We have seen, however, that it is quite conscious and awarely felt or sensed, both while living and when attending to feeling.

It is known that complex implications and connections exist "beneath" any simple human event, but these are viewed as sharp and defined entities that are just like cognitions, only outside awareness. We have seen, however, that there is an implicit texture, a wholistic living.

It is thought that "feelings" are important for psychotherapy, but the word is taken to mean emotions. We need a new word that will distinguish emotions from what I call "felt sense," feelings as sensed complexity. Above all, we need a new concept! Really, such a new concept for feeling would also require changing most of the related concepts in our theories.

What matters most in psychotherapy is "feeling" in the sense of being unclear and sensing an implicit complexity, a wholistic sense of what one is working on. This can be very quietly sensed, or it may be very emotional, but that is not the crucial question at all.

Emotions—recognizable joy, sadness, or anger—any of these may be part of such sensing, or it may not. Even when it is, the felt sense is more complex and less well known than such a familiar emotion.

Explicit cognitions emerge from a felt sense, but this is not to say that they were "in there," in explicit form, in a layer beneath. An implicit understanding sensed in living, and its implicit capacity for speech, must be understood as living-in-context.

We need a new conceptual pattern for our concept of "felt sense," one which has the more basic unity preceding the inner/outer split, the self/other split, the affect/cognition split, and the acting/speaking split.

Philosophical Note

Human beings *are* with an implicit felt understanding, that is to say, they *are* "ontologically" because this is an understanding of being—of their own being and the being of others, things, and tools involved in their own being-with and being-in.

Heidegger uses the word "ontic" for ordinary assertions of anything, and the word "ontological" for the understanding of the kind of being of anything. Thus, to say that I have a felt sense, now, of what I want to say, is an ontic statement. In contrast, to explicate the structure of how there is such an implicit sense of what I may later say at length, that would be ontology.

It needs to be clear that, although we distinguished the philosophical and ontological level from the ontic (for example, psychology), the two are about the same world, the same things, the same beings. One is an account of the basic structure of the other. If they were not about the same beings, there would have to be a separate realm of beings, just for philosophy to be about!

While Heidegger, when delineating *Befindlichkeit*, speaks of the basic structure of the human being-in-the-world, and thus of the world, and of any subject-matter of any science insofar as humans have access to it, this *Befindlichkeit* is nevertheless the same feeling or sensing studied in psychology.

This is so doubly. First, it is so because the "ontic" and the "ontological" are two ways of considering the same being. Secondly, it is so especially because humans *are* inherently ontological. While one seems only to understand some particular living one is doing, one is always implicitly understanding one's own manner of being—as being human, that is to say, as being-in-the-world, always already in the midst of situations, with *how one is* quite open to events and in play, in the living itself as ongoing.

Heidegger says humans are "pre-ontological" (B&T 12), insofar as this understanding of one's way of being is implicit, rather than articulated.

Later I will give many implications that follow if we restructure the psychological concepts.

To be sure, Heidegger, whom we will now let speak in his own words, speaks on the philosophical level. As I said earlier, implications follow not just for psychology, but for any science, and for life. But it will also be immediately clear from what Heidegger says, how—and exactly how—we might restructure theoretical concepts in psychology, especially the concept of feeling or affect.

It is an error to make of *Befindlichkeit* something different than the way humans are feelingly, as if in addition to that there were some other, mysterious, purely philosophical something. *Befindlichkeit* has been little understood just because as a merely abstract principle it makes no sense. Heidegger is somehow not believed, when he flatly insists that he is talking about how we live, and calling our attention to what we can directly sense. Then he is made to sound abstract and ununderstandable.

Not only does psychology and any science study the same being that ontology clarifies, also for ontology itself it is vital to begin with "Befindliches," with what is livingly sensed directly—and every statement of ontology lifts out something we can then directly sense, something which we already understood before in a pre-ontological way.

To understand Heidegger experientially (if I may call it that) is not at all to reduce ontology to psychology, it is the only way to do ontology, as he insists. The implications of so understanding him are of course much wider than just for psychology. To understand him experientially is to understand the inherent relation between living, feeling, understanding, and cognitions of any kind.

II. HEIDEGGER ON *BEFINDLICHKEIT,* UNDERSTANDING AND SPEECH

What we indicate *ontologically* by the term "Befindlichkeit" is *ontically* most familiar: the mood, or being moody. (134)[6]

The different modes of *Befindlichkeit* . . . have long been well-known ontically under the terms 'affects' and 'feelings'. . . . (138)

Dasein is always in some mood. A pallid, flat being out of sorts . . . is far from being nothing at all . . . to be has become a manifest burden. One does not *know* why. (134)

Befindlichkeit has always already disclosed one's being-in-the-world as a whole. . . . (137)

The possibilities of disclosure which belong to cognition reach far too short a way compared with the original and basic disclosure of moods. (134)

Even if Dasein is 'assured' in its belief . . . if in rational enlightenment it supposes itself to know . . . all this counts for nothing as against the phenomenal facts of the case. . . . (136)

So we see the difference between how mood discloses the whole of one's being in the world, and how the mood stays "phenomenally," regardless of what one might say to the contrary. What one believes "counts for nothing" as the mood goes right on being what it is. The mood discloses much more fully than one knows. Let us now see how this disclosing and its understanding differs from ordinary cognition.

> Disclosed does not mean known as such and such. (134)
> *Befindlichkeit* always has its understanding, even if only in holding it down. Understanding is always moody. (142)
> In *Befindlichkeit* Dasein . . . has always already found itself, not in the sense of . . . perceiving itself, rather as finding itself moody. (135)
> Understanding is never free-floating, rather always *befindliches*. (339)
> (There is) . . . an existential fundamental connection between *Befindlichkeit* and understanding. (340)

We must now see how Heidegger delineates this "being-in-the-world" which is disclosed in a mood, feeling, or affect. How is it that people *are* the being-in-the-world?

> In clarifying being-in-the-world we have shown that a bare subject without a world . . . never is, and is never given. And so, in the end, an isolated 'I' without others is just as far from being . . . ever given. The others are always already here with us in our being-in-the-world. (116)
> The human being's 'substance' is not spirit as a synthesis of soul and body; it is rather existence. (117)
> The world of Dasein is a with-world (*Mitwelt*). Being-in is being-with others. (118)
> And even when Dasein explicitly addresses itself as 'I, here', . . . this 'I, here' does not mean a certain special point of an I-thing; rather, it understands itself as a being-in, in terms of the overthere of the world. (119)

Humans are called "*Dasein*," which means being-*here*. This *here* understands itself as a being-*in* the world in relation to the *overthere* of the world. Humans aren't just in space, as if space were just given. The being-here in relation to the overthere generates being-in-the-world. It is one structure, one pattern. And this is also the structure of feeling:

> In being in a mood . . . the pure 'that it is' shows itself, the where-from and where-to remain in the dark . . . in everyday life the human does not 'give in' . . . to moods, that is to say, does not go after their disclosing. (134-135)
> Mood discloses in the manner of turning toward, or turning away from one's own Dasein. The bringing before the 'that it is' . . . may be authentically revealing or inauthentically covering up. . . . (340)
> Dasein, as essentially *befindliches*, has always already got itself into possibilities. . . . But this means Dasein is . . . through and through . . . possibility. (144)

Authenticity requires this bringing oneself before how one already is, how one is being-here as disclosed in a mood. Without going after what the mood discloses one cannot be authentic. Authenticity is fundamentally grounded in *Befindlichkeit* and its understanding, and requires bringing oneself before how one is disclosed in the mood.

Being-here (that is to say, the human being) *is* the possibilities insofar as it is *befindliches*. As we will see now, one's authentic possibilities are only those disclosed in *Befindlichkeit*, for only *Befindlichkeit* and its implicit understanding (which it always already has) discloses how we are thrown into the situations in which we find ourselves (into which we have lived ourselves).

Befindlichkeit always discloses being-in-the-world "as a whole," and the familiar emotions are, for Heidegger, "determined modes" of *Befindlichkeit*. He discusses fear and anxiety. Fear is inauthentic because we attribute the cause to the external world. Anxiety is authentic because it brings us before our own being, and before the essential nature of our own being, its unsubstantial character.

> . . . the phenomenon of the *Befindlichkeit* of Dasein shall be more concretely demonstrated in the determined mode of fear. (140)
>
> In what way is anxiety a distinctive *Befindlichkeit*? How, in it, is Dasein brought before itself through its own being . . . . (184)
>
> Anxiety arises out of the being-in-the-world as thrown being toward death. (344)
>
> The insignificance of the world, disclosed in anxiety, reveals the nullity of the things of our concerns, or in other words the impossibility of projecting oneself (*sichentwerfen*) on a can-be that is primarily founded in the things of our concerns. (343)
>
> Fear has its occasion in being concerned with the world. Anxiety, in contrast, arises out of Dasein itself. . . . Anxiety frees *from* possibilities that are nullities, and enables becoming free *for* authentic ones. (344)

Anxiety will thus be part (but only part)[7] of authentic action, since the authentic possibilities will still be in the world. If anxiety were all there is to authentic *Befindlichkeit*, death would be the only authentic action. But one "lives toward death" in a way that frees for authentic action *in the world. Anxiety is only one essential part of authentic action*, because it is always only one specific aspect of the wholistic *Befindlichkeit*:

> . . . fear and anxiety never 'occur' isolatedly in the 'stream of experiencing'; rather, they always determine an understanding, or, determine themselves from such an understanding. (344)

Understanding and *Befindlichkeit* are "equally original" and interlocked together.

> Understanding is never free-floating, rather always *befindliches*. The here is always disclosed equally originally through mood. . . . (339)

Understanding sketches out possibilities, or one can say (even in English) it "throws out" possibilities, as one throws out suggestions. The

German word "entwerfen" means to sketch, to outline. Part of that word is "werfen" which means throwing. As we saw before:

> Dasein, as essentially *befindliches* has always already got itself into possibilities. . . . But this means Dasein is . . . through and through thrown possibility. (144)

Let us now look more exactly at this "throwing"[8] of possibilities, and the "thrown" nature of humans. It is "moody understanding," or *"befindliches* understanding," which "throws" the possibilities, and as *Befindlichkeit*, we are always already "thrown."

> As thrown, Dasein is thrown into the kind of being which we call 'throwing out' (*Entwerfen*). (145)
>
> Dasein is not something . . . which as an addition also possesses that it can be something; rather, it is primarily being-possible. (143)
>
> Understanding inherently has the existential structure we call *throwing out* (*Entwurf*). (145)
>
> The character of understanding as throwing constitutes the being-in-the-world . . . as the here of a can-be (*Seinkönnen*). (145)
>
> Dasein is always more than it factually is . . . on the ground of . . . being constituted through throwing. (145)

One is always already engaged, in the midst of trying something, striving for this or avoiding that, going about something. If we ask, "What are you doing?" it is never just the actual. We are trying to bring about this, or going to that, or making this point or trying to achieve something that is not yet. But this being possible, this way we are the possibilities, is not conscious planning, neither is it unconscious. It is implicit.

> Throwing (throwing out possibilities, *Entwerfen*) has nothing to do with relating oneself to a thought-through plan. . . . The sketch character of understanding does not grasp the possibility thematically, . . . such (thematic) grasping would deprive the sketching precisely of its character as possible, and would reduce it to a given intended content. . . . (145)

Heidegger doesn't mean by possibility and sketching-throwing a mere not-yet, that is otherwise fully and actually known. Rather, it is the understanding which mood always has, the implicitly lived understanding which is this possibility-sketching. We "know" what we are about, how we came into the situation, but we don't "know" it in a sharp way, in the kind of "cognition" that is cut off from "affect." We know it, rather, in that way in which a mood always already has its understanding, and in which understanding (as Heidegger defines it) is always moody.

We have seen that in Heidegger's conception the person is not an "I-thing," but a being-in-the-world. But have we lost the person thereby? Is this being-in-the-world not just an extraverted, internally empty way of being only in relation? Heidegger says that this losing oneself in the world is indeed a constant pitfall. To be authentically, we must continually bring ourselves back from being dispersed.

It is in how we bring ourselves back that the authentic essential nature of the self becomes clear.

Authenticity has been largely misunderstood, in Heidegger's philosophy, just because *Befindlichkeit* has not been understood. Authenticity is frequently taken to mean nothing more than living by one's own originative possibility-sketching, rather than living by what the world says and the possibilities it defines. While this is true of authenticity, it lacks the essence. One could be merely capricious and still fit such a definition. Also, one could live oblivious to much of one's relations to others, and still fit the definition of authenticity. But Heidegger defines authenticity much more exactly, and his definition depends upon *Befindlichkeit*.

As we grasp his definition of authenticity, we will also understand feeling or *Befindlichkeit* much better. His conception of the person will emerge much more basically.

A human being is not a what:

> In understanding . . . the can-be is no what; rather, it is the being as existing. (143)
> We designate 'knowlege of the self' . . . not as a perceptual . . . viewing of a self-point, rather an understandingly grasping of the full disclosedness of being-in-the-world *through* its essential parameters, *on through* them. (146)

A human self is not a thing but a process, and a "self" is not a what, but a reflexive structure, the phrasing of which always requires that the word "self" be used twice. In bringing oneself before oneself (or in covering up), the human self *is*. The self is not, like a point *is*.

> Existing being sights "itself" only so far as it becomes transparent to itself as the constituting aspects of its existence, equally in its being-alongside the world and its being-with others. (146)

But how does this being, which *is* being-in-the-world, which *is* the sketching of possibilities that are in the world . . . how does it bring itself back from the world, how does it bring itself to itself?

Human beings cannot help being-in-the-world, for that is what they are. But we can continuously bring ourselves back from being lost in the possibilities themselves. But to do this is much different than just sketching out more possibilities. Then we would only be lost in those instead of these.

We are not the possibilities themselves, we are the sketching, the throwing, and also the being-thrown. Since we are the throwing and the being thrown, we are lost as soon as we identify with the possibilities themselves.

> And only *because* Dasein (being-here) is its here understandingly, *can* it disperse and mistake itself. (144)

Since "understanding" means throwing out possibilities, and being this throwing, therefore it is possible to be lost in the possibilities.

> And insofar as understanding is *befindliches* . . . Dasein has always already dispersed and mistaken itself. (144)

The mood is the possibilities we already are, as being thrown into them.

> . . . *Befindlichkeit* and understanding . . . characterize the original disclosedness of being-in-the-world. In the way of having a mood Dasein 'sees' possibilities from out of which it is. In the sketching disclosing of such possibilities it is always already in a mood. (148)

"Always already." The possibilities we are, are always already in the mood, and only in the mood are they seen, or known. But the mood, *Befindlichkeit*, has a special power. It brings the being-here before itself, it finds itself.

> Being in a mood brings Dasein *before* its thrownness, in such a way, however, that the thrownness is not recognized as such, but rather is much more originally disclosed in the 'how one is.' (340)

A special time relation is generated here. By going back to retrieve oneself one goes forward authentically.

We saw earlier how Heidegger views space not as a geometric container in which we happen to be, but as generated by the human being-here in relation to a there. Now we also see a new time-relation emerging, not the linear one thing after another, but a going back that is also a going forward, and the only authentic way of going forward.

All three times, past, present, and future are together, but not just merged. We must see the exact, sharp structure of their relations. Although the three are together, "understanding" grounds primarily in the future, as possibility.

> *Befindlichkeit* . . . temporalizes itself *primarily* in the having-been. (340)

Being moody, we saw, *brings Dasein before* its thrownness.

> The bringing before . . . becomes possible only if Dasein's being constantly *is* as having-been. (340)

That humans exist as having-been is just as true, whether we bring ourselves before it or not, since we *are* moody, we already are the having-been, we are it in the "how we are," as we just saw above. Heidegger says that this human way of existing as having-been

60

> . . . enables the self-finding (*Sich-finden*) in the manner of being *befindlich*. (340)

> The basic existential character of mood is a *bringing back to*. . . . (340)

> The authentic coming-toward-itself . . . is a coming back to the ownmost thrown self . . . (this) enables Dasein resolutely to take over that being which it already is. (339)

How is this "coming back" or "bringing back" of *Befindlichkeit* related to the sketching-forward of "understanding"? The exact relation of this "past" of the moody having-been, and the "future" of understanding, makes the authentic present. Let us see exactly how this is structured:

> The understanding is . . . primarily future . . . but equally originally determined through having-been and presentness. (337)
>
> In running ahead, Dasein brings (*holt*) itself again (*wieder*) forward into its own can-be. The authentic *being* the having-been we call retrieval. (*Wiederholung*) (339)[9]
>
> In resoluteness the present is . . . brought back from distraction with the objects . . . (and) held in the future and in having-been. (This is) the authentic present. (338)

Past, present, and future are thus not merely serial, as usually viewed, as if they were positions in a line. Instead, each involves the others, and they make one structure together.

Going back is also bringing before oneself. One goes back to "how one is," how one is already existing. One goes back to it, it is always already. It is a having-been. Only in so doing does one retrieve one's authentic possibility-sketching, so that a present is made in which one is ready to act authentically.

Mere caprices, however they may originate from me alone, are not authentic because they don't arise from the being I already am. I must take this being over. If I leave it covered, nevertheless, I am that existing, but inauthentically.

I can only take over the being I already am, by finding myself in my *Befindlichkeit*, and moving forward from this going back and self-finding.

We have now found the person, not at all as some notion of oneself, not at all as some "thing" or spot, or steady entity, but as this finding-oneself (in the inauthentic mode of not pursuing one's "how one is," or in the authentic mode of retrieving, going back to bring oneself before oneself).

It is the essential nature of Dasein, not to be a substantial "thing," but rather a being-in and being-with, that is therefore fundamentally open to events. What we are is our living, the existing, and that is how we *are affected* differently than a stone is affected. A stone isn't affected essentially. It is a stone, and then it may be changed in this way or that, while its stoneness continues. Humans *are* being affected. Our being, in

Heidegger's view, is always being affected and that is how we find ourselves. We *are* the living-in events with-others, our being rides on the events, is dispersed in what happens, is the being-in what happens. Only in so finding ourselves, can we constantly retrieve ourselves, so that there is a present in which our capacity to be is again and again our own. That is authenticity.

Being-with is a fundamental aspect of being-in the world. Our situations are always with others. That we can hear each other is inherent in this being-with.

> Hearing is constitutive for speech . . . listening to . . . is the existential being open of Dasein as being-with. . . . Indeed, listening constitutes the primary authentic being-open of Dasein. . . . (163)

> Dasein hears because it understands. (162) Speech is constitutive for the being of the here, that is to say, for *Befindlichkeit* and understanding. (163) *Speech is existentially equally original with Befindlichkeit and understanding* (Heidegger's italics). Understandability is always already articulated even before it is appropriately interpreted. Speech is the articulation of understandability. (161)

Just as Heidegger uses the term "understanding" for the implicit sense of our mood, that is to say, for something much earlier that pre-figures what we usually call by that name, so also he uses "articulation" (*gegliedert*) for the inherent speakability of mood and understanding, before we put it into actual words.

However, "articulation" is not a good translation. "Gegliedert" means having interconnected links and parts, being structured, having interlinked links, not like a snail or applesauce but like a skeleton or an animal with articulated limbs.

It is clear that Heidegger means that, in how we are as *Befindlichkeit* and understanding-sketching, which is not just applesauce-like but has structure. That is the inherent pre-condition of actual speech, and is equally original, equally basic, inherent in *Befindlichkeit* and understanding. This characteristic of people is inherent in what humans are as being-with. Understandability means not only that I understand implicitly what I am doing, but that others do, and that I am understandable to them and they to me. Thus the basis of communication lies in the nature of our being as being-with, and without it there would be no world, no situations for us to be-in.

This concludes my quotations of Heidegger on *Befindlichkeit* and its implicit understanding and communicability.

Earlier I said that in addition to the conceptual structure with which we must think about feeling, in psychology, *Befindlichkeit* also has important implications for method generally. Again, what he says is philosophical and examines how we can know anything. Specific sciences are specific ways of knowing some specific topic. What he says also applies to the sciences, of course.

Heidegger on Befindlichkeit *and Method*

> *Befindlichkeit* is a basic existential way in which Dasein (being-here) is its here. It not only characterizes Dasein ontologically, but because of its disclosing, it is at the same time of basic methodological significance for the existential analytic. Like any ontological interpretation whatsoever, this analytic can only, so to speak, 'listen in' to the previously disclosed being of something that is. . . . Phenomenological interpretation must give Dasein the possibility of original disclosing, to raise the phenomenal content of this disclosing into concepts. . . . (139-140)

Here Heidegger says explicitly that *Befindlichkeit* is the disclosing on which phenomenological method depends. Without the "possibility of original disclosing" there is no phenomenological method, for that is what this method raises into concepts. If the disclosing of *Befindlichkeit* isn't there as part of the method, it will be free-floating, and not phenomenological.

Every statement or interpretation, every "logos," must be in a direct relationship to this original disclosing of *Befindlichkeit* and its understanding. What we already sensed and understood, perhaps in the mode of covering it up, must be brought to concepts.

In explaining what phenomeno*logy* is, Heidegger discusses phenomena and then logos:

> The *logos* lets something be seen . . . and it does so either *for* the one who is doing the talking (the *medium*) or for the persons who are talking with one another, as the case may be. Speech 'lets something be seen' . . . that is, it lets us see something from the very thing which the speech is about . . . making manifest in the sense of letting something be seen by pointing it out. (32)

What phenomenological statements let us see is usually covered up, and emerges and shows itself only in response to such statement.

> And just because the phenomena are mostly not immediately given, phenomenology is needed. (36)
> As meaning of the expression '*phenomenon*,' the following is to be firmly *held on to* (ist daher *festzuhalten*): that which shows itself on itself. (28) (Heidegger's italics)

Thus phenomena in the primary sense of phenomenological method are not those which are immediately obvious anyway without method, but those which show themselves in response to the logos, the statement or formulation.

Heidegger, instancing what he is telling us, here gives a phenomenological interpretation of phenomenological interpretation. He has asked us to *"hold fast to"* the meaning of "phenomenon" as what shows itself on itself. Now he says:

> With a concrete having before oneself of that which was set out in the interpretation of 'phenomenon' and 'logos,' the inner connection between the two terms leaps into view.... Phenomenology means ... letting be seen ... that which shows itself, just as it shows itself from itself. (34)

Thus phenomenological method involves something quite different from statements only, something that, once the logos lets it show itself, shows itself independently. It is possible to have only "free-floating" statements without such an independent phenomenal aspect showing itself, leaping before us, in response to statement. Also, even if there once was such a concretely present self-showing aspect, it can be lost as mere statements are passed on without insuring that the self-showing aspect too is each time found by each person.

> Every concept and sentence drawn originally in a phenomenological way as a communicated assertion has the possibility of degenerating. It is passed on in an empty understanding, loses its grounding and becomes free-floating thesis. (36)

Thus Heidegger insists that he is to be understood experientially with something concretely showing itself from itself, for every concept and sentence of his. The ontological structure of the human being, and all other subject-matter that can be studied only in relation to it, can be grasped only phenomenologically, and never as "free-floating thesis."

> *Only as phenomenology is ontology possible.* (35) (Heidegger's italics)

It is often thought, wrongly I believe, that Heidegger's concepts and those of others, if repeated, are phenomenological or are phenomenology. Heidegger has himself said that this isn't so, they might be repeated as free-floating theses. Phenomenology is nothing, if it is not method, the method of grounding each assertion in something that then stands out.

> 'Phenomenology' names neither the object of its inquiries, nor does this title characterize the subject-matter of its inquiries. The word informs us only about the *how* of the presentation and mode of treatment. (34)

III. FURTHER APPLICATIONS AND IMPLICATIONS

Psychological

The essence of psychotherapy—when it is effective—is phenomenological, not perhaps in the conception of the therapist or the theory, but in the process of the patient.

As in the cited excerpt, any statements and interpretations are effective only when they lift out something from the directly sensed and pre-verbally "understood" felt complexity.

Even very sophisticated statements by patients and therapists alter nothing in the patient's living, unless there is the distinct effect of lifting something out. Many patients have gone to psychotherapy, so-called, for many years several times each week without much effect.

Such failure cases are found in all methods of therapy, and success cases are also found in all methods. The difference is not the ostensive method of psychotherapy, but whether the concrete experiential process described earlier occurs or not. Thus we can neither accept nor condemn one or another type of therapy.

Note that in our excerpt, at each step, one could apply Freudian theory (or Jungian theory) and explain the patient in terms of the theory. However, no theory could have predicted the next steps to which she was led by directly bringing herself before her felt sense. Similarly, if we wish, we can render the whole chain, now that it is explicit, in any of the theories.

In retrospect, it is always possible to construct a logical account for such steps of therapeutic process. In the actual process the steps come first. The statements are a kind of "listening in," as Heidegger puts it, to what is already disclosed pre-verbally in the feeling.

There is a back and forth movement between statement and feeling. Having verbalized something, what then leaps up is not the same as before, and enables a new listening in, which leads to a new statement.

In this role, the theories can be highly useful. Of course any inference is only a guess, a try, an attempt. The anticipated aspect (*or some other aspect*) leaps up in response; if not, then even the best theoretical inference happens just then to be useless. Even when it is corroborated, the inference is not the therapeutic process. The inference has helped, but only insofar as a directly sensed phenomenal aspect arises. It then guides the next step, not what one would have expected to follow theoretically. Notice: Even when the inferred statement is corroborated, the aspect lifted out as a result of it soon leads to something further and different than could be inferred from the very statement that led to it.

This being so, we see that the actual texture of living cannot be equated to any theory. All theory and language *can relate to* living (and to the feel of living), but cannot be equated to it.

Freud and Jung discovered depth psychology. They correctly saw that there is always a vastly complex texture involved in any human event, however simple and routine it might seem. In this they were right.

Freud and Jung erred in taking the symbolizations from a number of people (very much like the patient's symbolizations in my excerpt) and constructing from this a system of contents in terms of which we are all supposedly explainable.

The fact that there is more than one such theory should give one pause. All of them are effective to some extent, which contradicts the exclusiveness with which each is put forward. We cannot really accept any *one* of these theories as rendering us. If we change the way they were intended to function, we can use them all, Jung's, Freud's, and additional theories. The more ways of articulating human experience one knows the better. At a given juncture one or another of these vocabularies may enable us to make a statement that leads to a lifting out. This way of using theories changes the very essence of what theory is:

Theory, taken phenomenologically, relates to what it is about not as an equation or a rendering, but as a logos which lets something be seen *which is then seen on its own.*

The nature of human nature, of living and feeling, is therefore of a much finer texture than any theory or system of sharp cognitions. This is the opposite of saying that experience is indeterminate or vague; it is always very demandingly just exactly how it is, how we find ourselves, but *more organized*, structured, "gegliedert," than any system can equal. Also, it is not given in little pieces, but as a wholistic texture of sensing and living.

In recognizing this, we do not give up on theory; rather, we restore theory to its proper relationship to actuality. This proper relationship lets theory have its own great power. For as we lift out, more and more becomes possible. Theory further builds the world, develops life and gives further structure to anything to which it is applied, but of course it does not do this by itself. Only if theory is put in direct relation with what it is about, does it show its power there.

Words can help the patient lift out something only if the words each have *their own* sharp meanings (even though what is lifted out then has *its own* character). Theoretical words too can lift out, and again only if they have their own sharp meanings. In no way, therefore, does what I say lead to a loss of theory or theoretical sharpness.

If one says that an ax shows its power only on the wood, or whatever is cut with it, this wouldn't imply that one doesn't need to keep one's ax sharp. How much more is this so for the subtle further living and building when theory lifts out something.

Phenomenologists have not well understood all this. There has been a tendency for phenomenology to fall back into descriptions of what is obvious on the face of itself and needs no lifting out, needs no phenomenology. It has become popular to deny not just the concept of the "unconscious" (which, as a conception, deserved to be denied), but also what this concept (clumsily) points to. The implicit complexity, at first only sensed or felt, emerges in the kind of process I am describing. Then something further is felt. There are steps of an explication process. Phenomenologists have felt compelled either to insist on only the face value of human experiences, a hopelessly inadequate view, or—when put to it—they fall into the other extreme and cannot find their way out of accepting one or another psychological theory. This happens frequently, when the phenomenological philosopher as a person enters psychotherapy (for then the power of these theories is experienced directly), and also when the philosopher at last decides to think about psychotherapy. Avoiding the topic, not especially of psychotherapy, but more importantly the topic of feeling, has not well served philosophy.

Feelings were relegated to "tertiary" status in the eighteenth century. They appeared in the rear of philosophy books as "the passions," and had little or no role to play in the constitution of objects and objective reality. Humans were thought to be in touch with reality only in two ways: through perception and through reason. Reason was thought to give order to incoming bits of perception. (Of course this was not ever the only viewpoint during any period.) This view still structures most of our concepts, so that even if we wish to say something else, we cannot do it clearly. Our concepts themselves are still part of that outlook. "Feelings" are held to be internal, rather than a sensing ourselves living. It is then puzzling why there is so much implicit wisdom in feelings. They are also confused with sheer emotions, as I explained earlier. Most philosophers have stayed away from them, instead of clarifying our thinking regarding them.

There has also been another reason for this avoidance. We want to avoid the erroneous view that philosophical questions can be resolved by arguing from psychological factors, wrongly placed underneath as if they could determine philosophy. Freud, for example, thought he could give psychological reasons why philosophers say what they say. But when philosophy assumes Freudian underpinnings, it is no longer philosophy, for it omits at least the examination of Freud's kind of concepts and conceptual patterns.

Psychotherapy is essentially phenomenological—that does not mean phenomenology is psychotherapy. Phenomenology is a far wider category, and its most important meaning is philosophical. Precisely, therefore, it can provide a critique and re-structuring of the way we have been thinking about feeling in psychology and in everyday life.

Elsewhere I have presented a "Theory of Personality Change"[10] in which I formulate psychological concepts along the lines I presented in discussing Heidegger. I cannot go into them here. One concept only will be mentioned. A "direct referent" (I also call it "felt sense" or "felt meaning") is both felt and interactional, the feel *of* one's living in one's situations. It has the organization of this living before and without reflection. Facets can be lifted out and symbolized, which "were" how one was already living. This "were" is in quotation marks, because one changes in authentic explicating.

67

The very act of symbolizing is itself a further living and a further structuring. But only rare statements (and other kinds of symbolizing) have this lifting out character. As I said earlier, research can measure the extent to which this is part of someone's manner of approach.

Let us change our fundamental way of considering psychological theory. If we see clearly in philosophy that the human way of being cannot be reduced to, or undercut by, any system of concepts—why leave psychology to that false assumption? A quite different kind of psychology is possible, one that studies the process, rather than imputing a content-system.

Even to study process, certain concepts must be formed and used. Philosophy will always be on another level, and will always examine how concepts are made, and what different kinds of being are. But from philosophy implications follow for what kinds of concepts are needed in psychology. We need and have recently formulated concepts to study steps of process and even to measure them. With such concepts we can make clear how there is "content mutation"[11] through process-steps.

Theory must be considered in a new way. What I have said so far can be misinterpreted as if to imply that the differences between Freud, Jung, and others don't matter. Nothing of the sort follows! Words and theoretical concepts, too, have power only insofar as they are sharp and have their own clear structure and implications. Feelings without further symbolization are blind (and symbols alone are empty). The new view implies no denigration of theory and clear concepts—but a fundamentally new way of understanding what concepts and theory are, and how they may best be used in their proper relation and most powerfully. And that is in a process of steps of lifting-out.

Philosophical

Let me now turn to more philosophical implications, still bearing on this question. What is this "lifting out" relation between theory (and language) on the one hand, and living and feeling on the other? I ask this now not in the practical sense already described, but as the philosophical question how this relation is possible.

In Heidegger's sense, living is always already linguistically patterned ("gegliedert"). Speaking is an equally original emergence along with *Befindlichkeit* and understanding.

In my way of saying it, we live in linguistically structured situations. Even though what we will further say is new, that emerges from living-in our contexts. These contexts are differentiated by speakings (although, not only in this way). If we imagine speech gone, then a whole host of differentiations and intricacies of our situations is also gone. New further living restructures this implicit structure further.

We must therefore grant feeling *more* organization than that of our poor theoretical systems, vastly more. Given that we do, we can then also understand the power of theory to structure further. This is no small power! Poetry in a very different, and more obvious way, has a power of that kind. One would not need to think that humans are *made of* the kind of entities of which poems are constructed, in order to sense why poetry is powerful. Such a view would trivialize the obviously creative power of poetry. Neither are humans made of the cut entities the theoretical systems contain, and yet theories are immensely powerful new languages for living further what we already are.

But this line of thought leads to the question: How shall we think of this much more organized implicit patterning—if the theories are not to be taken literally? So far I have spoken of it as a persian rug, a fine texture, a capillary system (metaphors of intricacy, complexity, and fine patterning).

Homage to a great philosopher is best done by really seeing what the philosophy points to, and by going on further. The later Heidegger himself goes much further in this direction than he does in *Being and Time*, from which my quotations are taken. And his pointing becomes more powerful. For example, in *Vom Wesen der Wahrheit* he says that any true statement also hides truth, and formulation is thus also false.

Ultimately, that cannot be denied. It will apply to Heidegger's own work and to anything I said, or will say.

Heidegger brought forward a line of development from Schleiermacher and Nietzsche through Dilthey and Husserl, the founding of our assertions directly on our living, as we experience. Having seen how Heidegger does that, let us notice: Heidegger always goes only one step, from the living experiencing to his formulation of the structure implicit in it. The reader thereby has lifted out some aspect that "was" already being lived, but was not seen as such. But other authors lift out other aspects, or one could say, they formulate "the same" aspects differently. Different aspects of these "same" aspects are lifted out. My interest here is not in reconciling different philosophies, rather in the question I have been posing: How might we think about that much finer and different organization of living, such that "lifting out" is possible?

What is (or are) the relationship(s) between living and formulations, such that different formulations are possible? (And, such that each hides, as well as lifts out?)

As capable of giving explicit birth to all these liftings out, the character of the organization of living is much more fundamental than even the structure in *Being and Time*. And it can be studied!

This organization can be studied because we have transitions from one formulation to another, one mode of symbolizing to another, one step of this process of further symbolizing to another step.

Eugene T. Gendlin

Thus I said above that one could say either, that others lift out other aspects different than Heidegger's, or one could say they lift out "the same" aspects but somewhat differently and thus with different sub-aspects. One can see that our ordinary logical notions of "same" and "different" are offended by this situation. Put differently, what is lifted out by two systems is not the same, neither is it just plain different. "Same" and "different" have to give way to a kind of order that doesn't consist of sharp units, the kind of units that are only the same *or* different.

My own work for many years preceded my reading Heidegger. I came to him quite late. Both the Personality Change theory mentioned above, and the philosophical work I will now mention, were written before I read Heidegger. But I had read those philosophers that most influenced Heidegger, and so I emerged from the same sources, at least to some extent. I had also read Sartre, Buber and Merleau-Ponty, who were greatly and crucially following Heidegger. Hence my own work continues from Heidegger, and stands under his influence, although I did not recognize that until later. I have differences with him, too, but this is not the place to discuss them.

In *Experiencing and the Creation of Meaning*[12] I develop a way of studying, not unformulated being or experience, nor formulations, but rather the transitions from one formulation (of something lifted out) to another formulation (of "the same" aspect lifted out). It is easy to show negatively that in such a transition lived experience has no one scheme, and no one set of fixed units. Much more follows. Experience *in relation to further symbolizations* can be said to have quite an odd "structure." I call it the "metastructure." A different kind of "logic" arises to specify these transitions. There are a number of different kinds, each with specific dimensions. The resulting "characteristics" of experiencing in relation to further symbolizing are startling, and lead to a new way of thinking that can be sharp and clear, but with a very different logic.

NOTES

1 In Macquarrie and Robinson's English translation of *Being and Time* (New York: Harper & Row, 1962), "*Befindlichkeit*" is translated as "state of mind." However, it is neither state, nor mind. I mention this here only because the reader may be using the English translation. In addition, *Befindlichkeit* cannot be translated either as "mood" or "attunement," since Heidegger uses "Stimmung," which normally means "mood," and yet finds it necessary to use "Befindlichkeit" instead.

2 Heidegger told Joan Stambaugh, an editor and translator of his works in English, that in his later work *Befindlichkeit* becomes *wohnen* (dwelling). Personal communication from Joan Stambaugh.

3 E. T. Gendlin, "A Theory of Personality Change," in *Personality Change*, ed. Worchell and Byrne (New York: Wiley, 1964). Reprinted in: *Creative Developments in Pyschotherapy*, ed. A. Mahrer (Cleveland: Case-Western Reserve, 1971).

4 I use the term "felt sense" for one's feel of a wholistic texture. That is to be distinguished from an emotion like joy or anger. Such emotions are embedded in a "felt sense"—the sense of all of one's living involved in being joyful now, or angry.

5 Gendlin, Beebe, Cassens, Klein, and Oberlander, "Focusing Ability in Psychotherapy, Personality and Creativity," in *Research in Psychotherapy*, ed. J. Schlien, Vol. III (Washington, D.C.: American Psychological Association, 1967).

6 Unless otherwise indicated, all Heidegger quotations are from *Sein und Zeit* (Tübingen: Max Niemeyer Verlag, 1927). Throughout the quotations all italics are Heidegger's own.

7 "Equanimity (*Gleichmut*) . . . is also characteristic of authentic action." (345)

8 This "throwing out" is translated "projection" by Macquarrie and Robinson. That loses the inherent relation between the throwing out of possibilities and being thrown.

9 Although "Wiederholung" can mean "repetition" in German, it is an unfortunate translation. Heidegger carefully constructs the term in the above sentence from "holen" (bringing) and "wieder" (again). I translate it "retrieval."

10 E.T. Gendlin, "A Theory of Personality Change," in *Personality Change*, ed. Worchell and Byrne (New York: Wiley, 1964). Reprinted in: *Creative Developments in Psychotherapy*, ed. A. Mahrer (Cleveland: Case-Western Reserve, 1971). *See also* E. T. Gendlin, "Experiential Psychotherapy," in *Current Psychotherapies*, ed. R. Corsini (Itasca, Ill.: Peacock, 1973); E.T. Gendlin, "The Newer Therapies," in *American Handbook of Psychiatry V*, Chapter 14, ed. S. Arieti (New York: Basic Books, 1975): and *Focusing* (New York: Everest House, 1978).

11 *Ibid.*

12 E.T. Gendlin, *Experiencing and the Creation of Meaning* (New York: Free Press, Macmillan, 1962, reprinted, 1970). *See also* E.T. Gendlin, "Experiential Phenomenology," in *Phenomenology and the Social Sciences*, ed. M. Natanson (Evanston, Ill.: Northwestern University Press, 1973).

71

Madness and the Poet

JEFFNER ALLEN

. . . the madman. Does the word mean someone who is mentally ill? No. Madness [*Wahnsinn*] here does not mean a mind filled with senseless delusions. "Wahn" belongs to the old high German *wana* and means: without. The madman's mind senses—senses in fact as no one else does. Even so, he does not have the sense of the others. He is of another mind. "Sinnan" signifies originally: to travel, to strive for . . . , to drive in a direction; indogermanic root *sent* and *set* means way. The departed one is a man apart, a madman, because he is on the way in another way. From that other direction, his madness may be called "gentle," for his mind pursues a greater stillness.[1]

> God's own colors dreams my brow,
> Feels the gentle wings of madness.

The poet becomes poet only as he follows that "madman" who died away into the early dawn and who now from his apartness, by the music of his footfall, calls to the brother who follows him.[2]

I.

Why cite Heidegger in a study of madness and the poet? Surely his thinking on madness is other than we in the present age are commonly given to understand: The madman is without senseless delusions. This notion sounds strange to we who are accustomed to identify the "mentally ill" with those who engage in incorrect and/or inappropriate "reality-testing" owing either to a neurological defect causing a breakdown in physico-chemical processes and which is correctable by medical research and treatment or to a deformity of personality due to deviation from psychosocial and ethical standards and which is to be remedied within the therapeutic framework of the mental health movement.[3] Yet it is true that such quasi-medical methods of social control are often resisted by the madman. The madman at times defies, though rarely escapes, the scientific techniques which our present Age of Reason employs and propagates with ever-increasing frequency. Hospitals, insane asylums, mental health centers which wish to treat the "mentally ill" for their own good celebrate the power of our scientistic world view. Indeed, without the presence of individuals who have "lost their minds," who have lost hold of reason and repudiated its object, Reality, such shrines to the modern scientistic will to power would be radically thrown into question and, upon losing the objects of their all too frequent missionary zeal, would be rendered impotent. At the very least, the madman as one who is full of "senseless delusions" is necessary to us: without those who no longer function as "rational animals," whose loss of their "humanity" brings about their expulsion from our social order, our dualistic society of the sane vs. the insane, the rational as opposed to the irrational, of reason vs. madness, would lose its self-imposed identity and focus.[4]

72

MADNESS AND THE POET

Of course, one might well protest that such a view of psychology and psychiatry in the present Age of Reason is too critical, too negative, and "misses the boat" completely. One might even agree with Heidegger, at least to a certain extent: The madman is apart from the crowd of everyday life and is traveling on the way in another way. Existential literature, for instance, is often said to depict the solitary journey through dread as that of one who is mad. Tolstoy's "Diary of a Lunatic," Dürrenmatt's "The Tunnel" and Nietzsche's aphorism 125 of *The Gay Science*, "The Madman," are excellent examples of such an approach to the experience of madness. Existential literature also speaks of a relation between madness and creativity and of the poet as one who follows the madman:

> What is a poet? An unhappy man who in his heart harbors a deep anguish, but whose lips are so fashioned that the moans and cries which pass over them are transformed into ravishing music.[5]

Here Kierkegaard and the Aesthete tell us how the poet-existence transforms the dread experience into art. Yet, if we also listen to Kierkegaard and the Ethicist, we find that the poet-existence of which "A" writes is, according to "B," an existence which, in principle, necessarily fails to attain the metaphysical Infinite. The poet's existence is an "unhappy" one for it has a "false ideal": "it is higher than finiteness and yet not infiniteness." In a sense, the poet is not mad enough. By failing to choose despair, the poet falls short of the religious existence in which his spirit would attain its "true transformation."[6] Accordingly, a second glance shows that Heidegger's thinking on madness is also alien to such an interpretation. Kierkegaard's viewpoint stands on the peaks of a highly refined and subtilized metaphysics. While free of the scientism of our Age of Reason, it lies within the confines of that age's metaphysics. The human creator flees the finite and seeks the infinite, but since the poet-existence is not the religious-existence, the desire for artistic creativity obliges the poet to be nothing more than a "human sacrifice" to the will to power of Western metaphysics. The metaphysics of Kierkegaard's religious existentialism does not listen "from that other direction."

Thus our original question remains unanswered: Why cite Heidegger in a study of madness and the poet, especially when his statements are at variance with many of those made by modern science *and* by modern literature? If we look back to Plato's classical account of madness in the *Phaedrus*, we find that there are two types of madness, one arising from human ailments and one arising from a divine disturbance. The latter, divine madness (*mania*), or possession of an individual by a god (*enthousiasmos*), is of four types: Apollonian, or prophetic, pertaining to divination of the future (*mantikē*), the greatest of the arts; Dionysian, or mystical, belonging to one who is maddened and possessed by the gods (*entheos*, or *Begeisterung*[7]) and thereby delivered from one's troubles; that

73

of the Muses, or poetic, concerning which Socrates says, ". . . if any man come to the gates of poetry without the madness of the Muses, persuaded that skill alone will make him a good poet, then shall he and his works of sanity with him be brought to nought by the poetry of madness"; that of Aphrodite and Eros, or that of the lover of beauty, the best of all forms of divine possession. Above all else, Socrates tells us that the sound of mind do not always have an advantage over the mad, that it is not invariably true that madness is an evil: ". . . in reality, the greatest of blessings come by way of madness, indeed of madness that is heaven-sent."[8] To be sure, one might object that this reference is "out of date," that the modern understanding of madness has progressed beyond that found in the *Phaedrus*, as well as beyond that set forth by Democritus, "There is no poetry without madness."[9] But, then, might not what is deeply rooted in the past also be coming to us from out of the future—if only we can learn to listen to it? Elements of all four types of divine madness are undergone by the poet who, in Heidegger's thinking, feels "the gentle wings of madness."

Thus we will make reference to Heidegger in our study of madness and the poet precisely because Heidegger's understanding of madness is other than that of the most up-to-date theories of modern science and literature. Coming from out of the past, from out of the future and into the present, Heidegger's statements challenge us to listen and to think.

II.

To understand the relation between madness and the poet we must pursue the poet's journey into madness, we must see how the poet undergoes the experience of madness. By examining the fundamental dimensions of the poet's journey through madness we may come to see how the poet is "on the way in another way." We may also see that Heidegger's understanding of this venture is other than we are commonly given to understand precisely because Heidegger has learned from the poet who has journeyed into otherness, into apartness, and into divine madness.

> Since the end of the eighteenth century, the life of unreason no longer manifests itself except in the lightning-flash of works such as those of Hölderlin, of Nerval, of Nietzsche, or of Artaud—forever irreducible to those alienations that can be cured, resisting by their own strength that gigantic moral imprisonment which we are in the habit of calling, doubtless by antiphrasis, the liberation of the insane by Pinel and Tuke.[10]

Let us, then, also be guided by the "lightning-flash" of the poetry of Hölderlin, "the poet's poet," the poet who poetizes the essence of poetry.[11]

By what is the poet sent on the way in another way?

> . . . to each of us is allotted his own,
> Each of us goes and comes to the place that he can.
> Hölderlin, "Bread and Wine"[12]

Moira imparts the poet's destiny (*das Geschick*) to the poet. That destiny is sent (to send, *schicken*) in the sending (*die Schickung*). What is fitting (*das Schickliche*) is what conforms to that sending, or dispensation. Thus the poet does not independently devise the proper element of the poetic mission; rather, the poet is resigned to and follows that which is allotted, that by which the poet is sent.[13]

Whence is the poet sent?

> Within the Alps it is still bright night and the cloud,
> Poetizing the joyous, covers the yawning valley within.
> Hölderlin, "Homecoming/To Kindred Ones"[14]

The poet is sent from the "between," from that poetizing element which opens itself upward to the heavens and gods while at the same time covering the chaotic abyss of the earth and mortals. The "between" is the realm of the birth of the being of the poet and of the art of poetry. The poet, or demigod, is born, or cast out into the between in the wedding festival which celebrates the encounter of the gods and men. Cast out and alone, the poet abides in the supreme isolation of the poetic mission. In solitude the poet stands in the open which mediates the relations between all reality.[15]

Whither is the poet sent?

> What you seek, it is near, already comes to meet you.
> Hölderlin, "Homecoming/To Kindred Ones"[16]

The poet is sent from the "between" into the foreign, into what is far and yet is always already near: "The cloud must, of course, go beyond itself to what it itself is no longer."[17] Travelling in the direction of the foreign, the poet moves toward apartness, toward an encounter with the "fire of the sky" of the foreign land. However, by being sent away into the unfamiliar the poet also learns to become at home in nearness to the origin, which is still withdrawn. Such nearness brings near that which is near, while keeping it at a distance.

Where is the way?

> But where the danger is,
> There also grows the saving.
> Hölderlin, "Patmos"[18]

While underway on the way the poet goes into the saving danger. The poet's way is into the saving: the healing, the whole, the hale, the holy. The poet's way is into the danger of violating the essence of the poetic existence: the poet may be enticed to remain with the mortals and/or to become one with the gods.[19]

How is the way another *way?*

> . . . and as one says of heroes, I can well say of myself that Apollo has struck me.
>
> Hölderlin, "Letter to Böhlendorff," 1802[20]

The poet travels on the way in "another" way. The poet travels by undergoing a particular sort of experience, by being "struck" as it were: "To undergo an experience with something . . . means that this something befalls us, strikes us, comes over us, overwhelms and transforms us."[21] Such an experience is not invented by the poet; rather, it comes upon the poet who receives, endures and submits to it.

That which comes upon the poet is a "flashing," a lightning bolt, the "fire of the heavens." The flash opens, preserves and conceals what is lit up in the lightning. Illumination comes to presence only by concealing itself and so can be named only in a song without words, quietly or in silence.[22]

The poet brings to presence that which is undergone by talking "like a fool." Like King Oedipus, the poet-fool "has perhaps one eye too many," or, in other words, the poet "senses in fact as no one else does" and yet is blind.[23] Does that mean that the poet is of another mind or is endowed with a peculiar sort of seeing so that the poet can glance into the flashing and not be burned by seeing the high one? Or, does such a statement mean that the poet is of another mind in virtue of an abundance and excess of sight and sensing such that the poet's *hubris* leads the poet to desire to violate the limits of the "between" and to see the high one? In the former the poet's blindness is a special type of seeing, a third eye, which allows the poet to do what is fitting for the poet existence and to realize the possibilities of the "between." In the latter the poet's blindness results from the eye of *hubris*, which shatters the limits of the possible and in so doing is itself destroyed. Either way the poet "is of another mind," and so "feels the gentle wings of madness." In the former instance the poet becomes the poet by following the madman into otherness, but does so in such a way that the danger of any essential misfortune is overcome and the poet remains standing under favorable weather. In the latter, the poet follows, joins and becomes the madman who calls to the poet and the poet's soul perishes in the birth of the work. In either case the poet is always in some relation to madness, though in different ways and with differing consequences. Accordingly, by pursuing the poet's journey into madness we have found that the poet *as* poet is always in some relation to madness: to study the poet is also to examine aspects of madness and to analyze madness also leads to reflection on various aspects of the poet.

The poet is on the way in "another" way: that which the poet undergoes renders the poet of another mind, for it transports the poet into otherness, into apartness, into divine madness.

MADNESS AND THE POET

At this point one may well refer to Hölderlin's poem, "As When on a Holiday," the poem which perhaps best shows the otherness of the poet's path:

> So, as poets say, when she desired to see
> the god, visible, his lightning flash fell on Semele's house
> And ashes mortally struck gave birth to
> The fruit of the thunderstorm, to holy Bacchus.[24]

It would seem that the poet's fate can be akin to that of Semele: under the unbearableness of the flashing, the poet falls out of the "between" to which the poet is destined, loses all proper orientation to the whence, whither and where of the poetic mission and is lost in otherness. Like Semele, the poet is threatened with and finally succumbs to loss of that being which is fitting. Hölderlin simply offers the above stanza as an illustration of a possible fate of the poet. However, Heidegger writes to the contrary, "Semele's fate reveals in reverse how only the presence of the holy guarantees that the song truly succeeds. The recollection of Semele's fate, spoken by Euripides and by Ovid, is only introduced into the poem as a counter-theme."[25] Yet, Heidegger's claim suppresses the stanza without explanation and in so doing seems to ignore the very danger of the poet's task. Moreover, it would seem quite unnecessary for Heidegger to make such a claim since he writes elsewhere, "Excessive brightness has driven the poet into darkness. Do we need any further testimony in regard to the extreme danger of his 'occupation'? The poet's own fate says everything."[26]

Indeed, further examination shows that the similarities we have drawn between Semele and the poet are often supported by Hölderlin and by Heidegger. As Hölderlin writes in 1800, ". . . and that is why language, the most dangerous of goods, has been given to man, so that creating, destroying, and perishing, and returning to the ever-living, to the mistress and mother, he may bear witness to what he is."[27] And as Heidegger writes, "The end—being the end of the decaying kind—precedes the beginning of the unborn kind. But the beginning, the earlier earliness, has already overtaken the end."[28] The poet who perishes also returns to the everliving, the end is also already a beginning. In being possessed by the flashing thunderbolt, Semele gives birth to Dionysus, the mad god whose appearance sends humankind into madness and Hölderlin gives rise to one of his most thought provoking poems, "In lovely blueness blooms. . . ." Furthermore, just as Semele is brought back to life by Dionysus, perhaps the poet Hölderlin, who was similarly struck, may address us in a new way too. Birth in death, creation in destruction, poetizing in madness, already speak from the otherness of the poet's path.

What is the greater stillness?

> Gentle madness often sees the golden, the true.
> Trakl, "Corner by the Forest"[29]

77

As the poet listens "from that other direction," the poet cor-responds to a "greater stillness." We may think that stillness as the unaccustomed and awesome, the immediate, nature, the holy, Being.[30] By listening in another key, the poet mediates the immediate, whose immediacy resists any immediate intrusion by the mediator. Thus the poet, possessed by the flashing of the gods, divines the holy, for love of gods and mortals. The poet's madness is divine.

III.

Upon further reflection, to be sure, such a Heideggerian account of the relation between madness and the poet may be subject to several criticisms. One problem which arises is whether a Heideggerian view applies to all, or only to some, types of poets and madness. Is it a view that holds universally or is it merely a narrow romanticization of madness and the poet? Certainly it is not equally valid for every particular kind of poet and every particular instance of madness. Yet it does say something essential about the essence of the relation between madness and the poet and thus is invaluable to even the contemporary poet who seeks self-understanding, as well as to the contemporary non-poet who wishes to better understand the present-day poet. But, then, this also needs to be qualified. A Heideggerian approach does not speak by making a timelessly valid statement. Its statement belongs to a definite time. It belongs to the present age, not in the sense of conforming to the readily accepted ideas of our time but, rather, by speaking of that which comes to us from out of the past, from out of the future and into the unique time of the present. Earth, sky, gods and mortals, and even the flashing of the holy are appropriated by the contemporary poet in a way which cor-responds to how they are given to that poet in the present age. Nevertheless, one might still object that our account of madness and the poet reflects the thought of Heidegger's later writing, which adds little to what Heidegger wrote earlier (*Being and Time*, "What is Metaphysics?") concerning Dasein's encounter with otherness in the uncanny. There Dasein experiences Being as other than everything that is and does so in dread, from which Dasein may flee or into which Dasein may fall. The voice of that otherness is soundless and robs Dasein of speech.[31] It cannot be named directly. Yet, Heidegger's account of the poet's experience of the flashing differs from his understanding of Dasein's experience of dread. The poet-existence is, as it were, a unique mode of Dasein, a mode that abides in the "between" of earth and sky, gods and mortals, that has a primordial relation to language, and that thereby makes ready for our poetic dwelling on the earth. The poet's divine madness is a peculiar modality of *Angst*, one which allows us to think the mediated immediate from that other direction which has overcome the limitations of Western metaphysics.

MADNESS AND THE POET

In addition to such difficulties, however, a further problematic appears as open-ended: How may the thinker think the relation between madness and the poet? If the thinker is called to think the question of the meaning of Being and if the poet is struck in such a way as to poetize the holy, how can the thinker think the fundamental experience, the madness, of the poet?

> Only image formed keeps the vision.
> Yet image formed rests in the poem.[32]

The thinker's path, then, is to think the fullness of the image which keeps the vision of the advent of the flashing and which resides in the poem. We think the poet's images because our dwelling rests in the poetic, our existence is poetic in its ground. Or, in other words, by listening to the poet's images we may come to dwell poetically: "to dwell poetically means: to stand in the presence of the gods and to be struck by the essential nearness of things."[33] The danger for the thinker is, in part, that one may hear wrongly, but even more thought provokingly, that we may become altogether hard of hearing.

NOTES

1 Heidegger, *On the Way to Language*, trans. Peter D. Hertz (New York: Harper & Row, 1971), p. 173. The translation has been altered to correspond to the German text.

2 Ibid., p. 191, in which the poetry cited is from Georg Trakl, "Whispered into the Afternoon."

3 Thomas Szasz, *The Manufacture of Madness* (New York: Harper & Row, 1970), p. 121, and *Ideology and Insanity* (New York: Doubleday, 1970), pp. 12-16.

4 Szasz, *The Age of Madness* (New York: Doubleday, 1973), pp. 3, 4.

5 Kierkegaard, *Either/Or* vol. I, trans. Walter Lowrie (Princeton: Princeton University Press, 1971), p. 22.

6 Ibid., vol. II, pp. 214, 215.

7 Jean Wahl, "En familiarité avec le haut," *Centre Internationale d'Etudes Poetiques - Courrier*, no. 7 (1956), pp. 3-19.

8 Plato, *Phaedrus*, 244a-245d, 265a-b, trans. R. Hackforth, in *Plato: Collected Dialogues*, eds. Edith Hamilton and Huntington Cairns (Princeton: Princeton University Press, 1963).

9 Kathleen Freeman, *Ancilla to the Pre-Socratic Philosophers* (Cambridge: Harvard University Press, 1948), p. 17.

10 Michel Foucault, *Madness and Civilization*, trans. Richard Howard (New York: Random House, 1965), p. 278.

11 Heidegger, *Elucidations of Hölderlin's Poetry*, trans. Keith Hoeller, forthcoming, p. 34. In subsequent citations of this work the title of the book will be abbreviated *EHP* and only the German pagination will be given.

12 *EHP*, p. 183.

13 *EHP*, p. 12 and "Translator's Notes 'Homecoming/to Kindred Ones.'"

14 *EHP*, p. 15.

15 *EHP*, pp. 14, 46, 47, 61, 113.

16 *EHP*, p. 24.

17 *EHP*, pp. 15, 87.

18 *EHP*, p. 21.

19 *EHP*, pp. 18, 63, 104, 118.

20 *EHP*, p. 157.

21 *EHP*, 15; *On the Way to Language*, p. 57.

22 *EHP*, pp. 17, 43, 188-190.

23 *EHP*, pp. 25, 170; Heidegger, *Poetry, Language, Thought*, trans. Albert Hofstadter, (New York: Harper & Row, 1971), p. 228.

24 *EHP*, p. 70.

25 Ibid.; Paul de Man, "Les Exégèses de Hölderlin par Martin Heidegger," *Critique*, vol. 11 (1955), pp. 800-819.

26 *EHP*, p. 44.

27 *EHP*, p. 36.

28 Heidegger, *On the Way to Language*, p. 176.

29 Ibid., p. 175.

30 *EHP*, pp. 41, 58, 59, 63, 71.

31 Heidegger, "What is Metaphysics," trans. David Farrell Krell, in Heidegger *Basic Writings* (New York: Harper & Row, 1977), p. 103. See also Charles E. Scott, "Heidegger, Madness and Well-Being," *The Southwestern Journal of Philosophy*, vol. 4 (1973), pp. 157-177, with respect to an interpretation of the theme of madness in Heidegger's earlier writings.

32 Heidegger, *Poetry, Language, Thought*, p. 7.

33 Ibid., p. 22, *EHP*, p. 42.

Psychotherapy: Being One and Being Many

CHARLES E. SCOTT

My purpose is to interpret a fundamental aspect of therapy by attending to one of the central distinctions in Western thought: it may be called the part-whole distinction, the problem of the one and the many, or the issue of identity and difference. The distinction reflects a pervasive and experienced dimension of human awareness: that in being who I am in particular I am in my awareness beyond my particularity in common with all. I shall interpret this situation by focusing on how we occur in common. That *how* is a particular event that reflects non-particular commonality. I shall assume that the coming forth of beings, how things are available with us, is the place to look for a thematic understanding of how we are in common, i.e., I do not view form or matter or subjectivity as the key for understanding how we are in common. Hence, the experience fundamental for the part-whole distinction, not its various theoretical formulations, is my linkage with my great philosophical predecessors. And the meaning of that experience is our linkage together now as we, philosophers, psychologists, and therapists, work on an interpretation of the basis of psychotherapy. We shall be doing phenomenology as we examine the experiential occurrence of one and many: our aim is a descriptive interpretation of a central aspect of human awareness.

1. THEORY AND THERAPY

The relation of theory and therapeutic practice is seldom clear. When a philosopher speaks about therapy, the therapist is inclined, intuitively in the present cultural climate, to hear abstraction and intellectual exercise. And philosophers are inclined to discount as unsophisticated those ideas developed by non-philosophical therapists. Experiences, however, may link theory and practice. We practice out of basic experiences, and we think out of basic experiences. When, for example, the categories fundamental for our thinking have to do for the most part with explanation, with causes and results, we speak out of a desire for intellectual order and out of projects related primarily to conceptual structuring. Those desires and interests mean that thinking in an explanatory manner is separated from therapeutic practice in which people attend to meanings and events in terms of fundamental affections and affective relations. At least that appears to be the situation presently in that the meanings of affection and the meanings of explanation are usually ordered in highly different ways. But if the thinker and the therapist find common experiences to think out of and use discipline in attending to these common experiences, an accord of theory and practice can occur. In that accord, thinking enriches and guides practice and practice guides and enriches thinking. Our interpretative aim should be to find and attend to common events and to relate and speak out of those specific instances of commonness.

I shall use *event* and *experience* in these remarks. I am partial to the word *event*, because it can mean an occurrence that is its own meaning, its own relations, and may carry the connotation of disclosive world-relatedness free of the implications of subjectivism and privacy. But *experience* emphasizes affect, involvement, and individualized significance. *Event* can also have those meanings, but they are harder to hear. So I use both these words with the hope that *experience* will mean *event* and *event* will mean *experience* for you in the course of this discussion. We shall be dealing with how we are in common, and we shall try to think out of our commonality, which is central for therapeutic occurrence. Our commonality is eventful in the sense that we occur together in common. And our commonality is experiential in the sense that feeling, mood, and directions of awareness are aspects of how we are in common together.

When we attend to our commonality and see that commonality in relation to therapeutic events, therapeutic practice and thought regarding therapy will reflect each other in an area of growing awareness that is made up at once of theory and practice. That awareness is the aim of these remarks, and it is not attainable as a thought or as an object of thought. Rather, this kind of awareness comes as one listens to the events and experiences out of which the remarks arise and which are reflected in the remarks. As concepts reflect and speak of events common for us, our awareness develops and a level of communication is reached which is genuinely dialogical, whether the mode of speaking is philosophical or therapeutic. Then we may say that interpretation, in the sense of growth of understanding and development of common meanings, is going on.

2. PLATO, PARMENIDES, AND HERACLITUS

There is a relation between unity and order that has been experienced as not efficiently caused. Order is found not to be done by any particular direction of will. The Greek experience of destiny is an instance. Directions are ordained by the fabric of possibilities, nature, and particular human beings. Like the inexorable moving of a suspended wheel, like the seasonal course of the heavens, situations move toward fulfillment of directions, toward intrinsic completion, without regard for specific human interests or personal fulfillment. Destiny is a self-completing unfolding of a situation or setting that is not defined by its many participants. This notion of destiny has spoken out of people's awareness that the whole of the situation of which they are a part is not deeply informed by the strength and character of individual passion. That whole may be thought of as the

Cosmos all around a located human being, or it may be thought of as the non-personal dimension of human being. In either case, the person is deeply and sometimes terribly aware of an infinitely transcending region which is regardless of the individual's fulfillments and suffering.

My emphasis presently is to fall on how this non-personal and non-volitional region has been found. Finding and responding with this region defines the perimeters of my discussion.

I want to note, without developing further, how Plato, Parmenides and Heraclitus spoke of the immanent presence of a region which transcends individuals, is in some sense comprehensible by them, and which is present as a direction of non-personal unfolding in personal experience.

Plato speaks of the intimate and intrinsic link of unchanging beings to changing beings by saying that the unchanging "becomes in" the changing being or is "to be in," "to lie in" the changing being. The non-personal is definitive of what is personal, for example, as the non-personal "comes to be" in the individual's circumstances. A particular finite being is "in common with" its defining, but transcending reality. They are "in communion with each other," and finite being "imitates" or "is like" its present and transcending destiny as it lives out and toward what is given to be.

The defining reality of a given thing is not the specific, existing thing, but is its order, its particular unity. This unity is found to be different from the vicissitudes of the existing thing, but definitive of what the thing, in spite of itself, can be and become. It is an instance of destiny. And for Plato, unity means goodness. The unfolding of a being's destiny, its definitive reality, is a reflection of the unity and wholeness that enjoys sway over everything. I understand that to mean that Plato discovered that the present non-personal directions of his being, when thoroughly included in the individuality of his own way of seeing, inspired a fulfilling completeness that was good in its occurrence.

This experiential correlation between well-being and non-personal unity is also reflected in Heraclitus' and Parmenides' fragments. Heraclitus combines a method of reflection that "distinguishes each thing according to its own way of being" with an encompassing insight that "what is common to all," how we are in common, can guide us. *Guides* us in what sense? "Nature loves to hide," he says, and it is not usually available for direct knowledge. Things, however, find their "repose in changing," and "conflict" and "strife" provide direct access to the repose in common of all things. Such claims are paradoxical only if we view all things solely from the perspective of individuality. How we are in common guides us in how change occurs. The measure of kindling and dying down, waxing and waning, victory and defeat and so forth is defined by none of its instances.

83

Again we find the insight that order is an event of relation between individuals and non-individual aegis, a relation susceptible to sight, but not to explanation. The meaning of this aegis is found by Heraclitus in that soul that lives out its "inner law" to fulfillment as a "dry beam of light." Seeing for Heraclitus, as it is for Plato and Parmenides, is an occurrence in which one gives way to the seen and does not interfere with how it is. Only then can human awareness undergo an ordering in which it finds its partiality to reflect thoroughly that unity or wholeness which defines awareness without being that awareness.

"Gaze steadfastly," said Parmenides, "at things which, though far away, are yet present to your mind. For you cannot cut off being from being; it does not scatter itself unto a universe and then reunify." He found being to be one, common and utterly the same in all of its instances. This sameness is utterly compelling when seen, only and simply as it is; it is that without which differences could not occur; it is present always and always not an instance of anything. The intensity of Parmenides' experience of the meaning of the sameness of being should not be overlooked: the scattered is always in common and reposed in its being; the scattered is not to be denied, but the common repose is to be intimately known.

Plato, Heraclitus, and Parmenides each knew that order is found in a present non-object which need not will to be and which in its presence makes possible an accord among the many that need not overcome differences, strife, and relative agreements in order to be at one and deeply at peace.

3. DIFFERENCE AND DIVERSITY

We experience difference and diversity in terms of puzzlement, privacy, opposition, resistance, identity, and self-differentiation. The child discovers that he is not the same as his mother. The adolescent discovers he is not the same as his father. The adult discovers that he is not the same as life itself or being itself, i.e., he discovers that he is to die. We all discover that we are different from the world of which we are intimate parts, and I believe that puzzlement accompanies these discoveries. One may not think about the discovery. He may not ever know that the discovery is going on. He may simply see his mother or father or himself differently. He may feel pause or doubtful or set apart. He may laugh or fall quiet in his puzzlement, but an experience of question occurs as such transitions occur. The words *odd* or *remarkable* or *strange* would probably be appropriate for such experiences. I suspect that most of us at one time or another wish, out of our puzzlement, that we were more at one with things such that doubt and question were not so pervasively appropriate.

In the puzzle of being different, we are immediately aware of ourselves in our silence, in what we do not say, in how no one absolutely knows us, in our capacity to say yes and no. We occur as private in our differences. As private we are opposed. We can experience the "no" of others, their privacy, their differences, their refusal of us or of our intentions. And we have a sense of who we are in our difference and privacy. We are name and identity to ourselves in our being different with others.

But the most problematic experience presently appears to be self-differentiation rather than differentiation with others. We tend to think of ourselves exclusively in terms of our specific identities with others, which means not only that a backdrop of loneliness is particularly characteristic of our present manner of being together, but also that we expect to be just exactly who we are. I take this literalism of identity to be expressed in resistance to one's dreaming awareness, in remarkable conceptual stress on the ideas of personality and character when one wishes to understand human reality, in the identification of consciousness and conceptual mentality, and so forth. When we occur to ourselves as significantly different from the way we usually are, we may be surprised, shocked or traumatized. If I am this one identity, private and different from everyone else, how can I possibly also be different from myself? How can I be mother and father to myself? How can I be my own shadow? How can I desire what I abhor? And so forth.

I shall indicate later that this kind of literalism is lived as a refusal of one's sameness, of one's own being. Presently I want to stress that difference from everything else but oneself and difference from oneself are aspects of how we are in common. Consequently, doubt, question, puzzlement, and a thorough absence of sameness are given aspects of our world and of ourselves in our particular being.

4. INDIFFERENCE

Difference occurs by virtue of immediate interest and concern. As I feel desire, things distinguish themselves, and as desires change, foci and penumbra change. I am a region that is alert in desires and interests. I am aware of myself in relations marked by intricate and familiar networks of interests, commitments, concerns, i.e., networks of desires. Desires are living, aware directions which have the power of singling out and ignoring and which give energy in some relations while letting other relations fall out of importance.

As a person I am a self-aware region of desires. That region is subject to changes in the hierarchy of interests, to shifts in relations, satisfactions, failures, and so forth. But I am immediately aware of myself in desiring, in being interested, in seeking, avoiding, finding, struggling, etc. Differentiating in concrete relations is at the core of personality and character.

As I differentiate in desiring, I find all manner of things that are not what I am after. Intense desires are particularly powerful ways to distinguish things. Hatreds and loves, as we know so well, set things apart and bring things together, discover sames and not-sames, and give fundamental identities to things in their desiring contexts.

Not desiring at all might well seem like death to us, at least the death of our identifiable selves, our individuality, our character. Our being particular, that is, our specific way of being just who we are, occurs in distinguishing things. Our identity is intimately involved in the manyness of beings. In our desiring we find the world highly diverse, potentially fulfilling and threatening, filled with beings that come and go and change always.

Indifference has a puzzling quality about it. By indifference I do not have in mind ignoring something or someone. Ignoring is an attitude. I have in mind an absence of attitude. This absence of attitude is noted in the notions of one and whole. The whole context of all our many situations is not attitudinal or personal. What Heraclitus, Parmenides, and Plato knew, viz., that indifference is always an accompaniment of differentiation, that indifference is never resolvable into differentiation, that the one is not the many—that knowledge was partially recovered some years ago when nature ceased being viewed through the metaphor of mother and, after some initial, heated disappointment, was allowed to be impersonal, indifferent and yet beautiful. I say partially recovered because we have yet to appropriate fully in our contemporary setting the fact that indifference is the horizon of all differentiation. The nursing mother, for example, who provided so much meaning for people's experience of nature, is not only personally and uniquely related with her child. She is also mother. It is child. Feeding is occurring. The very quality of eternity which we might experience in the nursing situation is beyond all the individual caring and specific nurturing that is going on. The metaphor of mother nature can mean that mother is pervaded by indifference even as she particularizes and gives individual nurturance.

This absence of attitudes is a dimension of human awareness. It is constitutive of the world as we live it. A pervading sameness, a non-differentiated, non-individual unthing-like quality may be found with all instances of things. It is a non-caring, non-desiring, non-differentiating dimension that we are sensitive to when we know, for example, that we die without regard for our interests, that we change regardless of how we change, that meaning occurs in spite of what meanings there are, that being is regardless of our desires, that personality and character occur no matter what their content.

Indifference names one aspect of how reality is. It is important for our interests because it also names one way in which what has been called the one, the same, or the whole appears. In the course of my observations I shall interpret indifference by primary reference to the meaning of *event*, or the coming forth of things, which I shall also call *happening* or *occurrence*. Therapeutically indifference is important because it not only names a dimension of our own existence which can be terrifying, but it also names the wholeness of our being which can be refused or blocked only with enormous expense to our well-being.

If we absolutize the personal for psychotherapy either in our language or method, we shall leave out of account the very being of our existence, i.e., the event or the coming forth of things, in such a way that plurality and individualism will be perimeters for our understanding of health. Desire, in that case, would appear to be the foundation of human existence, and all experiences would be lost in which desire steps back of impersonal insight, uncaring contemplation, aimless intuition, and desire-free communion. Our refusal of indifference means insensitivity regarding not only nature in its difference from us, but also the very quality of seeing the undesired or the totally unexpected, as frequently happens in insight. Such refusal means that our appreciation for the non-personal, such as I-Thou occurrences, would be seriously damaged. It would also mean that we would tend to identify knowledge of objects with awareness as such. Indifference names the non-objective, non-particular, non-desiring dimension of our awareness, the immediacy of awareness, in which no person is found and on which personal well-being is founded.

5. AN INSTANCE OF PART/WHOLE: AWARENESS OF MEANING AND AWARENESSES OF MEANINGS

By looking at our sense of meaning in relation to our senses of meanings we shall take one example of the simultaneity of particular and whole, and that will give us at least some orientation toward understanding the meaning of our being at once one and many. My aim is to direct us toward an interpretation of human being in which we can see that oneness or wholeness is a fundamental state, not an accomplishment, and that as that state is lived in denial it is accompanied by psychological illness. I choose the occurrence of meanings as an exemplary focus in order to stress, in the process of this part of our discussion, that meanings are events of world-relation which are not to be understood by reference to any type of a priori structure or to any type of subjective processes. Our community of being is found in how things occur, and their occurrence provides us direct access to the sameness, or oneness, or wholeness of being.

I want to focus on how meanings reflect the sheer event of meaning, how a meaning is a phenomenon of an event of which the particular meaning is a part. "Participate" won't do to speak of this relation of part-whole, because that notion tends to mean two separate things which are characterized by one thing's being in the other thing. We would have thereby begun with a primordial separation of realities which means that the whole would be taken as an entirety of the parts. The basic words which I shall use to name the part-whole presence are *event* or *occur*. The advantage is that these two words may say how we are aware of whole and part without meaning that part and whole are separated things.

Whole is not experienced as a thing or as a part of a larger context of experience. When Heraclitus, for example, spoke of Logos as the unity of all change I do not think he had reference to an entity posited by intelligent guesswork or to a particular thing in his experience. He addressed by his notion of Logos a non-objective awareness of sameness, a wholeness which happens as diversity happens.

This starting point is significant for us here insofar as we want to understand how therapy happens with two or more persons. We might want to speak of our sharing common properties or of our participating in a common process or of our privately enjoying experiences that are similar. But such manners of understanding assume from the outset a separateness that takes no account of being same together in its point of departure. Such accounts make wholeness either something to be accomplished or to be found from a particular perspective. Particulars are not received, from the beginning, as phenomena of sameness when we speak of participating in a common process, privately enjoying similar experiences, or sharing common properties. In such instances, we give a virtually unchangeable primacy to particular perspective.

But meanings precede perspectives in a linear as well as in a founding sense. When we speak as though particular perspectives are primary for either meaning or awareness, we misstate in a deeply forgetful way the primacy of meaning with respect to all particular points of view.

A point of view is always a meaningful part of a meaning event. Shall we say that that event of meaning is like a body of water that contains a particular drop of water which we note particularly? I believe that such a physical analogy would mislead us. Meaning is not like a body that holds and contains. Meaning is an event of relatedness that allows for identification. Things are already together in certain ways such that we may occur in particular ways regarding them. Our regard, our awareness in our particular manner, is our being related in certain ways with things that are already together with us in certain non-perspectival ways.

So-called 'existential analysts' such as Binswanger have located the general characteristics of human experience in the a priori structure of human experience. We, however, are following those who locate such aspects in the 'world', that is, in the identifiable relatedness of things and not in an a priori structure of mind or experience. And we are noting that world-relations themselves constitute our awareness as the foundation of our perspectives. How things are together and how we are with them is the region of awareness, as distinct to a posited, interior brain structure. Further, the wholeness or the sameness of the event of many fluctuating particulars is to be found in the already together quality of the event itself. Things being apparent in their own relatedness is the region for inquiry when we want to understand our experiences of part-whole.

Meanings are world-relations, not primarily private experiences. Meanings are constitutive of human awareness. How things are together, how they occur with each other, constitutes a basic dimension of individual consciousness. This dimension is cultural, social, historical, and so forth. What concerns us, however, is that *meaning* names an occurrence that tolerates an apparently immeasurable range of differences. Things are good, bad, indifferent, threatening, inviting, or whatever. But in any case they are present as something: they are nameable and related. Meaning seems to be an horizon that cannot be transcended, even in radical experiences of meaninglessness, since these experiences are founded in nameable world-relations which are experienced as disconnected or falling apart. Meaning, though not like a physical container, is pervasive, an immeasurable sameness that tolerates an infinite range of differences and opposites. And human awareness occurs as meaning event: it is at once a situation free of the individual, an individual stance in that situation, and a pervasive occurrence of meaning regardless of the contents of the meanings.

We may consequently speak of an awareness of meaning as well as of awarenesses of certain meanings. One is always found with the other, but neither is the same as the other. An awareness of meaning happens indifferently vis-à-vis which meanings occur, and that awareness is defined without regard to which desires, interests, comedies, or tragedies are going on. And yet, without an awareness of meaning as such, the world would be totally absent, i.e., 'we' would have no sense of relatedness, identity, or particularity.

6. METAPHORS FOR THE EXPERIENCES OF WHOLENESS

Metaphors for the experiences of wholeness are frequently ones of depth or of light; down deep, underneath, back behind, feelings of depth and descent; translucent, pervasive shades, light of lights, like the light of the sun, and so forth. Metaphors of hearing could be used just as well, if not better; pervasive sound, backdrop of silence, unsounding harmony. In any case, pervasiveness and distance without objectivity are important aspects of the meaning of the experiences of wholeness.

Wholeness is being one's own event. We are never finally circumscribed by any one particular situation or by any one set of factors which identify us particularly. Being whole is, as classically seen, transcendence of that particularity which is also real. Parmenides doubted the reality of particularity and, closely related to Parmenides' doubts, Plato doubted the reality of change and changing things. None of us can share these doubts now, in the way they seemed unavoidable to Plato and Parmenides. We are more inclined to doubt whatever casts relativity on change and on a presumed absoluteness of particularity. We are more inclined to doubt the wholeness of being our own event than we are to doubt the idea that change is absolute.

In our classic, metaphysical tradition the reality of wholeness or the one tended to be identified as a permanent kind of thing. The very notion of wholeness may connote a circumscribed being which is all that and none of this: identical with itself. We must disassociate, however, the idea of wholeness from the context of permanent and changing things if we are to be attuned to the experiences of wholeness. It does not occur as something permanent or as something changing. It does not occur as a thing at all. We experience wholeness as an alertness that pervades and casts an horizon vis-à-vis all present things. We could call it non-voluntary readiness for experience in the midst of experiences, awareness that pervades opposites, a sense of the limitedness of identity, the mood of finiteness, alertness that goes beyond and beneath all that I reflect and know, a sense of sameness with all the differences of my experience. It is like light that illumines all lighted things as far as one can see. It is like darkness that cannot be grasped or seen through: dark into dark. It is like a tone reaching the limits of audibility and seeming not even to stop there. It is like a silence that is heard with sounds. It is like an unfathomable and unreachable source that is as it is, but does nothing in particular.

7. WHEN I AM AFRAID OF THE EVENTFULNESS OF MY BEING

My relation with my own eventfulness, my own being, always involves a sense of the limitedness of who I am in particular. When I identify my being with my particular way of going about things by crystallizing myself into patterns that I take to be absolute for me, the eventfulness of my being will be deeply and inevitably threatening at every level of my particular awarenesses. My self-understanding will need to be protected. What I possess will need to be guarded and defended. Ownership will foreshadow repeated crises of danger and attack. My sense of place will need constant reinforcement to make clear its fortification against change. Peace will seem to be the opposite of open freedom. Definition will need the enforcement of strong commitments. Fixity will need guarantee. Guarantee will need defense. My very eventfulness will be a constant taunt of the particularities of my life. My life might feel deeply and vaguely decayed, like there is something gnawing at the core. Death might feel like a hand taking away something precious. The horizons might seem like boundaries under imminent attack. The danger of loss, defeat, and perhaps poverty will pervade my successes, fulfillments, and affective riches. I will be utterly at odds with my own being.

When I am at odds with my being in that way, and when I am with you, I will be inclined to attack or defend or hide or control. But I will not be inclined to be together with you in the horizons of awareness where who I am in particular fades back of our being together. I will immediately and non-reflectively define our relation in terms of interests and intentions. I will want to build or tear down or change or keep things as they are, that is, I will want to do something. But I will not seek touch with that non-particularity of the event of being together which happens in the aims and interests of our relation, but which is itself neither aim nor interest.

Being out of touch with my eventfulness, my wholeness, is like being out of touch with any other dimension of my own reality in this sense: I cannot feel close to it even when I focus on it or think about it. It will seem distant even when I know about it. It will feel foreign in my relations with it. It will seem inappropriate or suffocating or emptying in its closeness. I will seek to protect myself from it, and in whatever protection I find I will be solidifying an opposition to dimensions of my own being.

When I am opposed to the eventfulness of my own being I will be predisposed to blocking openness and pervasiveness at all points in my existence. I will want to control my bowels as well as my children. I will feel the threat of merger and loss of identity in all dimensions of relating with others that do not involve clarity of intention and a sense of control. I will want to exercise a maximum jurisdiction over the details of my death. I will tend to define consciousness in terms of structures of knowledge, and I will tend to define my psyche in terms of volition. I will tend to find the meaning of my life solely in projects and accomplishments. I will find open and free listening difficult. I will find deep serenity, as distinct to happy relaxation, impossible, and I will seek, perhaps compulsively, confirmation of the value of the particulars of my life.

The oppositions which are part of my existence will, in this situation of refusal, tend to seem unnatural or wrong or contradictory. If my tendency is toward moral judgments, I will feel wrong and guilty to be different from the favorable aspects of my being. If my tendency is toward literalism, I will tend to deny the existence of my own self-differences. I will generally think of truth as different from contradiction and opposition, such that I will be unprepared to face the enormous range of opposites and differences that make up being human.

8. WHEN I WELCOME THE EVENTFULNESS OF MY BEING ONE AND MANY

I am swaying back and forth among the words *oneness, unity, wholeness,* and *eventfulness* because *wholeness, unity,* and *oneness* traditionally have named the region of pervasive non-diversity. But I have used *event* and *eventfulness* in an effort to set our thinking apart from the traditional inclination to attach to *wholeness* or *unity* the meanings of either changelessness or sole claim to being or the characteristic of being a separate thing in relation to other things. And I have said that *wholeness* is not an object of awareness, but is a dimension of awareness that is immediately and non-personally self-aware. The eventfulness of human being is the occurrence of awareness in its pervasive immediacy.

We have seen that this dimension of our occurrence is an experience in the sense that we live it unavoidably and with non-objective sensibility. It pervades all aspects of our lives. But we are free to assume various stances regarding it. Among those postures, we may reject it or welcome it in all manner of ways.

Therapeutically, when you address and confirm the claims of my being, you may need to remain silent regarding the claims of my personality. My particular way of being may well be opposed or hostile to how my being is. I may fear my own occurrence as whole and non-personal. I may be angry over my own inevitability of change, given my desire to keep what I like. I may deeply resent and view as evil the inevitability of my death, given my enjoyment of me and my life. I may hate the pervasiveness of loss even when loss means the growth of my children or of a friend or the maturation of possibilities in a situation which I like in its nascence. I may not like being limited, and I may seek to defy the limits of my being. Or I may not like the intangible and indeterminate presence of possibility and seek to eliminate as much indeterminacy as possible. If any of these situations are true of me, and I am your patient, I shall want you to confirm and support me in my usually non-conceptualized refusal of my being. I shall want you to attend to my particular way of being at a distance from my being. In a word, I shall want you to support my refusal of my own occurrence. What will you, my therapist, do? Won't you hear the claims of my being, the occurrence of deathliness, limitation, possibility, indeterminacy, intangibility and change? Won't you be at peace with them and welcome them as you hear me and my disturbance? Won't you remain silent when I seek you to confirm me, in order that you may give place and time for my event, my occurrence as human?

And yet you always address me in my partiality as you address the claims of my being. I may be divided against myself in hostility to the claims of my being. I may be tight and pinched and blocked in my fear of the claims of my being. I may be so distant from those claims that I dash madly about at times in which slowness is appropriate and am hardly capable of movement when speed is most appropriate for the aims of a given situation. So as I seek your confirmation for the sake of justifying or confirming my way of being, you, whom I trust, let us say, remain silent. And yet you admit, allow, and accept me in my particularity. No resistance from you, no denial, and so forth. In admitting me freely in our way of being together, you have allowed me my denial of myself, my hostility or fear regarding how I occur, or whatever the case may be. Your non-confirming allowance of my particular way of being admits at once the claims of my being and how I am in particular. When depth therapy occurs, I am freed for my being in acceptance of how I am denying it.

Perhaps I now overplay the obvious when I say that in welcoming the eventfulness or wholeness of my being, I find myself free for diversity, difference and opposition as characteristic of my own existence in my being with others. I may now be open to be as I am in my particularity as well as to be transcendent of my identity in the very occurrence of my reality. I occur as part/whole, or—and I intend to say exactly the same thing as part/whole—I occur as an event of awareness that is in a particular way.

The wholeness of human being is not an achievement, and when I welcome it I am in that welcome free from the necessity of validation of my being by means of accomplishments. The wholeness of human being is not a specific situation; and when I welcome it, I am free from the demands, responsibilities, and opportunities which also define my place and position. As I allow it, i.e., do resist and refuse it, the freedom for being whole pervades these demands and opportunities and is lived as my not being enslaved or destroyed or finally defined by them. I am then deeply free for change, in those particularities and consequently in my self-understanding and identity. The difference of wholeness vis-à-vis particularity is my freedom in my being from the identity of a particular way of being. This difference may be lived, for example, as hope when one's life is desperate or as the capacity to change even when one's life is happy, or as an uninhabited desire for growth when one feels generally satisfied with the particulars of his life or as what we name vaguely, but significantly, *soul* and the German language names *Mut*, i.e., that disposition which is the desire to be as distinct to the desire to be one thing in particular. I believe that Freud made reference to this difference made by freedom for the wholeness of one's being when he spoke with Binswanger about resistance to therapy. He noted that there is often a time in therapy when the patient may turn toward a healing process or away from it, and that, he said, is a time over which the therapist has no control. I believe that is a time when one is faced with the experiential meaning of welcoming or turning away from the eventful quality of his own being.

I might turn away because I am deeply and precognitively convinced that I will simply pass away if I do not affirm absolutely the *way* that I am alive. Absorption might be the primary object of my fear. Or I might be terrified of a total insignificance which might come if I do not second by second insist upon my way of being. Welcoming the wholeness of my being might well feel like opening my arms to dying or like sinking into a deep sea or flying endlessly and aimlessly with no control. These terms are founded in my immediate awareness of the difference between being partial and being whole. The positive direction of the terror is my sense that if I cease being partial in the way in which I now am, I cease to be. The meaning of the pathological direction is my ignorance of wholeness as compatible with intense partiality.

If you are my therapist and seek to respond with my terror in such instances, you will have the difficult task of hearing my being with my particularity. I will need to learn in my relation with you that I can welcome my wholeness without dying or totally losing my sense of myself. Perhaps I will make this non-intellectual discovery as I find myself repeatedly accepted by you in many diverse or opposing ways. Or in your freedom for whatever I am unfree for in myself. Surely there are uncountable ways in which such awareness occurs. But whatever its mode, I shall be able to welcome the wholeness of my being with you only as you and I touch or hear with and behind our words and silences and feelings and aims that occurrence pervasive of all that happens: the wholeness, the occurrence, the happening itself, which is always with, but never the same as what is going on.

When I welcome the happening of my being, its event, I am open with the oneness of existence. I am immediately in touch with the strangeness that there are beings, that this and this and this *is*. As Parmenides, Heraclitus, and Plato knew, the wonder of things is not found exclusively or even primarily with reference to their idiosyncrasies. Their particularity is necessary in their occurrence, i.e., that's the way these things are, but there is also an occurrence of reality, an event, the very opposite of a vacuum. It is the coming forth of what is there, its being there, not absolute dissolution, but coming out as things; not total darkness, but lighting up; not absence, but being. Welcoming the happening of my being is my being open with this unfixable region of awareness which I have named the wholeness or the event of being. When this welcoming openness is a part of my particular way of being, I suspect that I will no longer need extensive therapy with you.

The Mirror Inside:
The Problem of the Self

WILLIAM J. RICHARDSON

"Everyone is born different, and when we look in a mirror for the first time what we see is an image of ourselves not as ugly but simply as different from everyone else." The low-keyed voice came over CBS radio at about 7:45 a.m. one Sunday morning as part of an "all news all the time" program. Was it a news item? Was it a sermon? Was it a paid advertisement? As recalled in retrospect, the voice continued in the following vein: "We are not born ugly, but we can make ourselves ugly by lying, cheating, stealing, or simply by the way we live. Then sometimes to forget that ugly image we take drugs. But when they wear off the image is still there, even uglier than before. Then we either face the ugliness or take more drugs; the cycle starts all over again, and things go from bad to worse. Are you on drugs because of that ugly image in the mirror inside you? Then *Project Return* is for you. Let *Project Return* help you clean up that image in the mirror inside. Try *Project Return*! Make your life drug-free—it's the only way to fly."

It was, then, clearly an advertisement—a straight pitch to young listeners urging them to get help with their drug problem. What effect it had on them at 7:45 on a Sunday morning is anyone's guess, but it brings to focus a problem that—partly for philosophical, partly for psychological, partly for situational reasons—is worth discussing here. The philosophical reason is the suggestion of a classical problem: how can we better understand the nature of the human person to whom such an appeal can be made, namely, one in which the self appealed to for a free response is other than the self perceived by reflection in one's interior mirror? The psychological, or perhaps meta-psychological, reason is that the most prominent Freudian theoretician in Europe, Jacques Lacan, has been insisting for the past 30 years on precisely this kind of distinction between self and self-image in terms of the distinction between the human subject and its ego. How, then, does so pedestrian an advertisement crystallize so sophisticated a problematic? The situational reason is offered by the circumstances in which these reflections appear, for they follow upon, and to a certain extent find their point of departure in, the preceding essay of Charles Scott, "Psychotherapy: Being One and Being Many."

For Scott's essay is a sensitive phenomenological analysis of what he calls "one of the central distinctions in western thought": "that in being who I am in particular I am in my awareness beyond my particularity in common with all" (p. 81). Although this analysis is a personal one, it has deep roots in the same philosophical soil that has nurtured much of the so-called "existential" approach to psychotherapy in recent years, i.e., the thought of Martin Heidegger, for Scott's distinction between "commonality" and "particularity" in our experience recalls Heidegger's distinction between the self (*Dasein*) and the ego-subject. This raises the question as to whether a Heideggerian concept of the structure of man might offer a philosophical context within which to think Lacan's psychological/metapsychological/structuralist distinction between self and ego. At any rate, the following pages propose the thesis that this indeed may be the case.

To give the discussion a clinical context, let us talk about Craig, a 20-year-old college dropout who comes into treatment because of a chronic complaint of "loneliness" and "inability to relate" to people that has led to severe depression, relieved by the regular use of marijuana, compounded recently by an increasing dependence on alcohol. Although he had done well in grammar school, even to the point of skipping the third grade, and had proven to be a successful athlete, he was not prepared for the rigors of junior high school. He had matured early and was physically attractive to the girls in his class, but he felt shy and embarrassed in their presence—unable to respond to their interest in him. Despite an increasing attraction to girls during the high school years and a longing to touch and be touched by them, he was unable ever to feel sufficiently at ease to have any satisfactory relationship to them. Nor did his athletic ability win him any friends among his male companions, for a severe case of osteochondritis kept him for the most part inactive in sports. He was introduced to marijuana while working in a gas station during the summer after tenth grade and soon became a regular user.

The social isolation and severe loneliness of high school only became intensified when he began college at the nearby state university, and slowly he began to "come apart." He would try very hard to relate to girls on occasional dates, but the more he tried the more he would awake the next morning filled with doubts and guilt. He would then run from them with intense, bottled-up feelings. He dropped out of college in February of his freshman year and took a job as an assistant mechanic in an automotive shop, spending all of his spare time passionately preoccupied with his own car. He became more and more depressed, soon was plagued with suicidal thoughts followed by stomach cramps and diarrhea. When all physical tests proved negative, he finally, at the urge of the examining physician, sought psychiatric help.

In treatment, Craig's pathology found suggestive expression in an early dream: He was starting up his truck to go somewhere. But when he started his engine, he noticed the oil pressure reading very low. He didn't trust the gauge—but the risks would be too great to continue on, so he got out to see what was wrong. The danger was that the engine would cease while he was in motion with an explosion that would send pieces flying apart—breaking out of the engine block, hurling through the air, injuring people, or at the very least disabling the vehicle completely. So he stopped and checked, looked into the engine, started pulling a piston out, found he was pulling this out of his own chest and abdomen. The machine was himself. He pulled the piston out, put it back, repeated this several times— in and out, in and out. Couldn't see what was wrong. All he noticed were the signs of normal wear and tear.

Diagnostically, what does the psychological test report say of him? "Narcissistic personality [the *Diagnostic and Statistical Manual of Mental Disorders, II* terminology would say 'schizoid personality'] with obsessional features and an underlying depression." Fair enough— provided that we understand what a narcissistic personality is. But narcissism is one of the notions that Freud left ambiguous. Its general sense, of course, is clear: Referring to the myth of Narcissus, the fair youth who fell in love with his own image in the water and pined away while contemplating it, Freud understands narcissism to be love directed toward the image of oneself. But does that mean that Narcissus fell in love with his own ego? Here is where the ambiguity appears, for Freud's conception of the ego (and with it the notion of "narcissism") fluctuates over the years from meaning a simple image of oneself to meaning an agency differentiated from other agencies of the subject, such as "id" and "superego," whose fundamental task is adaptation to the "real."[1] Lacan, for his part, resolves the ambiguity by opting clearly for the first sense. How, then, would Lacan understand Craig's narcissism in terms of such a conception of the ego?

But first, who is Jacques Lacan?[2] Now in his seventies, he is probably the best known and certainly the most controversial psychoanalyst in France. His early training culminated in 1932 with a doctoral thesis entitled, *On Paranoiac Psychosis in its Relationship with Personality.* His earliest researches had left him convinced that no physiological phenomenon could be considered adequately, independent of its relationship to the entire personality that engages in an interaction with a social milieu.[3] And it was to ground this conviction in an exhaustive case study that the doctoral work was undertaken.

The nub of the matter, of course, is the word "personality." He speaks of it in the loosest terms as a kind of "psychic synthesis,"[4] "the ensemble of specialized functional relations that establishes the originality of man-the-animal, adapting him to the enormous influence exercised by the milieu of mankind, or society, on the milieu of his life."[5] As Lacan's own thought began to take shape after the doctoral thesis, two themes in particular intrigued him: the role of the image and the role of milieu in personality formation. The first, the role of the image, found articulation in a paper given at the Fourteenth International Psychoanalytic Congress in 1936. The second theme, the role of milieu, found articulation in an article on "The Family" in de Monzie's edition of the *Encyclopédie française,*[6] where Lacan maintains quite explicitly that the family is more significant as a social milieu than as a biological fabric out of which the subject is cut. The first theme was treated again in a much revised version at the Sixteenth International Psychoanalytic Congress in 1949. The second theme, the role of milieu, was to find a completely new mode of expression under the inspiration of Lévi-Strauss' structural studies of the late 30's and 40's.

For our present purposes, let us focus on the famous paper of 1949, entitled, "The mirror stage as formative of the function of the 'I' as revealed in psychoanalytic experience."[7] Here his thought is polarized by the notion of "image" which he takes to be a principle of in-*form*-ation, i.e., of giving form to the organism in the sense of guiding its development. Starting from what he takes to be the aforementioned ambiguity in Freud's conception of narcissism, Lacan argues this way: The newly born human infant, initially sunk in motor incapacity, turbulent movements, and fragmentation, first experiences itself as a unity through experiencing some kind of reflection of itself, the paradigm for which would be self reflection in a mirror. This normally occurs between the ages of six and 18 months. This mirror-like reflection, then, serves as the form that in-forms the subject and guides its development. So it happens that there is an "identification" between infant and its reflection ". . . in the full sense that analysis has given to the term: namely, the transformation that takes place in the subject when he assumes an image. . . ."[8] It is this reflected image of itself with which the infant identifies that Lacan understands by the "I," or as we would normally say, the "ego." To be sure, this "mirror" experience is no more than a "convenient symbol" of what takes place here. The essential is that there be some human form, some external image that the infant takes to be a "reflection" of itself. Presumably this human form could also be—and in the concrete is more likely to be—the mothering figure. In any case, the image is "other" than the subject, and identification with it constitutes a primordial alienation of the subject. The consequences of this, of course, are enormous.

Let us focus on only one of them. What precisely does the infant discover in experiencing his form reflected in the mirror? First of all, a unity that replaces his prior experience of fragmentation.[9] This unity becomes idealized into a model for all eventual integration. This model, however, although it "fixes" the subject in a certain permanence that contrasts with the "turbulent movements that the subject feels are animating him,"[10] does so through a form that initially (i.e., prior to the subject's assumption of it through identification) is "other" than the subject, exterior to it, hence an "alienation" of it. The stability of this form, contrasting as it does with the instability of the initial fragmentation, assumes a tensile strength that eventually becomes rigid and armour-like—the basis of "the inertia characteristic of the formations of the I," i.e., its defense mechanisms.[11] That is why the author can speak of the process as the "assumption of the armour of an alienating identity, which will mark with its rigid structure the subject's entire mental development."[12]

If Lacan were to look at Craig, then, he would find in him, one suspects, a clear example of the alienated, objectified ego stretched to the age of 20. If he were to hear Craig tell of some of his fantasies (e.g., his flash-like vision of fingers cut off, his forearm amputated) or read in his psychological test report that "what he tries to connect up are spatially distant, separately perceived body parts (of insects, rodents and crabs)," Lacan almost certainly would say that this is a fantasy of the body "in bits and pieces" (*image du corps morcelé*) "bound up with the elucidation of the earliest problems of the patient's ego."[13] This would be confirmed by the dream in which he finds himself "suspended in a metal frame over a body of water, rocking back and forth in the wind, trembling with terror," for Lacan tells us that "this illusion of unity, in which a human being is always looking forward to self-mastery, entails a constant danger of sliding back again into the chaos from which he started; it hangs over [an] abyss . . . in which one can see perhaps the very essence of anxiety."[14] And Craig's preoccupation with his car would simply exemplify for Lacan another of his remarks: "The relations between *Homo psychologicus* and the machines he uses are very striking, and this is especially so in the case of the motor-car. We get the impression that his relationship to this machine is so very intimate that it is almost as if the two were actually conjoined—its mechanical defects and breakdowns often parallel his neurotic symptoms. Its emotional significance for him comes from the fact that it exteriorizes the protective shell of his ego, as well as the failure of his virility."[15]

But if all this is said about Craig's ego as the initial alienation of himself, what of his true self-hood and how can it be salvaged? Surely it is more than the sheer physical organism of the infant that finds itself reflected in its mirror image, but strictly speaking it is no more than an inchoative subject at that point. True subjectivity, according to Lacan, begins when the human infant has entered the domain of language and becomes capable of speech. But how he understands this needs some explanation.

To be sure the self is the one who says "I," but Freud's greatness, Lacan tells us, consists in having discovered once and for all "the self's radical ex-centricity to itself."[16] He arrives at that statement after dallying with the notion of the self implied in Descartes' *cogito* by posing the conundrum: "The place that I occupy as the subject of a signifier, is it in relation to the place I occupy as subject of the signified concentric or ex-centric?—that is the question"[17] (1977, p. 165). In other words, does the self have another center than that of its conscious discourse? His answer with Freud is, of course, "yes." But how is this ex-centric center of the self to be conceived? Here we have to back up a little.

William J. Richardson

For Lacan, Freud's basic insight was into the nature of the "talking cure" and a close reading of Freud's early work, principally *Interpretation of Dreams* (1900), *The Psychopathology of Everyday Life* (1901) and *Jokes and Their Relation to the Unconscious* (1905) all convince Lacan of the importance for Freud of language and speech in psychoanalysis. Scientifically trained, however, Freud wanted to make his insights scientifically respectable, but the only scientific model available to him at the time was that of nineteenth century physics. In our day—and this is something that the early structuralist studies of Lévi-Strauss helped Lacan appreciate—we have available another scientific model (a more characteristically human one) for understanding the psyche: the science of linguistics—a science that explores the structures discernible in the one phenomenon that is coextensive with man himself, i.e., human language. Linguistics has already thrown light on other disciplines, particularly anthropology (e.g., the work of Sapir and Whorf in America as well as of Lévi-Strauss himself) and Lacan's intention, following the stimulus of Lévi-Strauss, is to let it throw light on psychoanalysis.

To appreciate what the structuralists see in linguistics that leads them to take it as a paradigm for their work, recall for a moment Lévi-Strauss' explanation:

> ... Among all social phenomena language alone has thus far been studied in a manner which permits it to serve as the object of truly scientific analysis, allowing us to understand its formative process and to predict its mode of change. This results from modern researches into the problems of phonemics, which have reached beyond the superficial conscious and historical expression of linguistic phenomena to obtain fundamental and objective realities consisting of systems of relations which are the products of unconscious thought processes. The question which now arises is this: is it possible to effect a similar reduction in the analysis of other forms of social phenomena? If so, would this analysis lead to the same result? And if the answer to this last question is in the affirmative, can we conclude that all forms of social life are substantially of the same nature—that is, do they consist of systems of behavior that represent the projection, on the level of conscious and socialized thought, of universal laws which regulate the unconscious activities of the mind? . . .[18]

The answer for Lévi-Strauss is "yes."

It is "yes" for Lacan, too. His task becomes, then, to explore the "universal laws" that regulate the "unconscious activities" of the mind, where these "universal laws" are the laws of language and the "unconscious activities" are those processes that Freud discovered and which he designated simply as "the unconscious." What is meant here by the "universal laws" of language? We know well enough that since Saussure in modern times language has been considered a system of signs and that these signs are composed of a relationship between a signifying component (a sound image) and a signified component (a concept), the relationship itself being arbitrary, i.e., non-necessary (e.g., there is no necessary connection

100

between the word "horse" and our idea of horse—*cheval, Pferd, equus,* will do as well). In one of his essays, Lacan speaks of these signifiers as composed of "ultimate distinctive features" that are the phonemes, i.e., the smallest distinctive group of speech sounds in any language. These signifiers in turn are combined according to the "laws of a closed order," i.e., laws of vocabulary and of grammar according to which the phonemes are grouped into units of meaning of increasing complexity (e.g., words, phrases, clauses, sentences, etc.).[19]

Now the units of meaning composed out of phonemes (words, phrases, clauses, etc.) relate to one another along one or other of two fundamental axes of language: an axis of combination and an axis of selection. Here again the pioneer work was done by Roman Jakobson (1956, pp. 53-87). Along the axis of combination, linguistic units are related to one another insofar as they are co-present to each other. Thus the words used in this very sentence, even though stretched out in a linear sequence that suspends their full meaning to the end, are related to each other by a type of co-presence, i.e., they are connected to each other by a certain contiguity in time. The second axis along which linguistic units relate to each other, however, is the axis of selection. This means that they do not relate to each other by reason of a co-presence, but rather by some kind of mutually complementary non-presence, i.e., of mutual exclusion, whether this is because one word is chosen over another as being more appropriate (e.g., we speak of Lacan as a psychoanalyst rather than simply as a "physician") or because one word implies the rejection of its antonym, (e.g., by calling him a "structuralist," we imply that he is not an "existentialist," etc.). Thus, to select one unit is to exclude the other, but at the same time the excluded other is still available to be substituted for the first if circumstances warrant. The axis of selection, then, is also an axis of possible substitution.

These two principles of combination and selection permeate the entire structure of language. Thus, Jakobson was able to analyze the nature of aphasia according to whether the patient was deficient in terms of the axis of combination or the axis of selection.[21] Now, when these two axes of combination and selection function in terms of the relationship between signifiers, we find that signifiers either may be related to each other by a principle of combination, i.e., in terms of some kind of contiguity with each other (e.g., a relationship of cause/effect, part/whole, sign/thing signified, etc.), in other words, by reason of what the old rhetoric of Quintilian called "metonymy"; or they may be related by reason of similarity/dissimilarity, hence by a principle of selection in virtue of the fact that one is substituted for the other—in other words, by "metaphor." For example, on the morning following the first Nixon-Frost interview, the CBS radio news headline announced: "Nixon discusses Watergate; Australia has its own Watergate." Here, "Watergate" is twice used as a signifier, and the signified is both times the same, i.e., a political scandal. But in each instance, the relationship between signifier and signified is different: in the first case ("Nixon discusses Watergate") the signifier ("Watergate") signifies "political scandal" by designating the place where it first began to be uncovered, hence by contiguity along the axis of combination, i.e., by metonymy; in the second case ("Australia has its own Watergate"), the signifier "Watergate," already clothed in metonymic associations, is used to substitute for the term "political scandal," hence is plotted along the axis of selection and functions as a metaphor. If we say, then, that signifiers are related to each other under the guise of either metonymy or metaphor, this is simply to transpose the laws of combination and selection into another key. Let this suffice, then, to indicate the sort of thing that is meant when we speak here of the "laws of language."

But how do these relate to the nature of the unconscious as Freud experienced it? It is Lacan's thesis that Freud's insight into the nature of the talking cure was an insight into the way the laws of language work in a relationship between signifiers that may be described as either metonymy or metaphor. Let us be content with mentioning two ways in particular by which this may be understood so as to gain some appreciation of the flavor of his thought: the first concerns the principle of free association as the "fundamental law" of psychoanalysis; the second concerns the function of dream work in shaping the manifest dream.

To be concrete, let us recall the analysis Freud makes of one of his own dreams, the "Dream of the Botanical Monograph":

> Content of the Dream. — "I had written a monograph on an (unspecified) genus of plants. The book lay before me and I was at the moment turning over a folded coloured plate. Bound up in the copy there was a dried specimen of the plant."
>
> The element in this dream which stood out most was the *botanical monograph*. This arose from the impression of the dreamday: I had in fact seen a monograph on the genus Cyclamen in the window of a bookshop. There was no mention of this genus in the content of the dream; all that was left in it was the monograph and its relation to botany. The "botanical monograph" immediately revealed its connection with the *work upon cocaine* which I had once written. From "cocaine" the chains of thought led to my friend Dr. Königstein, the eye surgeon, who had had a share in the introduction of cocaine. . . .
>
> Not only the compound idea, "botanical monograph," however, but each of its components, "botanical" and "monograph" separately, led by numerous connecting paths deeper and deeper into the tangle of dream thoughts. "Botanical" was related to the figure of Professor Gärtner [Gardener], the *blooming* looks of his wife, to my patient Flora and to the lady of whom I had told the story of the forgotten *flowers*. . . . So, too, "monograph" in a dream touches upon two subjects: the one-sidedness of my studies and the costliness of my favourite hobbies.[22]

Here we see Freud associating freely to his own dream. Now for Lacan, the flow of associations is a flow of signifiers. Each signifier has what Saussure would call a corresponding conceptual content (signified), but for Lacan the signifier does not refer to its individual signified but rather to another signifier/association, and this in turn to another in a chain of signifiers. Lacan describes this "signifying chain" as "rings of a necklace that is a ring in another necklace made of rings."[23] Surely the complex concatenation of Freud's thoughts here may be described in such terms: "Rings of a necklace that is a ring in another necklace made of rings." It is important to note that the meaning (signified) of this series of associations resides not in any association in particular but in the whole sequence. As Lacan puts it, "it is in the chain of the signifiers that the meaning 'insists' but . . . none of its elements 'consists' in the signification of which it is at the moment capable. We are forced, then, to accept the notion of an incessant sliding of the signified under the signifier."[24] In any case, the signifiers in this stream of associations relate to one another along the great axes, namely, combination and selection, which are typical of the laws of the unconscious.

Perhaps this will become clearer if we look at the second way in which Lacan sees the "laws of language" structuring the operation of the unconscious, namely, in that operation by which the raw materials of the dream, such as the dream thoughts or day residues are transformed (usually with distortions) into the manifest content of the dream, i.e., by the "dream work." The distorting process according to Freud's economic theory has two basic modes: "condensation," where a single idea represents several associative chains insofar as it is located at the point where they intersect,[25] and "displacement" where the intensity of an idea is "detached" from it and passed on to another idea/ideas of less intensity but related to the first by a chain of associations.[26] Now Lacan, following the suggestion of Jakobson but developing it in his own way, claims that condensation is a form of substitution, grounded in the principles of similarity/dissimilarity, hence to be located linguistically along the axis of selection: in other words, it is basically metaphor. Displacement, however, functions by reason of contiguity, hence is to be located linguistically along the axis of combination: in other words, it is metonymy.

The dream of the botanical monograph Freud himself presents as an example of both condensation and displacement. First, as condensation:

> This first investigation leads us to conclude that the elements "botanical" and "monograph" found their way into the content of the dream because they possessed copious contacts with the majority of the dream-thoughts, because, that is to say, they constituted "nodal points" upon which a great number of the dream thoughts converged, and because they had several meanings in connection with the interpretation of the dream.[27]

What Lacan adds to Freud here—or explicitates for Freud—is that these "nodal points" function as such because the laws of language (in this case the axis of selection/substitution) first make their metaphoric structure possible.

Again, according to Freud the same dream from a different point of view is an example of displacement, too:

> In the dream of the botanical monograph, for instance, the central point of the dream-content was obviously the element "botanical"; but as the dream-thoughts were concerned with the complications and conflicts arising between colleagues from their professional obligations, and further with the charge that I was in the habit of sacrificing too much for the sake of my hobbies. The element "botanical" had no place whatever in this core of the dream-thoughts, unless it was loosely connected with it by an antithesis—the fact that botany never had a place among my favourite studies.[28]

If Lacan says that the unconscious is structured "like a language,"[29] the sense is that its processes follow the axes of combination and selection as all language does. As such, it is "that part of [our] concrete discourse, insofar as it is transindividual, that is not at the disposal of the subject in re-establishing the continuity of its conscious discourse."[30] "Transindividual" (I take him to mean "beyond my particularity in common with all"), it is "other" than individual consciousness (I take him to mean "being who I am in particular"), i.e., "the other scene" or simply the Other. Other, it is yet discernible, namely:

> —In monuments: this is my body. That is to say, the . . . nucleus of the neurosis in which the hysterical symptom reveals the structure of language, and is deciphered like an inscription . . .;
> —In archival documents: these are childhood memories . . .;
> —In semantic evolution: this corresponds to the stock of words and acceptations of my own particular vocabulary as it does to my style of life and to my character;
> —In tradition [understand: all traditions and natural languages], too, and even in the legends [understand myths] which, in a heroicized form, bear my history.
> —And, lastly, in the traces that are inevitably preserved by the distortions necessitated by the linking of the adulterated chapter [of my life] to the chapters surrounding it and whose meaning will be re-established by my exegesis.[31]

As Lacan understands Freud, then, the unconscious is the transindividual structure of language that we have "in common with all," filtered, however, through "who I am in particular" with my own personal history. It is in this sense that the subject is "radically ex-centric to itself" and it is in terms of such a conception that the psychoanalytic method takes on its full import: "Its means are those of speech, insofar as speech confers a meaning on the functions of the individual; its domain is that of concrete discourse, insofar as this is the field of the transindividual reality of the subject; its operations are those of [the subject's] history, insofar as history constitutes the emergence of truth in the real."[32]

But our concern at the moment is not so much with the psychoanalytic method as with the "radical heteronomy" of the unconscious in the "ex-centric self."[33] Lacan speaks of the "other to whom I am more attached than to myself, since, at the heart of my assent to my own identity it is still he who agitates me."[34] How, then, does Lacan conceive of the process by which the infant as inchoative subject still-to-be-achieved becomes exposed to this other center within himself? How is he, to use Lacan's own phrase, "born into language."[35]

Lacan himself takes as the paradigm for this experience a famous anecdote of Freud's that is, I presume, familiar:

> ... This good little boy had an occasional disturbing habit of taking small objects he got hold of and throwing them away from him into a corner, under the bed, and so on, so that hunting for his toys and picking them up was often quite a business. As he did this, he gave vent to a loud, long drawn out "o-o-o-o," accompanied by an expression of interest and satisfaction. His mother and the writer of the present account were agreed in thinking that this was not a mere interjection but represented the German word *fort* ["gone"]. I eventually realized it was a game and that the only use he made of any of his toys was to play "gone" with them. One day I made an observation which confirmed my view. The child had a wooden reel with a piece of string tied round it. It never occurred to him to pull it along the floor behind him, for instance, and play at its being a carriage. What he did was to hold the reel by the string and very skillfully throw it over the edge of his curtained cot, so that it disappeared into it, at the same time uttering his expressive "o-o-o-o." He then pulled the reel out of the cot again by its string and hailed its reappearance with a joyful *da* ["there"]. This, then, was the complete game—disappearance and return. . . .[36]

For Freud, the meaning of the game was obvious. "It was related to the child's great cultural achievement—the instinctual renunciation (i.e., the renunciation of instinctual satisfaction) which he had made in allowing his mother to go away without protesting..." (p. 15). For Lacan, the "cultural achievement" here did not consist simply in the child's "renunciation of instinctual satisfaction" but rather in his experience of desire for the mother precisely in separating from her and in dealing with his frustrated desire through the little game of which inchoatively verbal sounds were an essential part. It is in this context that he tells us that the moment "in which desire becomes human is also that in which the child is born into language."[37]

How "born into language"? Lacan tells us: ". . . The child begins to become engaged in the system of the concrete discourse of the environment by reproducing more or less approximately in his *fort!* and in his *da!* the vocables which he receives from it."[38] Let us note, then: that given a matrix of possible phonemes, it is the environment of the natural language that determines which ones are assimilated by a child; that the pair that is assimilated expresses the experience of presence through absence; and what characterizes this moment for Lacan is the fact that although the natural language has surrounded the child from the beginning of life, it is only now that the child actively begins to make the language his own.

But how the child passes from this moment of incipient speech into the domain of language as a social institution is for Lacan much more than what it is, say, for a Piaget, simply a matter of "self-regulating equilibration." He sees here a profound evolution from a dyadic relationship with the mother into a profoundly pluralized relationship to society as a whole. The father, then, is more than the third member of the Oedipal triangle—he is the symbol and representative of the social order as such into which the child by the acquisition of speech now enters. The social order is governed by a set of relationships that determine all forms of human interchange (e.g., the forming of pacts, gift-giving, marriage ties, kinship relations, etc.). This mapping of human relationships with its symbolic arrangements Lacan speaks of as "law," to suggest in all probability the patterning, compelling quality of it. In any case, this law is characteristically human, for, Lacan writes, ". . . In regulating marriage ties [it] superimposes the kingdom of culture on that of nature abandoned to the law of copulation. The interdiction of incest is only its subjective pivot. . . ."[39] This law is what Lévi-Strauss has called the "symbolic order," an order of signs designating the primordial arrangement of society itself. Lacan, following Lévi-Strauss here,[40] finds that this primordial law that sets the pattern for human relationships is the same law that sets the pattern of human language. ". . . The law of man has been the law of language, he writes, since the first words of recognition presided over the first gifts. . . ."[41]

In any case, the symbolic order represented by the father is the field, or domain, in which the child becomes an active citizen when he acquires the power of speech. The essence of Freud's discovery, Lacan claims, was to see the relationship between the individual psyche and the symbolic order in terms of man's unconscious dimension. "Isn't it striking," he writes, "that Lévi-Strauss, in suggesting the implication of the structures of language with that part of the social laws which regulate marriage ties and kinship, is already conquering the very terrain in which Freud situates the unconscious"?[42]

At this point one would be tempted to ask how it is that this moment of "birth into language" is also the moment when "desire becomes human," but that would take us too far afield. For it would be necessary to show how the basic dynamic of the human subject for Lacan is not libido, as it is for Freud, but desire, as it is for Hegel; how this desire e-rupts in the infant in the rupture of the dyadic, quasi-symbiotic relation with the mother by which the infant experiences in its separation from her the negation of itself, hence, its *manque à être*—its own lack of (or, better, want of) being, out of which its wanting (its desire) is born; how this desire is essentially a desire to be desired, i.e., to be recognized as an object of desire by another; and, finally how the child's desire—its endless quest for a lost paradise—

must be tunnelled like an underground river through the subterranean passageways of the symbolic order—passageways whose labyrinthine involution resembles in its complexity the "rings of a necklace that is a ring in another necklace made of rings." All of this is too far-reaching for adequate treatment here.

For now it must suffice to situate Lacan's conception of the ex-centric, i.e., de-ego-centered self, in a philosophical context that is not Hegelian but rather Heideggerian, as this is suggested by Scott's distinction between "who I am in particular" and "my awareness beyond particularity in common with all." That Lacan needs a philosophical base presumably need not be argued here. That such a base is conveniently a Heideggerian one is suggested by Lacan himself. The "force" of the unconscious comes from the "dimension of Being: *Kern unseres Wesens* are Freud's own terms."[43] It is this Being-dimension of the self for Lacan that is the ground for those experiences common to all men such as are captured so often in myth, the ground even for neurosis in the sense that "a neurosis is a question which Being poses for a subject 'from the place where it was before the subject came into the world' (Freud's phrase which he used in explaining the Oedipal complex to Little Hans)."[44]

How are we to understand Being here? Lacan answers: "The 'Being' referred to is that which appears in a lightning moment of the void of the word 'to be' and I said that it poses its question for the subject. What does that mean? It does not pose it *before* the subject, since the subject cannot come to the place where it is posed, but it poses it *in place of* the (*à la place du*) subject, that is, in that place it poses the question *with* the subject, as one poses a problem *with* a pen. . . ."[45] But this is certainly Heideggerian language, and Lacan acknowledges the influence explicitly. In fact, at one point in his career he personally translated into French and published an essay of Heidegger—the essay on *Logos* in Heraclitus (1956).[46] In any case, we have reason to find in Heidegger some paradigm for Lacan's notion of an ex-centric subject.

The basic parameters of Heidegger's thought are familiar to the readers of this *Review*. It is commonplace knowledge now that Heidegger is not at all concerned with a cheap "existentialism" that was often attributed to him in the past but is in search of the meaning of Being (*Sein*). Choosing phenomenology as his method, he considers the phenomenon par excellence for examination to be man, (i.e., *Dasein*), because man obviously has some vague awareness (*Seinsverständnis*) of what Being means inasmuch as he can and does speak, say "is." Heidegger begins the analysis by taking *Dasein* as he is found with other *Daseins* in his everyday condition as Being-in-the-World, analyzing first the meaning of World, then the nature of Being-*in*-the World with its four existential components of *Verstehen* ("understanding"), *Befindlichkeit* ("state of mind"), *Rede* ("discourse"), *Verfallen* ("fallenness"). He then tries to see this complex

Being in its unity (*Sorge*: care), and in its totality, (i.e., as defined by its ultimate limit [death]). After this, he explores the sources of this unified totality in the still deeper unity of time, with everything that this implies concerning historicity, history, and all that goes with it. All of this, I take it, is well known. I suggest that we focus our attention on those aspects of it that pertain to the notion of the de-centered self.

In Heideggerian terms, *Dasein* is an ex-centric, de-centered self insofar as its own Being consists in its openness to the Being of all beings (including itself)—that mysterious process that lights up all beings from the inside and lets them present themselves to man as what they are. As such, *Dasein* can indeed relate to other beings as a conscious ego, for it can and does say "I." This is called its "ontic" dimension, and it is on this level that it becomes possible for *Dasein* to "occupy a place as subject of the signifier," and to view itself in a mirror image, in experiencing itself as an alienated, objectified ego. Be that as it may, *Dasein* is more than a conscious ego—it transcends all beings to their very Being—this is called its "ontological" dimension, and, since the center of *Dasein*'s ontological movement is Being (*Kern unseres Wesens*), and Being is "other" than the beings that surround *Dasein* and form the lateral center of its day-to-day direction, *Dasein* is a genuinely de-centered, ex-centric self.

The details of Heidegger's existential analysis are sufficiently familiar. It is important only to call attention to the fact that an essential part of *Dasein*'s ontological constitution is the component of *Rede*, often translated "discourse," though perhaps better translated back into the Greek word that it translates into German, i.e., *logos*. Logos, as an "existential" component, is that element in *Dasein*'s structure by which *Dasein* "lets be seen" in human words what the disclosive power of *Verstehen* ("understanding") reveals. Let us recall, too, that different modes of this process of "letting be seen" include "attend-ing" (*Hören*), on the one hand, and "keeping silent" (*Schweigen*) on the other.[47] This attending may be either to others or with others to the insinuations of Being itself. Remember as well that this constituent element of *Dasein* is prey to the finitude that marks its fundamental condition, one important aspect of which is described in terms of "fallenness"—the ground of *Dasein*'s inauthentic everydayness.[48] Fallenness permeates the existential component of logos, too, and accounts for that propensity in *Dasein* by reason of which human speech tends to lose its basic character as revelatory of beings and to become a mutually interchanged verbalism, more concealing of beings than revealing of them. The result is what Heidegger calls merely "idle talk" (*Gerede*),[49] and it is here, perhaps, that one should look for the ontological foundation of what Lacan calls "empty speech."[50] Be that as it may, the existential component of logos is the ground in *Dasein* that makes all dia-logue, hence the psychoanalytic method of attend-ing to the unconscious, possible.

Dasein, then, ontologically equipped for the articulation of speech by reason of the existential component of logos, is open to Being. But what is the nature of this Being to which *Dasein* is open? Initially, it is discerned as the Being of beings encountered within the World, then as more than this— as the World itself, experienced as a matrix of relationships (Total Meaningfulness) interior to which these beings find a place and have a meaning. But this is the perspective of the early Heidegger, of *Being and Time* (1927), which took man for the starting point of the analysis. Later on the focus shifts, and Heidegger attempts to meditate the sense of Being by thinking it, so to speak, for itself as it reveals and conceals itself in and as history. He returns to the early Greeks to meditate their ways of bringing their experience of Being to expression in words like *Physis* (nature), *A-lētheia* (truth), and, in Heraclitus, *Logos*. We restrict our attention here to the *Logos* of Heraclitus. For the early Greeks, according to Heidegger, the word *Logos* came from *legein*, meaning "to gather, collect, bring together, lay out in the open," etc. As *Logos*, then, Being was experienced as a gathering process that collected all beings together within themselves and in relationship to one another.[51] Above all, it is a process that lets beings appear as what they are, a letting-them-lie-forth in all the freshness of their original presencing.

How, then, did such a term ever come to mean "speech" or "language"? Heidegger's claim is that speech, long before it became an instrument of communication, is that process in man by which he responds to, corresponds with, the gathering process (*Logos*) in beings and through the functioning of the logos within himself lets *Logos* lie forth in words. To name something properly, for example, is to call it forth, in the sense of laying it out in the open, in such a way that the being can shine forth as what it is. ". . . The process of naming (*onoma*) is not the expressing of the meaning of a word but letting-something-lie-forth in that light wherein it takes its stand [as a being, simply] inasmuch as it has a name."[52] To speak in this way, of course, is the special privilege of the poet, but all of language is a derivation—or a degeneration—from this primordial experience.

The way from the conception of language as correspondence with the *Logos* by calling beings into presence to the conception of language as a system of signs or code of communication (as in Saussure) is, of course, a long and winding road that cannot be followed here. For the moment, let us infer at least this much: an experience of Being-as-*Logos*, the One that gathers the many unto themselves and lets them relate to one another, is an experience of language in its origins, of aboriginal Language. As such, it is also the source of the cohesiveness of all things that are, hence the principle of all Order, and specifically the foundation for the symbolic order as such, the ontological base of language as social institution and code. If Jakobson and his colleagues in their researches discover the laws of phonemes or the two great axes of language that Lacan then sees to be structuring the unconscious as it permeates man, then these are historical modalities, discernible by scientific scrutiny, of the promordial *Logos* as such. Primordial, it has a certain priority over man. That is why Lacan can speak of it as "agitating us," of "Language speaking man" rather than the reverse.

Some will argue, perhaps, that the correlation suggested here between Heidegger's experience of aboriginal Language and Lacan's conception of the Freudian unconscious is too farfetched, for the latter is "ontic," the former "ontological"—and "never the 'twain shall meet." But *Logos* as we are proposing to conceive it is only the structur*ing* process that gives rise to the structur*ed* ("like a language") phenomenon—albeit ontic—that Freud discovered. And the conception of *Logos*-as-Language is only a later development in Heidegger of his lifelong effort to think the meaning of Being as the structuring dimension *of beings*, one of which, of course, is language as it is studied by the linguists. The meditation on *Logos* published in 1951 is clearly an effort to grapple with a question already bothering him in 1925, i.e., even before the publication of *Being and Time* (1927). In his Marburg lectures of 1925-26 he wrote:

> . . . Because *Dasein* in its very Being gives rise to meaning (*bedeutend*), it lives in meanings and can give expression to itself in these terms. And it is only because there are these locutions (*Verlautbarungen*) accruing to meaning, i.e., [inchoative] words (*Wörte*), that there are [the] words (*Wörter*) [of ordinary speech]. That is, now for the first time speech forms (*Sprachgestalten*) can become separable from the meaning that first shaped them [and signifier from signified?]. A totality of such locutions in which to a certain extent the comprehension of a *Dasein* grows and in the existential sense is—this is what we designate as *language* (*Sprache*). However, if I speak here of the totality of *Dasein*, I do not mean the individual *Dasein* [i.e., "who I am in particular"] but [*Dasein*] in its togetherness with others (*Miteinandersein*) (i.e., "beyond my particularity in common with all") as an historical [phenomenon]. What manner of Being this phenomenon that we call language has is up to now fundamentally obscure. The language that day by day grows and decays, that changes from generation to generation or even lies dead for centuries—this peculiar Being of language itself is still totally unexplained. In other words, the manner of Being of what is theme for all philology and linguistics is, ontologically speaking, completely enigmatic. . . . [What is clear is] that the phenomena of language itself, taken here in the narrower sense of speech form in a kind of separation from the content of meaning— all these structural complexes (*Strukturzusammenhänge*) of a speech form itself can be understood only in terms of the historicity of *Dasein*. . . .[53]

How Heidegger passed from these reflections on the relation of *Dasein* to language early in his career to the *Logos* meditations of 25 years later is a question that may be left aside for the moment. It suffices here to remind ourselves that this long and tortuous path was but a single way. This is what permits us to suggest that in an effort to discern a Heideggerian base for the perspectives of Jacques Lacan, both moments of Heidegger's development may be thought together.

For the genuine psychoanalytic dialogue will consist in attend-ing with the other to the Other (the *Logos*) in its self-manifestation and bringing it appropriately into words. But this mutual attend-ing takes place in a manner that is profoundly marked by *Dasein*'s historicity, more precisely by an effort to retrieve (*Wiederholung*) the patient's past. Thus Lacan can say: ". . . In Heideggerian language one could say that [properly psychoanalytic] types of recollection constitute the subject as *gewesend*— that is to say, as being the one who thus has been. . . ."[54] In any case, "it is certainly this assumption of his history by the subject, insofar as it is constituted by the speech addressed to the other, that constitutes the ground of the new method that Freud called psychoanalysis. . . ."[55]

How this "new method" might help Craig experience himself as ek-sistent *Dasein* (Lacan would simply say "subject"), how it might in effect help him come to grips with his own fallen condition and pass from the articulation of "empty" to "full' (i.e., authentic) speech and thereby appreciate his true self as more profound and re*source*full than the rigidified mirror-reflection of himself as an objectified ego suggests—all this would take us farther into his clinical case history than the circumstances of our present situation permit. Let it suffice to say that from a psychoanalytic point of view the work to be done here must be done without the help of *Project Return*—or rather through a "project return" (*Wiederholung*) of quite another kind.

NOTES

1 J. Laplanche and J. B. Pontalis, *The Language of Psychoanalysis*, trans. by D. Nicholson-Smith (New York: W. W. Norton & Co., 1973), p. 256.

2 The following sketch of Lacan's fundamental perspective condenses a much more adequate exposition to be found in J. P. Muller and W. J. Richardson, "Toward Reading Lacan: Pages for a Workbook," *Psychoanalysis and Contemporary Thought* (Fall, 1978). Portions of that exposition are repeated here through the courtesy of the International Universities Press.

3 J. Lacan, *De la psychose paranoïaque dans ses rapports avec la personnalité*, suivi de *Premiers écrits sur la paranoia* (Paris: Éditions du Seuil, 1975), p. 400.

4 *Ibid.*, p. 14.

5 *Ibid.*, p. 400.

6 J. Lacan, "La Famille" in A. de Monzie, ed., *Encyclopédie française*, 8, sec. 40 (*La vie mentale*), (Paris: Librairie Larousse, 1938), pp. 3-16.

7 J. Lacan, *Écrits: A Selection*, trans. by A. Sheridan (New York: W. W. Norton & Co., 1977), pp. 1-7.

8 *Ibid.*, p. 2.

9 *Ibid.*, p. 4.

10 *Ibid.*, p. 2.

11 *Ibid.*, p. 7.

12 *Ibid.*, p. 4.

13 J. Lacan, "Some Reflections on the Ego," *International Journal of Psycho-Analysis*, 34, 1953, 11-17, p. 13.

William J. Richardson

14 *Ibid.*, p. 15.

15 *Ibid.*, p. 17.

16 J. Lacan, *Écrits: A Selection*, p. 171.

17 *Ibid.*, p. 165.

18 C. Lévi-Strauss, "Language and the Analysis of Social Laws," in *Structural Anthropology* (New York: Basic Books, 1963), trans. by C. Jacobson and B. Schoepf, pp. 58-59.

19 J. Lacan, *Écrits: A Selection*, p. 153.

20 R. Jakobson and M. Halle, *Fundamentals of Language* (The Hague: Mouton, 1956), pp. 53-87.

21 *Ibid.*, pp. 63-75.

22 S. Freud, *The Interpretation of Dreams* (1900), in *The Standard Edition of the Complete Psychological Works of Sigmund Freud* (London: Hogarth Press, 1953), 4, J. Strachey, ed., pp. 282-283.

23 J. Lacan, *Écrits: A Selection*, p. 153.

24 *Ibid.*, pp. 153-154.

25 J. Laplanche and J. B. Pontalis, *Language of Psychoanalysis*, p. 80.

26 *Ibid.*, p. 121.

27 S. Freud, *Standard Edition*, 4, p. 283.

28 *Ibid.*, p. 305.

29 E.g., J. Lacan, *Écrits: A Selection*, pp. 159-164.

30 *Ibid.*, p. 49.

31 *Ibid.*, p. 50.

32 *Ibid.*, p. 32.

33 *Ibid.*, p. 172.

34 *Ibid.*

35 *Ibid.*, p. 163.

36 S. Freud, *Beyond the Pleasure Principle*, in *Standard Edition*, 18, pp. 14-15.

37 J. Lacan, *Écrits: A Selection*, p. 103.

38 *Ibid.*, p. 103.

39 *Ibid.*, p. 66.

40 *Ibid.*, pp. 61-62.

41 *Ibid.*, p. 61; cf. p. 66.

42 *Ibid.*, p. 73.

43 *Ibid.*, p. 166.

44 *Ibid.*, p. 168.

45 *Ibid.*

46 M. Heidegger, "Logos," trans. by J. Lacan, *La Psychanalyse* (1956), pp. 59-79.

47 M. Heidegger, *Being and Time*, trans. by J. Macquarrie and E. Robinson (New York: Harper and Row, 1962), pp. 206-208.

48 *Ibid.*, pp. 222-224.

49 *Ibid.*, p. 213.

50 Lacan, *Écrits: A Selection*, pp. 40-46.

51 M. Heidegger, *Introduction to Metaphysics*, trans. by R. Manheim (Garden City, N.Y.: Doubleday & Co., Inc. [Anchor Books], 1961), pp. 108-111.

52 M. Heidegger, *Vorträge und Aufsätze* (Pfuellingen: G. Neske Verlag, 1954), p. 223. Writer's translation.

53 M. Heidegger, *Logik. Die Frage nach der Wahrheit* (Frankfurt am Main: Vittorio Klostermann, 1976), pp. 151-152. Writer's translation.

54 J. Lacan, *Écrits: A Selection*, p. 47.

55 *Ibid.*, p. 48.

The Opening of Vision:
Seeing Through the Veil of Tears[1]

DAVID MICHAEL LEVIN

Psalm 115: They have mouths, but they speak not; eyes have they, but they see not.

Psalm 116: Thou has delivered my soul from death, mine eyes from tears.

Psalm 119: Open Thou mine eyes, that I may behold wondrous things out of Thy Law.

Heidegger: Wherever man opens his eyes and ears, unlocks his heart, and gives himself over to meditating and striving, shaping and working, entreating and thanking, he finds himself everywhere already brought into the unconcealed. ("The Question Concerning Technology")[2]

Heidegger: [M]ight not an adequate look into what enframing is, as a destining of revealing, bring the upsurgence of the saving power into appearance? (*Op cit.*, p. 310)

Heidegger: Therefore we must consider now . . . in what respect the saving power does most profoundly take root and thence thrive even where the extreme danger lies—in the holding sway of enframing. In order to consider this, it is necessary, as a last step upon our way, to look with yet clearer eyes into the danger. (*Ibid.*)

SUMMARY INTRODUCTION

Topic: Heidegger writes: "Perhaps what is distinctive about this world-epoch consists in the closure of the dimension of the hale [*des Heilens*]. Perhaps that is the sole malignancy."[3] Our topic is the pathology and potential health of our eyes, i.e., the well-being of our customary experiencing of visual perception.

Question: Heidegger dedicates thinking to its ultimate concern when he tells us that, "Thinking conducts historical eksistence . . . into the realm of the upsurgence of the healing."[4] Our question, then, is: By what process of change, of growth, can we transcend the pain, frustration, and suffering, and ultimately, that terrible loss of meaningfulness, brightness and clarity, characteristically involved in how we normally experience seeing?

Aim: In *Democracy and Education*, John Dewey says that "there is perhaps no better definition of culture than that it is the capacity for constantly expanding the range and accuracy of one's perception of meanings."[5] Bearing this in mind, our aim here is to contribute to our understanding of the essential nature of seeing as an experiential process intrinsically open to profound, even unfathomable regions of awareness. It is hoped that such understanding may help us get more in touch with the primordial, latent endowment of the eye-organs, so that we can open up and appropriately develop their innate, or intrinsic capacities, still mostly unrecognized, for a much more wholesome and fulfilling way of

113

functioning, more in keeping with the potential thrust of their essential nature.

Heidegger investigates the nature of this potential, as well as the difficulties we experience in realizing it, in what he calls, looking back toward *Being and Time*, "an analytic of human being which keeps itself ecstatically open . . . to Being."[6] This essay attempts to carry forward his analytic project by focusing on our experience of vision. If "meditative thinking" (*Andenken*) is ever to become our way of life, our way of being, we must understand what it means to embody it, and indeed, to embody it in the fullest and most satisfying manner. Our focus on feeling, and on the way we experience perception, meets a need I have long felt in the movement of Heidegger's thinking. The embodiment of thinking should not any longer be pushed to one side. It helps to remember, first of all, that human beings are necessarily embodied; second, that we, as human beings, can experience our embodiment in many different ways; and third, that *how* we *experience* our embodiment affects the modifiable nature of the human body as an everchanging process. Thus we ask: Is there any *alternative* to our so-called "normal" way of being embodied? Is it possible for perception and feeling to be more thoughtful in relationship with Being? If so, what needs to change, what needs to be done?

Methodology. According to Herbert Guenther, however, we are moved by an "inveterate tendency" to conceal from ourselves, and from others, those *inborn normative demands upon us* which originate in the fact that human beings have been granted a bodily nature whose innate perceptual resources are capable of a much more wonderful development, a much more spacious unfolding, than we (would like to) acknowledge. This is why we feel struck by a bolt of lightning when Heidegger helps us to hear, in the German word for perception (*Wahr-nehmen*), the call to "take into preservation" the *Ereignis* of truth which it is granted us to perceive. If it is the very essence of perception to be, as he claims in "The Anaximander Fragment," a "securing which clears and gathers," how can we long deny that our everyday perception, which we consider to be normal and healthy, *falls far short* of its essential fulfillment? However, because the healing metamorphosis is extremely arduous, and because the process of unfolding is so frightening for Ego, there is a strong temptation for us to cling to our confusion and pain, and to maintain, very defensively, our old fictitious conceptualizations about the "essential nature" of our perceptual organs and the inherent limitations to their experiential growth and health. We maintain this reductive delusion of sanity and health even while listening to ancient religious teachings, which tell us that vision participates in an ever-changing cosmic drama of unimaginable beauty and meaningfulness. Thus, we need to develop a fearless *trust* in the primordial, pristine healthiness of our embodiment, while sustaining, at the very same time, an unshakeable methodological *suspicion*, or skepticism (*epochē*), in regard

114

to the conventional wisdom, the "natural attitude," which we are all too easily persuaded to accept, and which tells us what (limited) kind of perceptual health (sanity) we may dare, even beyond our fears, to hope for.

In the passage cited at the very beginning of this paper, Heidegger asks us to consider with him in what respect the saving power takes root and thrives even where the extreme danger lies. Our answer is that the healing process of the saving power takes root and thrives to the degree that we recognize, and penetrate with the sharpest thinking and understanding, *the repetitive cycle of pain, frustration and suffering which characterizes our experiencing of the embodiment determined by enframing* (*das Ge-stell*).

This essay is an essay in *experiential* phenomenology. The sole criterion for the truth of what I have to say is its success in helping us to realize our ownmost human potential for growth and fulfillment. Phenomenology should enrich our lives. Heidegger's words, "openness toward Being," help us to stay openly *focused* on this potential. Since the potential for greater openness is *latent*, however, within the dynamic *depths* of our experience, a "prosaic" phenomenology which addresses itself only to the "normal" ontic *surface* of our experience fails to meet its one and only responsibility; it is false, and cannot be trusted. Consequently, we shall proceed, here, with the conviction that a phenomenological proposition is true if and only if it releases, and tends to complete, or fulfill, the deepest *wholesome* tendencies that are inherent in our experience by addressing this experience so truthfully that it opens us up to new realms of meaningfulness—realms in which we are helped to realize our abiding resources of being. Because our phenomenology works in this normative manner, combining a deep-seated suspicion of the immediate and the apparent with a deep trust in the spontaneous thrust toward health of our inborn, pristine, experiential wisdom, we will call our method a *hermeneutical* phenomenology.

We shall read Heidegger experientially. Among other things, this means we must accept his metaphors and, in general, his poetic language as irreducible, irreplaceable, and literally *truthful* evocations of his experience. If we read his metaphors as stirring fictions rather than as profound truths, that simply reflects the shallowness of our own experience—and our discomfiture, our defensiveness, when confronted by a human existence fearless enough to risk madness itself in order to enter the labyrinth of meaningfulness in which our human experience has been situated.

Let me attempt to make somewhat clearer, now, with the help of some specific textual exemplars, just what I mean by an experiential interpretation of Heidegger. This will also serve, at the same time, to sharpen and elucidate what I mean by an experiential understanding of, and experiential work with, the process of vision as a process of human embodiment.

115

First of all, it is crucial that we get in touch with our everyday experience of seeing. In "Metaphysics as History of Being," and in his "Sketches for a History of Being as Metaphysics," Heidegger carefully traces for us, in the most rigorous hermeneutic manner, what he calls the "narrowing down" and "distortion," both in our experiencing and in the philosophy which reflects it, of the "primordial essence of Being."[7] Thus, for example, he follows the experience of *aletheia* (truth as unconcealment) as it becomes, for mediaeval thought, the *adaequatio ad rem*; follows the path from Being as *Logos* to Being as *ratio*; follows the primordial grounding *archē* as it becomes *aitia* (a very complex matter in Aristotelian thought) which eventually becomes, through translation, the modern notion of causation; follows the overwhelming emergence of Being as *physis* through its understanding as *energeia*, and then to its loss of meaning in the notions of *ergon* (which becomes work, product, energy, and effect) and *actualitas* (which eventually becomes actuality, act, existence, and the here-and-now fact); follows, too, the fateful destiny of the shining appearance of *physis* as it is reduced, first to *eidos*, then to *idea* (Latin), and finally, to what in English we call ideas, concepts, and representations. And he shows how the awesome powerfulness of Being as *physis* becomes, in Leibniz, the *vis primitiva activa*, and then the *causalitas* which so easily reduces to the technological notion of physical causality and the contemporary scientific notion(s) of energy. Likewise, he retraces with us the historical steps from openness to Cartesian certitude, a course which brought along with it the substitution of re-presentation for presence.

According to Heidegger, these metamorphoses are "distortions," "covering up the primordial essence of Being" and involving a certain "transposition," or "misplacement," of "the word of Being."[8] Thus, the history of Being, which is metaphysics, shows us a very clear historical progression, viz: a progressive narrowing and tightening, a progressive restriction and foreclosing, of our privileged, primordial experiencing of the essential human relationship with Being, the Being of beings. "In the beginning of its history, Being opens itself out as emerging (*physis*) and unconcealment (*aletheia*). From there it reaches the formulation of presence and permanence in the sense of enduring (*ousia*). Metaphysics proper begins with this."[9] More precisely, "as soon as the fundamental characteristic of representing and being represented comes to power in the essence of reality, the constancy and persistence of what is real is narrowed down to the sphere of presencing in the presence of the re-presentation."[10]

The history of Being does not take place, however, solely in, and solely as, metaphysics. For the abstractions of metaphysics are, after all, and despite their profound originality, but the reflections and echoes of our typical everyday understanding. Thus, we must ultimately be willing to recognize this narrowing down in, and also as, the progressive closing and freezing of our experiential processes—the process of seeing, for example.

Heidegger cites Leibniz's "Twenty-Four Statements," two of which read, in English translation:

> 17. And it follows, in general, that the world is a *cosmos*, fully adorned, that is, so made as to give the most satisfaction to the perceiver.
> 18. For the *pleasure* of the perceiver is nothing but the perception of beauty, order, perfection. And every pain contains something of disorder, but only with respect to the perceiver, since absolutely all things are ordered.[11]

I doubt very much that we are hearing these thoughts exactly as Leibniz himself must have heard them. In fact, I'm not at all sure that Heidegger heard in them the same powerfully *experiential* meaning which I hear very clearly in their ring of truth. In any case, I believe that we *can*, in fact, experientially so prepare ourselves, that our eyes truly become "une concentration et un miroir vivant de tout l'univers, suivant son point de vue." (See Leibniz's fifth letter to Clarke.) Heidegger certainly comes quite *close* to a crucial experiential understanding of this mirroring, since he hears Leibniz's phrase to mean "allowing it to shine."[12] And he goes on to characterize Leibniz's metaphysics in these enchanting, evocative, almost Kabbalistic words: "In this continued fulguration from moment to moment of the divinity of the god, sparks originate striving toward light, and correspondingly let the light of the divinity continue to shine, and copy it."[13] What happens when we *hear* these words as *concretely true phenomenological characterizations*, sharing with us a wonderful way of experiencing what we behold?—Do you feel a *shift* in your way of seeing?

In his short essay, "Recollection in Metaphysics," Heidegger states: "Only from human beings, that is, from the manner in which man grants the word of response to the claim of Being, can a reflection of its dignity shine forth to Being."[14] For Heidegger, then, "Being needs the reflection of a radiance of its essence in truth."[15] Are we able to hear, thanks to Heidegger, what perhaps even he himself may not have heard, viz., that the sensuous radiance and beauty of Being, as it comes forth in unconcealment (truth), cannot be appropriately reflected and disclosed without appreciative human eyes to behold and respond?

In that same essay, recollection of the history of Being is a kind of thinking which Heidegger describes as,

> the listening response which belongs to the claim of Being, as determination attuned by the voice of that claim . . . Recollection of the history of Being returns to the claim of the soundless voice of Being and to the manner of its attuning.[16]

For the sake of brevity, let us assume, for the time being, that we have in some unmistakable way *felt* this "claim of Being." If so, we are, in all likelihood, initially somewhat confused, unsure, and ill at ease. Even if we are able to enjoy the experience, we are unsettled by questions and needs: What *is* this claim? And *what* is Being? We *can't* seem to get a conceptual handle on them: the "claim of Being" resists, or eludes, our anxious striving to grasp and secure it. And yet, the feeling remains with us, not only stronger than ever, after our failure to re-present what we feel in standard concepts, but also, mysteriously, it *persists as unquestionable*, even in its vaguely felt plenitude of meaning. What can we do, once our conceptualizing discourse has broken down, overwhelmed by the way that the claim of Being holds us in its power?

Well, we can begin, instead, with our unmistakable feeling, the overall feeling of being "claimed" in some special way by the powerful presence, or truth, of Being. And, in particular, we can *focus* on the qualities, the character, of our *responsiveness* to this claim, since we can enjoy the "felt meaning" of our relationship to the claim, even if we do not (yet) adequately (i.e., very clearly) understand it. If we follow Eugene Gendlin's technique of focusing, fully defined, step by step, in his new book, we can achieve *a felt sense* of the *whole* of this claim on us; and, while we rest on the ground of this felt sense of the whole, we can gently focus, more and more thoughtfully, more and more carefully, on *how we are responding*.[17] In this manner, we can work on, or work with, our responsiveness, deepening it, expanding it, nurturing it, and giving it the kind of spaciousness it needs to become more open and receptive to the original claim.

What we need to "do" and "say" will then spontaneously *come* to us, like an unexpected gift, from our felt sense of this claim on us as a whole. We cannot hope, nor should we willfully strive, to *say* this whole, fastening it to our ready-made concepts in order to make it "our own." But, the more openly and willingly we respond, the more we *will understand* the claim, and be able to respond to it in an *appropriate* way. As Heidegger says in a passage closely following the text just cited, "It must remain unsaid, because what is sayable *receives* its determination from what is not sayable." This "unsayable" is not, and cannot ever be, our personal "possession, for it belongs, rather, to Being, whose transmission thinking *receives* in its projects."

For Heidegger, then, the task of thinking centers on "how he [i.e., the human kind] is claimed by Being for history and cor-responds to this claim."[18] From what Heidegger says, moreover, we may infer that the claim is experienced, first of all and for the most part, as a "feeling." More specifically, a feeling of need: the recollection of Being is, he tells us, a "need," an undertaking which Being allows "to become [for us] a needful necessity."[19] And, at the very close of this same text, he gives us what I take to be an intimately shared, and therefore decisively precious, sense of how *he* personally has experienced a "glimpse of the history of Being" while tarrying a while on his destined path of thinking: "only," he avers, with a touching harmony of openness and restraint, "only in the form of an essential need which soundlessly and without consequences shakes everything true and real to the roots." In §VIII and IX of "Overcoming Metaphysics," an essay from the decade 1936-1946, and included in *The End of Philosophy*, Heidegger further characterizes this need as an experience of "pain"; but he carefully stresses that the "deformation of essence" (§XXII) exemplified by the "metaphysico-technological" sensibility prevailing in the modern epoch makes it extremely difficult for us to *get in touch* with our pain, our vaguely felt neediness, and even more difficult to *focus* on it in a way that would grant us a radically liberating understanding of our experiential relationship to the ontological difference and the Being of beings. Difficult though it is, a meditative focusing, relatively autonomous with respect to the "metaphysico-technological" sensibility, is, I think, possible. Such focusing could help us to "overcome" (*überwinden*) the ruling sensibility and powerfully *move* us into a more spacious realm of experience, the realm of the "ontological difference," the *open* space *between* moments of visual fixation and settled visual habits, where we might be able to descry, for the first time, a dawning, shimmering disclosure of the Being of beings.

Strategy: This paper is part of a much larger essay, already written, which is concerned with the process of opening as it lays claim to our vision. Limitations of space, however, permit us to present at this time only Parts I and II, corresponding to the first two dialectical "moments" in the experiential process. The third "moment," which I have named, echoing Heidegger himself, "the splendor of radiant appearing," and which I have analyzed experientially into three subordinate dialectical movements (*das Gestell*, the lightning flash of Being, and *das Geviert*), cannot be included here.[20]

In Parts I and II, we will undertake to think phenomenologically about our experiencing of the two-fold functioning of the eyes, seeing and crying, and about our experiencing of their dialectical relationship. Part I will concentrate phenomenologically on how we experience seeing in the everyday life-world (*Lebenswelt*), while Part II will concentrate phenomenologically on our experience of crying.

Whereas Parts I and II are, in essence, *psychologically* oriented, *ontic* studies, Part III (not included here) involves a revolutionary shift which carries our thinking *beyond* its ontic meaning and into what, for lack of a more suitable word, I shall call the "ontological"; and it reinterprets the original problematic within the *openness* of the field of Being as the question of a distinctly extreme step in the process of realizing, or healing, our vision.

It will be appreciated, consequently, that the wholesomeness and health of the eyes must not be *reductively* understood as nothing but a psychophysical state. Rather, whatever the difficulties and perils, we must attempt to understand the healing metamorphosis of the eyes at once much more experientially and also much more spiritually, as their pristine worthiness to be the organs whereby (to speak, still, in the traditional language we are also trying to break out of) the presencing of Being, in all its splendor and immeasurable intrinsic value, may be beheld and fully enjoyed.

I. THE EMPIRE OF EVERYDAY SEEING

What are the eyes for? What is their function? What is their "virtue"? Well, where are the philosophers who have *paused* to reflect on these questions before repeating the received wisdom? Despite their numerous and very intense points of conflict, rationalists and empiricists seem able, apparently, to agree at least on this: that our eyes are for seeing; that being able to see *this and that* is their sole function and special virtue; and that our everyday manner of experiencing this function leaves nothing special to be desired, so long as mirages, and other optical illusions, do not threaten the elemental trust of vision. Our thinking, here, will attempt to call this tradition into question. We might start by considering whether or not protection against the possibilities of illusion would completely satisfy, or fulfill, the innermost *needs* of sight.[21]

According to Heidegger, human being (*Dasein*) is, in its essence, what he calls "openness-for-Being": the capacity we may enjoy of entering into, and dwelling within, an essential, and essentially fulfilling, relationship (*Grunderfahrung*) with the Being of beings. This paper is intended as a small contribution to our understanding of the process through which our eyes may be opened to, and for, such a relationship.

Perhaps we can get a sense of the problem when we consider that, with a definition that unwittingly reduced and concealed an openness which surely must have made, against their eyes, a frightening experiential claim, the rationalists asserted that the spirit's wonderful *lumen naturale* is nothing but our "capacity to reason." Is this the case? I think not. And yet, what once was called by the strange words, *lumen naturale*, does now seem to be *sealed* within us, a faint *shadow* of what it must once have been.[22] Can we do nothing to restore this light to its radiance? Can we do nothing to return it to its natural openness? Well, we *can* work on opening our eyes, opening these windows: in one simple gesture, to *release* the inward light of reason and *receive* the surrounding light of Being, and to realize how, for us, the exterior light in which we are bathed is *not really different* from the *lumen naturale*, interior light of the human mind. (What we call "reason" *is* a *natural* light, sealed, for a certain protection, within the enclosure of the human body. Depending on the intensity of our enlightenment, the flesh which seals in this reflective luminosity will be more or less translucent, more or less radiant, more or less open. Philosophers have forgotten that the light of reason, being a natural light, is not essentially different from, not necessarily closed off from, the exterior light of our world: whether exterior or interior, this light is the light of Being.) Heidegger writes: "Philosophy does speak about the light of reason, but does not heed the opening of Being. [However,] the *lumen naturale*, the light of reason, *needs* it [i.e., the opening] in order to be able to illuminate what is present in the opening."[23]

Experiential work with the *affective* perceptivity of our eyes (e.g., their susceptibility to being touched and moved, even at a distance, by what they see) is, I believe, just the sort of thing Heidegger has in mind when, heeding "the call of conscience," he meditates on how human beings may get underway, fulfilling, or realizing, the ontological openness of their ownmost nature.[24] *Werde, was du bist*! Heidegger hears that. I hear that, too. But, for me, these words *call into question* our nature as bodily beings: our nature, for example, as beings who see, and who are capable of authentic vision. To begin with, this requires a proper understanding of embodiment. Heidegger writes: "The human body is something essentially other than an animal organism."[25] But, lest we stray into the opposite error, still caught in the web of dualism, he observes: "Just as little as the essence of man consists in being an animal organism can this insufficient definition of man's essence be overcome or offset by outfitting man with an immortal soul, the power of reason, or the character of a person."[26]

Fundamentally, and indeed as something of decisive importance, we are, each and every one of us, claimed "in seinem Freisein"[27] by the experiential truth that our embodiment is an on-going *process* capable of very significant *changes*, by virtue of which our bodily functioning may be progressively "perfected:" "perfected" as the appropriate and necessary embodiment, or expression, of our fully realized, fully opened essential nature as human beings, beings essentially living in, and for, the openness of Being. In regard to the perceptivity of our eyes, then, the question, very precisely, is this: How may we endeavor to become, by grace of our eyes, what *Dasein* essentially is, namely, a joyfully healthy, radiant being, whose wholesome joy is the opening of vision to the luminous presencing of Being?

In "The Turning," Heidegger writes: "But we do not yet hear, we whose hearing and seeing are perishing . . . under the rule of technology."[28] Now, I have no wish to deny our everyday eyes their rightful claims to (veridical) sight. But I do think that we need to be reminded that eyes which "see" may yet be blind. Is this not the teaching of the Oedipal tragedy? Are we ourselves blind, to the degree that what we see through the eyes, and what we experience of their essential nature, is only their seeing in its everydayness (*Alltäglichkeit*)? The philosophies and therapies of the West reflect this blindness. And, if we may judge by the pain and frustration which surround our visual experience, there is ample evidence that our blindness portends our plunge into a hellish darkness even more painful, and perhaps fatal. Thus I want to ask: What would an insightful philosophy of visual perception be like? What would it involve? The radicality of our therapeutic practice depends, in part, on the preparatory thinking of an ontologically appropriate philosophical groundwork.

So that the urgency of these questions not be slighted, nor missed, it will be necessary to consider, at least briefly, the nature of what Heidegger calls, in his discussion of the Parmenides fragment on *Moira*, "the everyday perception of mortals." To be sure, we do not experience our everyday seeing as predominantly and intensely painful. Nor can we deny that our everyday experience of seeing, and of its instrumental extension, for example, through telescopes, cameras and microscopes, not only has granted us visual satisfactions and even some intense visual pleasures, but has also immeasurably enriched our lives. In this essay, however, we will focus on the more stressful, more needful aspects of our everyday visual experience. Our focus will be justified if it encourages us to respond more thoughtfully to the manifest symptoms of need and deprivation in our everyday experience.

Of "metaphysical thinking," Heidegger writes: "starting from what is present, [metaphysical thinking] re-presents it in its presence."[29] In Part III, we will examine in some detail the ontological significance of our tendency to re-present what is present. (Re-presentation: *Vor-stellung*) For the time being, though, it may suffice to observe that our everyday manner of seeing *embodies, and tends to perpetuate*, precisely this re-presentational attitude, which Heidegger finds reflected in our "metaphysical thinking."

As Hans Jonas has shown with such philosophical skill and care, the eyes are wonderful organs for long-range sensing: functioning at a distance, without the need to touch, we acquire re-presentative knowledge which is already, in a certain rudimentary way, abstract and idealized.[30] It is inherent in the nature of seeing, as *Vor-stellung*, that it easily encourages us to develop its detached, dispassionate power to survey and encompass with the sweep of a glance. This is what Erwin Straus calls the "gnostic" power (in contrast to the "pathic"), which enables us to analyze and discriminate, and to anticipate and predict. Accordingly, the everyday powers of seeing are enjoyed not only for their natural role in our everyday life, but also for their decisive role, brilliantly analyzed by Husserl, in preparing the ground for the flowering of natural science as an axiomatized, hypothetico-deductive system of knowledge.[31] Likewise, seeing is also the often invisible accomplice of industry and technology. As Heidegger points out, our visual capacity to encounter beings in a detached, calculative, instrumental way, a capacity which is unique among our perceptual organs, makes it possible for us to organize, integrate, and standardize whatever the eyes may behold: "Every place [is] equal to every other place."[32]

Visual detachment grants us such significant and desirable opportunities that we may easily settle into habits of *powerful* seeing which will prevail in diverse kinds of circumstance, whether or not they are appropriate, whether or not they are satisfactory. Everyday seeing now takes place under the archetypal sign of the partriarchal male. We should not overlook the role of the eyes in situations of mastery, authority, and dominion. And Heidegger recognizes the threatening aspect of this subtle visual tyranny: "Every event [e.g., a flower appearing within my visual field] must be fitted into this ground plan of nature."[33] But we, because we still do not question the reign of science and technology, we blindly praise the eyes for their incipient geometry, their rational power, never giving thought to the ways in which the *one-sided nurture* of a capacity so fruitful, not only, of course, in science and technology, but also in the conduct of our daily lives, can painfully close off the healing nurture of certain other potentialities: potentialities in crying need of recognition and acceptance. (Above all, as we shall see in Part II, we need to develop more compassionate, more tender, more loving relationships with what we see. We need to develop the open, embracing, archetypally feminine, and receptive side of vision.)

Just as Husserl, in the *Crisis of European Sciences and Transcendental Phenomenology*, undertook to trace phenomenologically the *Sinnesgenesis* of certain fundamental concepts in geometry and modern physics, so Heidegger attempts, in "Science and Reflection," to trace the process by which, beginning with the investigation of Nature among the early Greek thinkers, scientific theorizing has progressively, and almost imperceptibly, affected our Western experiencing and understanding of the essential nature of the seer, the process of seeing, and the thing which is seen. It was Husserl, I believe, who first pointed out the irony: that the science of vision, which not only originates in, but continues to depend upon, the powers of everyday seeing, should charm us into measuring our natural powers against its own. Pain is what happens when the objectivity of science arrogantly claims for itself the sole standard of human vision.

"Science and Reflection" cuts through cultural delusions and obsessions to unmask the way that "theory entraps objects in order, for the sake of re-presentation, to secure those objects and their coherence in the object-area of a particular science at a particular time."[34] But Heidegger attempts to do even more than this. He wants to understand the nature of that process whereby the theoretical approach, to which our everyday seeing itself gave birth, rises to a position of unquestionable dominion, turns against certain vital, but still unrecognized (archetypally feminine) potentialities in our capacity to see, and affects them to such a degree that it is not only theoretical science, but our everyday seeing itself, which, charmed and enthralled by the scientific world-view, begins to function in this very same hostile and aggressive manner.

123

Heidegger notes that our word "theory" refers, according to its root meaning in the Greek language, to "the outward look, the aspect, in which something shows itself."[35] To "theorize" *originally* meant "to look at something attentively, to look it over, to view it closely."[36] "Thus," he concludes, "it follows that *theorein* is . . . to look attentively on the outward appearance wherein what presences becomes visible and, through such sight — seeing — to linger with it."[37] It hardly needs to be stressed that this original sense of what it means to undertake a "theoretical observation" of Nature, a sense which, if we are silent and very attentive, we may still hear resounding in the ancient Greek words, is completely missing today, buried and forgotten long ago under many sedimented layers of errant and narrowed awareness.

For the Greeks, the "theoretical life" (*bios theōretikōs*) is "the way of life of the beholder, the one who looks upon the pure shining-forth of that which presences."[38] It involves a "pure relationship to the outward appearances belonging to whatever presences: those appearances that, in their radiance, concern man in that they bring the presence of the gods to shine forth."[39] But, when the wonderful *experience* treasured by the word "theoria" was passed on and entrusted to the Latin word *contemplatio*, an *experiential shift* of earth-shaking importance took place: "there comes to the fore the impulse, already prepared in Greek thinking, of a looking-at that sunders and compartmentalizes."[40]

However, what the Romans and mediaeval schoolmen experienced through contemplation cannot easily be recognized in what, beginning, perhaps, with the work of Sir Francis Bacon and continuing until the revolutionary work of Heisenberg and Einstein, the English-speaking world experienced through the notion of "observation": "theory as observation," says Heidegger, "would be an entrapping and securing refining of the real." [41] So Heidegger argues that our modern (patriarchal) science "challenges forth the real, specifically through its aiming at objectness. Science sets upon the real. It orders it into place to the end that, at any given time, the real will exhibit itself as an interacting network, i.e., in surveyable series of related causes. The real thus becomes surveyable and capable of being followed out in its sequences."[42]

It is at this point in his analysis that Heidegger touches on a momentous development in the science of Nature, the strangeness of which he is, I think, the first to have clearly noticed and pondered. Stating that "classical physics maintains that nature may be unequivocally and completely calculated in advance, whereas [contemporary] physics admits only of the guaranteeing of an objective coherence that has a statistical character,"[43] he then calls our attention, first, to "the way in which, in the most recent phase of atomic physics, *even the object vanishes*," along with the self-forgetting and vanishing of the inquiring subject, and second, to "the way in which, above all, the subject-object relation as pure relation

124

thus takes precedence *over* the object and the subject, to become secured as standing reserve."[44]

Why? Well, let us consider the subject/object polarity from an *experiential* standpoint. The better we understand the polarization process in general, the better we will understand how seeing specifically contributes to, and functions in, a process which intensely *polarizes* dynamic differentiation and constitutes the existential situation (*Befindlichkeit*: the way the seer is, and can be, with that which is beheld) as the narrow and painful duality of subject and object.

Merleau-Ponty writes: "To say that I have a visual field is to say that by reason of my position *I have access to, and an opening upon, a system of beings*, visible beings, that these are at the disposal of my gaze *in virtue of a kind of primordial contract and through a gift of nature*, with no effort made on my part; and from which it follows that *vision is prepersonal*."[45] Subject/object duality is in essence, then, a freezing, or narrowing, of the dynamic process, *originally open*, of experiential growth. The polarization is well under way once insecurity and anxiety inhibit the openness and receptivity of our response. The more restricted and distant our response, the more the being of that which we have encountered, be it a person or a thing, will be *confined* within the limitations and endistancing of our response. This confinement is, in effect, a *reciprocal* subjugation. When we feel threatened by the person or thing we have encountered, either because we are attracted and fear being dispossessed or because we want to avoid that being and are distressed by its presence, then the person or thing is caught up in the web of our anxiety, as we ourselves are caught: it is transformed, as are we, and reduced to the being of an object.

Objects emerge out of the openness of being, emerge in correspondence with the struggle of a "subject" for dominion. But, once this person or thing has been subjugated and turned into an object, it can no longer enter the field of our experience in a whole-some way. So we are, in turn, subjugated, subject to the evil, tyranny, and rage of the object, in a tight dialectic of reciprocal and simultaneous co-emergence, when we cannot just *let something be*: when we must object to persons and things just being what they are.

This objectifying objection to being originates, as Buddhism tells us, in one of two basic experiential patterns: either aversion or attraction. But both, as Buddhism can easily prove, are patterns of egological attachment; and they always initiate a very destructive (karmic) cycle of events. Attraction, no less than aversion, will ultimately motivate a sequence of very hostile and aggressive responses. For, as a form of attachment, there is an inveterate tendency for our attraction, which is inherently insecure, to struggle, blindly, for possession and control. Whether attracted or averse, we oppose, threaten, abuse and destroy. Or we resist, refuse and attempt to repress. Do we not see that, as we have seeded, so shall we reap?

David Michael Levin

When we focus closely on our *experiencing* of everyday seeing, we will notice that, and how, we tend to objectify the persons and things we visually encounter, easily falling into such habits as, for example, staring and fixation, stereotyping, and overlooking through bored familiarity. Even such vital perceptual processes as isolating and abstracting can become habitual patterns of response which foreclose adequate and satisfactory encounter. When, giving thought to what we are experiencing through our eyes, we find ourselves settling into such everyday habits, we will begin to realize that the persons or things we are involved with can no longer be seen—appreciatively—as they are: instead of *releasing unto itself* what we have beheld and *letting it be what, and as, it is*, we have seized or captured it with our eyes, and it has become a mere object, an object to which, despite ourselves, we are finally subject. In "The Age of the World Picture," Heidegger accurately describes what happens: "That which is, is no longer that which presences; it is rather that which, in re-presenting, is first set over against, that which stands fixedly over against, [and] which has the character of object [*das Gegen-ständige*]. Re-presenting is making-stand-over-against, an objectifying that presses forward and masters."[46]

What, then, is the difference between beholding persons and things (as what they are) and experiencing their reduction to the status of visual objects? Fundamentally, the difference lies in the fact that the presence of persons and things is profoundly *gratifying*, while their absence, i.e., their replacement by the *object* (which is merely a *simulacrum*, a re-presentation of the thing), is not. Life literally loses its color: whatever our gaze reaches appears to be dull and inert; paltry: not glowing and vibrant, with intimations of depths that yield great significance. In fact, presence, as such, is *always* experientially satisfying, even when it is also, in some respect, displeasing or terrifying: satisfying, I mean, in a way that re-presentational substitutes never can be, since what is ultimately most satisfying is not what is most pleasant, but rather what is most *meaningful*.

Heidegger always listened carefully to the sounding of the language his thinking inhabits. And, when he focused on his experiencing of "es gibt," what he heard, resounding in these plainest of words, was the granting of "it gives" as the long silent truth of "there is."[47] That is what, thanks to the mindfulness of his listening, the German language granted to his ears. Beings are a gift: that was a gift from a language, which his hearing, filled with joy, gratefully received.

Vision is a form of sensibility: our susceptibility to the visible, a way of being *affected* by what is given. Persons and things are what is given, presented to our eyes. The eyes do not create what they behold; although whenever they are open, they are *present* in a field, and at the site, where a vast and colorful spectacle arises, unfolds. The eyes are receptive organs. But how do they receive? How do they greet and welcome? What is the feeling, the mood, of their reception? The persons and things we behold are gifts to our eyes, gifts our eyes could enjoy. But a gift cannot be enjoyed unless it is properly received, accepted as such. And it cannot be received or accepted so long as we deny that it is a gift—so long as we deny, and cannot thankfully accept, the fact that persons and things are indeed given, granted to our eyes, *as persons and things*, and never, primordially, as *visual objects*. (And yet, the philosophers' "sense datum" conceals, and thus denies, precisely this present, this presence. Indeed, both empiricists and rationalists loudly proclaim the reasonableness of their replacement: the sense datum is to *replace* the present of presence. Is it any wonder that their eyes are always clouded by tears of loss and mourning?)

Speaking to us, as does Heidegger, from the depths of his experiencing of the eyes' ontological dimension, Padmasambhava, called Tibet's Precious Guru, joyfully declares: "*Whatever* I behold is my Wish-fulfilling Gem."[48] And he compassionately adds, for our benefit: "I contemplate the Three Jewels *without averting my gaze*."[49] (The Three Jewels are: Buddha, or the grain of one's own true nature; Dharma, or the supportive ground of Being; and Sangha, or the community of kindred beings who carry on the Dharma tradition.) Padmasambhava's teachings (*circa* 775 A.D.) provide concrete experiential interpretations for Heidegger's more hermetic utterance, that "it is Being itself, whose truth will be given over to man when he has overcome himself as [ego-logical] subject, and that means when he no longer [aversively or aggressively] re-presents that which is as object."[50]

Earlier, we heard Heidegger tell us that contemporary physics pressed the process of objectification so far and with such intensity that the object finally *vanished*. This is fascinating, because we can experience a corresponding process in the objectifying of visual perception. The person or thing we behold is that which *gives* itself to us, unlike the object, which *objects* to this (this "free" manner of givenness): in keeping with its essential nature, *the object will not give itself, by itself, to us*; it stubbornly refuses our need, refuses to come forth and meet our visual need; it refuses to give itself *wholly* to our desire. When our eyes cannot be open to, or cannot accept, persons and things as they are, as they give themselves, then what they give us, instead, are their objections. The person or thing we tried to behold has in effect vanished, leaving to our gaze nothing but a flimsy image. (Consider, in this light, the eventual result of extremely intensive staring: the eyes start to tear and cry, while the thing our eyes objectified begins to shift and then jerk, in order to tear itself away, violently leaping, and perhaps finally vanishing, as it dances into freedom.)

Are we not at all distressed over the absence, or loss, of the wonderful gifts of being granted our eyes? Our objection to the object is already contained in the notion of re-presentation (*Vor-stellen*). So we need only to look into it for instruction. What, then, does this notion tell us about such absence or loss? Well, first of all, the willful re-presenting of what we behold is a symptom of anxiety: it always entails the postponement, and perhaps even the failure, of sensuous visual satisfaction. *Re-presenting* is always a strategy of *delaying, or deferring, presence; it is a willful unwillingness to be in and with the present*. Persons and things fulfill need and desire; the object invariably disappoints, refusing to fulfill us, to grant us the wholesome *gift* we would need in order to become, in that situation, essentially hale and whole.

Heidegger writes, in his essay on "The Thing," that "The first step . . . is the step back from the thinking that merely re-presents to the thinking that responds and recalls."[51] I take him to mean that our reflection on the nature of everyday seeing must eventually *respond* to the question of our basic sanity, our health. And it must also *recall* us to ourselves, reminding us of our crying need, hidden within an inborn, pristine nature, to enjoy the radiant ecstasy (*ek-stasis*) of vision: vision healed of all the dualities that block ecstatic openness. If true vision is the harmony of opposites, we need to be reminded, first of all, that eyes are not only for *seeing*. Opposite seeing, there is crying. Then we may be moved to the point where we will experience not only the *unsatisfactoriness* of our everyday seeing, but also, beyond this, the fact that there are *resources of healing* primordially *entrusted* to our eyes. Thus, our existential challenge is to recognize and accept these resources, nurturing them with thought and practice, but always mindful that, as Heidegger says in "The Anaximander Fragment," the destiny of vision is finally held in the keeping of Being: "Seeing is determined, not by the eyes, but by the lighting of Being. Presence within the lighting articulates all the human senses."

II. CRYING: THE BREAKING OPEN OF THE VESSELS[52]

Xenophanes: "It is the whole that sees, the whole that thinks, the whole that hears."[53]

Heidegger: "And the ear of our thinking, does it still not hear the cry?"[54]

Our eyes are also the organs, the site, of crying. Is this merely an accidental, or contingent fact? Or is crying, rather, in the most intimate, most closely touching relationship with seeing? We are wont to see crying and seeing only in their customary pattern of polarization (opposition). But what Herbert Guenther points out in regard to the apparent duality of heart and mind may be said here, too: "In splitting these, we have made them quite inadequate as a means of dealing with our self-imposed problems."[55]

But what is crying? Like seeing, it is a process of intentionality, an intense energy which structures a life-world: structures it as a painful mood. Although crying inhabits a shrunken world, the heart of the mood is the *need* for a healing openness and wholeness. Experientially considered, crying is a moving, meaningful process of opening and disclosure, which embodies what Eugene Gendlin calls "an experiential shift" or "step."[56] (As he observes, what really matters is the shift, the opening itself, and not so much the "cognitive content" of the disclosure.)

Our eyes are capable of three kinds of seeing: everyday seeing, which can differentiate and articulate what it beholds only in a dualistic, objectifying, re-presentational (i.e., endistanced) manner; seeing which cries, immersed in painful feeling, immersed in the process of its will-conditioned subjectivity; and finally, a joyful seeing, clear, bright, and penetrating, capable of being moved and deeply touched, even at a distance, by what is seen.

In the mood of crying, we move through two phases. The first can be extremely painful, for in getting in touch with our feeling, we feel the pressure of a need to see in a way which cries out to be more fully recognized and accepted. But our seeing is veiled in tears. Crying is the breakdown and vulnerability of our false ego-logical composure. Like the breakdown of a tool (see *Being and Time*), crying is a process of "exposure to the disclosedness of beings," which calls into question our comportment toward the being of whatever we behold.[57] It is hard for the one who is crying to avoid seeing his insecurity, his defensiveness, his craving for habitual certitude: "Man clings to what is readily available and controllable."[58] But crying *denies* us the comfortable (masculine) illusion of mastery and control, of certainty.

In the second stage, however, we are moved into a phase of integration and resolution. After the break-down, there is some sense of a significant break-through: not only the *relief* of finally hearing, and finally recognizing, the painful presence of a crying need for relationship, but also, and perhaps more importantly, the *ego-logical* release, the *opening*, of the crying as such. When we break down and cry, we let a crying need break through. Crying is the breaking open of our ego-logical masks, the veils which hide, and cloud over, the eyes. This may, at first, be very painful; but, as we begin to experience some satisfaction in the release, we may find that the process can really feel very whole-some and good.

Discussing the ontological understanding behind meditative and devotional practice in Buddhist *Vajrayana*, Guenther writes: "in the difference that is set up between subject and object, all the torment that usually accompanies the rift in Being asserts itself."[59] Heidegger says: "Pain rends. It is the rift." But he adds that, "Pain is [also] the joining of the rift." It is, in his words, "the difference [experience of duality] itself."[60] (I take it that, in this last remark, he means that, *from an experiential standpoint*, the rift is, at bottom, nothing other than the painfulness, intensified in proportion to our awareness, that inheres in our experiencing of the alienation from Being characteristic of our everyday seeing.)

Crying, as the *breaking down* of Ego's rigid defenses, and as a *breaking open* of the perceptual organs customarily enthralled by Ego's masks, can help us to abolish this painful difference which polarizes subject and object. For, as we experience Ego's eyes dissolving into tears, we are *moved closer* to an elemental, nurturing *rooting* of the entire process of seeing, a carnal integration of the seer and that which is beheld, which will *heal* the rift in Being, and make us whole and hale.

Merleau-Ponty says: "My eye for me is a certain power of making contact with things."[61] To be sure. But we know also that the eyes can be responsible for rifts and alienations that are deeply painful. What happens when this pain becomes unbearable? What happens when we become conscious of our detachment, and feel an overwhelming need for contact? *Crying is an opening of our eyes to their original rootedness in the primordial non-duality of subject and object.*

Why do I say that crying is the *root* of seeing? What don't I say, speaking in more Kantian terms, for example, that crying is the transcendentally necessary condition for the possibility of seeing? Of course, the Kantian formulation *approaches* the ontological truth of the matter. But what I want to say is meant to move us even closer. First of all, what we are trying to understand, namely, the connection between sight and crying, is not an a priori principle of pure understanding, but rather, in words that Merleau-Ponty might have used, an "organismic a priori" of the human body as we live and feel it. Second, what we are concerned with is much more primordial, much more fundamental, than a condition born in, and borne by, the faculty of pure thought. In keeping with its very essence, crying is not, and cannot be, articulate; thus, it is essentially different from Kant's a priori principles. Third, it is important to bring out the special nature of the connection: specifically, this means that it is more fruitful to understand the connection as a process of sensuous rooting, rather than as a process of cognitive synthesizing in accordance with certain rules. Fourth, the spontaneous, involuntary crying of the eyes, which expresses their compassionate destiny, attests a *pre-personal, pre-objective bond of communication, a sort of primordial communion*, which always already exists between the world and the gaze.[62] (See Merleau-Ponty's essay, "The Child's Relations with Others.") Thus, crying is an ontologically induced disclosing of the ontological mood of the eyes, in the sense that crying "reveals [the essential nature of] beings as a whole" — in a certain way, a certain light.[63]

But crying, as such, is only the *rooting* of our eyes and not itself their *full openness and flowering*. Crying does not, and cannot fully *resolve* our crying need to see in the most satisfying, most fulfilling, most meaningful manner. (When we cry, our eyes cloud over; and our vision is veiled, unclear. Moreover, although crying is a process of opening, crying eyes cannot see far: the horizons of the visible world temporarily contract in dark embrace. The openness of vision is still deferred.) Crying, then, is simply *a transitional stage* in the process of opening and clarifying our vision. Still, crying has much to teach us in regard for this process. For crying is non-conceptual; *it is a breakdown of the re-presentational way of thinking* and our "first," preliminary experience of the alternative: the gift of *visual presence,* dissolving duality into the vulnerability of openness. Borrowing Merleau-Ponty's words, here, to clarify our point, we find that crying "discloses subject and object as two abstract 'moments' of a unique [pre-personal] structure, which is presence."[64] Thus, when we give thought to the experience of crying, our thinking, "instead of furnishing [ready-made] re-presentations and concepts, experiences and tries itself as a transformation of its relatedness to Being."[65] (These are Heidegger's words.)

Crying, then, is the compassionate, but still painful face of seeing. It is the face with which we face and envisage that which would really meet our need for a closer, more sensuously fulfilling, and more openly touching relationship with whatever our eyes may behold. Our seeing, in its everydayness, tends to be aloof; instead of balancing its inherent skill in objective discrimination and distantiation against our need for a touching, but not grasping, relationship, we encourage a one-sided capacity. When we realize that the re-presentational attitude is an attitude not only of willful temporal deferment, but also of willful spatial endistancing, we may understand how the distancing power of our eyes is easily captured and pressed into the service of an ego-logical strategy, which employs visual representation for its own defense. When this capture takes place, re-presentation becomes at once aversive (closed off) and aggressive. But sometimes, our seeing makes known its inborn need, and cries out for a more open kind of seeing: a vision open, somehow, to touching things invisibly and intangibly, and being deeply but invisibly touched by what it beholds at a distance. Crying teaches that there is a nearness and a farness which are *experientially* real: not objectively calculable, yet not merely subjective, either.

Now, in his *Phenomenology of Perception,* Merleau-Ponty describes how "the senses communicate with each other."[66] According to him, "The senses intercommunicate by *opening* onto the structure of the thing. One sees the hardness and brittleness of glass, and when, with a tinkling sound, it breaks, this sound is conveyed by the visible glass. One sees the springiness of steel, the ductility of red-hot steel, the hardness of a plane blade, the softness of the shavings."[67] This is, certainly, the *basis* for a seeing which is wholly "in touch," even at a distance, and radically open to being touched, likewise at a distance, by what is beheld. But what Merleau-Ponty described is only the *beginning stage of a process of deepening perceptual awareness, capable of unlimited development. Could our vision be even more closely* in touch, and *even more open* to being touched? If so, how? If we understood better how to work on this, perhaps we could deepen the compassion of vision.

Merleau-Ponty writes, very helpfully:

> we cannot withhold from the sense of touch spatiality in the sense of a grasp of co-existences. The very fact that *the way is paved to true vision through a phase of transition and through a sort of touch effected by the eyes* would be incomprehensible unless there were *a quasi-spatial tactile field, into which the first visual perceptions may be inserted.*[68]

Elsewhere, he says that, "The task of radical reflection, the kind that aims at self-comprehension, consists . . . in recovering the unreflective experience of the world. . . ."[69] Perhaps crying grants us just such a radical, pre-reflective experience, by way of which we may recover a genuinely holistic kind of vision. Crying is the painful beginning of *responsive* seeing, rooting and immersing our vision in its sensuous element. Crying expresses and renews our eyes' "elective affinity" (Goethe's *Wahlverwandtschaft*) with the flesh of the visible world. Whereas everyday seeing tends toward the focused abstraction of "objective" *Gestalt* figures, *crying stresses our continuing need for a more visually satisfying holistic relationship with the non-objectifiable elemental ground of the Gestalt.* (The wholeness which crying helps us to experience is very different from the unwholesome totalizations achieved, for neurotic ends, by sheer willfulness.) And, whereas everyday seeing easily tends toward the articulation of a dematerialized ideality perfect for scientific speculation, crying stresses our perpetual need for the nurture of a more sensuous, communicative kind of vision, more closely in touch with its elemental origin. Just as there are, for Heidegger, certain poets whose voices "sing the healing whole in the midst of the unholy,"[70] so there are, too, for all of us, certain moments when our eyes are wonderfully opened, flooded with cleansing, elemental tears that can teach us the healing — and, above all, the healing compassion—of vision.

Now that we have interpreted the nature of crying, we need to return to our diagnosis of everyday seeing and deepen our understanding of how the experience of crying holds the power to move us through a process of healing. Consider how often crying expresses our pain, our natural objection, in seeing the loss, the disappearance, or the withdrawal of the persons and things our eyes are strongly attached to. An infant cries, for example, when its mother disappears from sight. (In *Beyond the Pleasure Principle*, Freud diagnosed this experience, which he recognized in the child's *fort-da* game, with great insight.) But it seems clear that *our way of seeing itself induces this pain*: in our attractions and aversions, Ego's two forms of attachment, coloring vision, set up situations which prepare, not for the most meaningful fulfillment of visual desire, but, on the contrary, for its inevitable frustration. For Ego's willful attachments, and its consequent gestures of anxiety and defense, work through our eyes to ground the vectors of our field of vision precisely on the dualities of loss

and enrichment, presence and absence, here and there, near and far —
dualities which will move us to tears.

Ego-attachments and anxiety (insecurity) are inseparable, and in fact
so interdependent, that it is impossible to determine which is the cause and
which the effect. But one thing is clear: that objectification is Ego's
defensive attempt, deluded and doomed to fail, to avoid the shadow of
uncertainty which stalks its attachments. Let us listen to Heidegger, who
tells us: "Objectification blocks us off against the Open. The more
venturesome daring does not produce a defense."[71] Authentic existential
security, which is serenity, "exists only outside the objectifying turning
away from the Open,"[72] in the joyful surrendering of our attachments (e.g.,
the anxieties and defenses we become attached to for protection). The
alternative to ego-logical attachment, however, is *not* an attitude of
renunciation and detachment, which would still ensnare us in an Ego-
pattern of willfulness and in no way diminish anxiety, but it involves rather,
an attitude of *non-attachment*, which is a daring openness, or willingness,
that transcends the painful, and sometimes even terrifying dualities of ego-
logical will.

In a surprising and thought-provoking passage, Merleau-Ponty
writes:

> What protects the sane man against delirium or hallucination is not
> his critical powers, but the structure of his space: objects remain before
> him, keeping their distance and . . . touching him only with respect. What
> brings about both hallucinations and myths is a shrinkage in the space
> directly perceived, a rooting of things in our body, the overwhelming
> proximity of the object, the oneness of man and the world, which is, not
> indeed abolished, but repressed by everyday perception or by objective
> thought, and which philosophical consciousness rediscovers.[73]

I would like to tarry here, but the scope of this paper will not permit this.
Let me simply raise some questions and leave you to follow your own
ruminations. (i) What is sanity? Are we so sure that we know who "the sane
man" is? (ii) Once we question the assumed identity of "the sane man," we
must also question the nature of his "protection." Does he *need* such
protection? Could the "need" for protection be rooted, at least in part, in a
paranoia which visualizes its own threats of delirium and hallucination?
(iii) Is the vision classified as "delirium and hallucination" always
undesirable? Could it be that the basic problem with such experiences
stems from the ego-logical attitude of the seer? (iv) Is it desirable, or
healthy, for objects (*Gegen-stände*) always to remain *before and against us
(vor-gestellt*: re-presented), "keeping their distance," and touching us "only
with respect"? (v) Why is "the oneness of man and world" unfortunate? Is it
necessarily *madness* to experience "a rooting of things in our body"? (vi)
Finally, to what extent, and in what ways do our eyes, the eyes of everyday
sight, *structure* a space for living which needlessly defends us against, and

needlessly represses, solicitations within our space to *open up* the field of vision and be moved by the very openness of the field of Being, whence the things we behold come forth?

Our seeing is blind to the presence of the present, the present of presence. For the coming-forth and giving-of-itself of what we behold is, ontologically considered (i.e., from the standpoint of our hermeneutic experiencing and understanding of Being), an event (*Er-eignis*) which solicits a reciprocating response of which our eyes may not be (entirely) capable. How shall we characterize an *appropriate* response? It may be helpful to allow ourselves a visualization, here, in order to awaken certain slumbering feelings. Imagine, then, that crying is the eyes' first libation, their first sacrifice, their heartfelt gesture of celebration and thanksgiving, for the blessing of vision. Can our eyes respond in this same mood, but without tears? Let us visualize accepting and receiving the sparkling jewels our eyes have been granted, by the grace of lighting, to see; let us visualize giving thanks, as it were, through thoughtful eyes which radiate and communicate the reflected light of their joy in vision. But such openness, of course, will always be extremely frightening to the sentinels who guard the Ego.

Now, in *The Ego and the Id*, Freud documents *the stages of development* whereby Ego progressively captures the function of perception, which originally belonged to, and manifested, the spontaneous, melodic, polymorphously libidinal energies of the id. (He called these energies "the primary processes." Unfortunately, even though he understood that Ego is at first the *product* of anxiety and later the compulsively repeating *source* of anxiety, he failed to draw the inevitable conclusion that, under Ego's authority, our perception tends to *lose* the qualities of its original, pristine nature and becomes, instead, the source of great anxiety, frustration, disappointment and deception. For example, whereas *original* vision enjoys a "limpid and pristine awareness" (Guenther's translation for the Tibetan Buddhist notion of *ye-shes*), *everyday* visual perception, functioning in, and as, the absence, the deferment, the *différ-ance* (Derrida) of re-presentation, tends to be very dull: not as bright, lively, refreshing and sensuously satisfying as it might be.[74] And, since objectification depends on repeated visual delays and fixations, our eyes continuously suffer from a tension and strain which are not only unnecessary, but visually restricting.

However, that we not fall right here into an abyss of despair, let us note that Heidegger insists that the ego-object relationship is "only an historical variation of the relation of man to the thing, so far as things can become objects."[75] And he adds that, "The same is true of the corresponding historical change of the human being to an ego."[76] This means that the process of visual objectification is in a sense historically contingent: we *could* enjoy a very different, non-dualistic (i.e., holistic) kind of relationship with that which we behold. There *is* an alternative to seeing which leaves us feeling bereft of meaning and satisfaction. But, as long as we are *bent* on *objecting* to the persons and things we behold, they will *object* to us. Perhaps they will resist and withdraw—or conceal from our eyes their most precious sensuous (i.e., visual) qualities, their most precious treasures. Or they may even turn toward us, instead, their most wrathful, most hellish, most terrifying face, thus mirroring the extremity of our paranoia. This is the sense in which we are responsible for the painful repetition of loss and renunciation, delirium and hallucination, which ends each cycle of vision, as it began, in crying.

Crying, as an experience of the process of opening, can move us beyond the anxieties, the paranoia, and the defensiveness which cause us to avert or needlessly restrict our gaze. Moreover, by *immersing* us in an experience that immediately breaks down the feeling of subject-object duality, crying helps to restore our original pristine awareness of their primordial, non-dual kinship, an androgynous kinship which constitutes the true existential situation of vision. In the self-abandonment of crying, we touch the very *root* of vision, which entwines the copulation of subject and object; and we leave them to cry in bliss.[77] Crying renews a crucial feeling, lost, perhaps, since early childhood, that it is the heart of vision to embrace, with its playful, androgynous gaze, every being upon which it alights. In precisely that spirit, Padmasambhava, Tibet's Precious Guru, described his way of seeing by declaring, with unquestionable phenomenological honesty, "I give myself as spouse to all beings."[78]

Merleau-Ponty, writing about our experiencing of space, echoes this wonderful awareness, asking: "is it not of its essence to embrace every being that one can imagine?"[79] And he fleshes out his own answer in phenomenological terms:

> The thing is inseparable from a person perceiving it, and can never be actually in itself, because its articulations are those of our very existence, and because it stands at the other end of our gaze, or at the terminus of a sensory exploration which invests it with humanity. To this extent, every perception is a communication or a communion, . . . or, on the other hand, the complete expression outside ourselves of our perceptual powers, and a coition, so to speak, of our body with things.[80]

Nevertheless, it is his contention that, "Perception has lost its erotic structure."[81] I sadly concur. But I would like to call attention to the fact that crying, as a powerful dimension of our experience of visual perception, really *can* teach us "how a thing or a being begins to exist for us through desire or love."[82] We can recover, even if only slowly and painfully, the non-dual, androgynous, erotic global intentionality (*Stimmung*) which underlies our visual perceptivity and which, in its undeveloped latency, constitutes the norm (*conatus*) for the spontaneous growth and flowering of true vision.

David Michael Levin

In India long ago, and even before the time of Padmasambhava, one of the eighty-four *mahāsiddhas*, Saraha by name, was moved to sing, out of his compassion for our suffering, that, "When body, speech, and mind become indivisible and one,/Spontaneity's actuality is there and [is] beautiful."[83] He also taught the need to transfer our perceptual processes from the archetypal sign of the master (Ego) to the sign of the mistress (id), as a stage on the way to non-dual experience: "When the master of the house has been devoured, the mistress/Is enjoyed." And he specifically interpreted this in regard for the eyes, telling us, very simply: "Whatever you may see you may then enjoy."[84] How is such joyful abandon possible? Again consider crying. Is it not true that, when we cry, tears well up and flow *uncontrollably* (i.e., in a way that Ego *cannot control*)? Thus, as a stage in the healing of vision, crying may serve to dissolve the dualities which we *willfully projected* into the indivisible *Gestalt* of the visible, giving us thereby a preliminary experience of unwilled wholeness, which our vision, seeing through the veil of tears, may later make its own: a preliminary experience, namely, of the fact that "spontaneity's actuality is there and [is] beautiful."

Now, we may be feeling that this spontaneity is especially manifest when we cry in joy, say, at the return of a beloved friend long absent. If so, I think it important that we recognize the experience and cherish it for its intrinsic value. However, it is equally important that we understand *why* we are moved to tears. Isn't the joy too great, or too simple, for our words? Isn't it too vast for the eyes to encompass, too deep for them to penetrate? We cry because the ontological "claim" (*Anspruch*) on our eyes overwhelms us: we are *not capable* of opening our eyes to receive this joy in its fullness. Our eyes are moved by intense feeling; but we still cannot harmonize their responsive, global feeling (com-passion) with their crucial need to see clearly. Whereas our everyday seeing involves focusing that tends to fixate what comes forth to be seen, crying involves seeing that is moved, even at a distance, by an aesthetic, appreciative *feeling-for-the-whole*. But, precisely for this reason, crying touches our *need* for a lucid, articulate vision gracefully encompassing the whole: vision which can focus meditatively and without fixation; vision which can let the *Gestalt* ground be what, and as, it is, while also letting the figure stand out as figure; vision which can move with articulate skill and care, but also, as it were, with promiscuous, erotic freedom, liberated from the spell of pain.

The egoless spontaneity and non-defensive opening which we may experience in crying can help us to *work* with our everyday seeing, so that our inveterate tendency toward visual objectification, a dualistic process which involves the Ego's aversive and defensive willfulness, becomes, transmuted, the willingness-to-see which Heidegger calls "releasement" (*Gelassenheit*).[85] In his "Conversation on a Country Path," he understands this to mean a mood of openness "beyond the distinction between activity

136

and passivity": a willingness (*Entschlossenheit*) even beyond the experience of the difference between willing and not willing, since *both* of these are still manifestations of Ego's willfulness. Such openness (called, in Buddhism, *shunyata*) is certainly an existential challenge. Fully appreciating this, Heidegger says, speaking through the Scientist: "The transition from willing into releasement is what seems difficult for me."[86] Indeed, it is for everyone! But perhaps we may now appreciate how crying can be not only an experiencing of the difficulty of this *transition* in the process of healing our vision, but also a very significant experiencing of the *shift*, the *movement* of our vision, from the narrow fixity of "the will to power" into the very spacious mood (*Stimmung*: harmony, attunement) of *Gelassenheit* (releasement).

Let us conclude this essay with a brief "repetition." Basically, crying responds to the need of our eyes *to see close relationship*. But wholesome relationship cannot be seen under the (patriarchal) sign of Ego. Crying, as the (archetypally feminine) opening of feeling, moves us through an insightful, if rudimentary experiencing of releasement. Heidegger writes: "Releasement toward things and openness to the mystery belong together. They grant us the possibility of dwelling in the world in a profoundly different way. They promise us a new ground and foundation upon which we can stand and endure in the world of technology without being imperiled [and brutalized] by it."[87]

(i) With regard for *the human personality and its growth* (its humanization), crying is a first response to our crying need for grounding in wholesome *self-acceptance*. What the eyes cry out for is a new way to see, a way that is possible only insofar as we are able to see ourselves (see who and how we are) with honesty and self-acceptance, and without the painful experiential dualities that self-hatred always entails. (Above all, this involves being open enough to seeing the archetypally *feminine* aspect of our human nature in an appreciative and responsive way. In a patriarchal culture, openness in this direction is, as Jung understood, especially difficult, especially threatening — for males and females alike.)[88]

(ii) What about vision and our relationship with Nature? Even Francis Bacon, for whom Nature is to be mastered and ruled, had to concede that, "Nature to be commanded, must first be obeyed." We have followed Bacon's urge to command; but we have forgotten even *his* sense of wonder and humility. Now, in "The Age of the World-Picture," Heidegger writes:

> Nature, in its objectness for modern physical science, is only *one* way in which what presences—which from old has been named *physis*—reveals itself and sets itself in position for the refining characteristic of science. Even if physics as an object-area is unitary and self-contained, this objectness can never *embrace* the fullness of the coming to presence of nature. Scientific re-presentation is never able to encompass the coming to presence of nature; for the objectness of nature is, antecedently, only *one* way in which nature exhibits itself.[89]

Are there, then, alternatives? If so, what are they? How else could we envision Nature?[90] Do we even *dare* to dream of a technological power of seeing transformed to the point where we are neither commanding Nature nor sacrificing ourselves to her caprice, and where "our relation to technology will become wonderfully simple and relaxed?"[91]

"Man," says Heidegger, "is the shepherd of being."[92] "Man is not the lord of beings."[93] How might we *develop* our capacity to "spare and protect the thing's presence in the region from which it presences"?[94] Is there any hope that our (predominantly patriarchal) eyes may learn to behold the world as their motherly dwelling, "so that we will belong primally within the fourfold of sky and earth, mortals and divinities"?[95] In other words: "Will we cor-respond to that insight, through a looking that . . . becomes aware of Being itself within it"?[96] Will we realize the crying need of our eyes to be able to see the "lightning flash of Being"?[97]

The world we behold is, of course, very attractive and colorful: it is even, as Heidegger says, a very dazzling spectacle, colored by the projections, the delirium, and the hallucinations of Ego.[98] But are the colors we see the "true" colors of Being? Are they as enchanting as they might be? Are they warm and bright and glowing and healing? Do we feel that they are as rich as we dream they might be, vibrant and radiant with a fullness of existential meaning? (The *meaningfulness* of a color manifests as, and is, in part, a function of, its sensuous depth, warmth, and vivacity.) Our world seems to have lost some of its wonderful color — the color with which it originally glowed and sparkled when we were still living within the magical world of the child. Our eyes are duller, now; correspondingly, what they *see* is (felt to be) much more dull, as if enshrouded with a certain gloom and mourning.

What is the *ontological significance* of the fact that we see the world in colors? Describing the *Jñānamudrā* experience (*Dohākośa*, verse 18), Saraha advises us:

> Do not create duality, create unity!
> Without setting up distinctions between patterns,
> Colour the whole triple world
> In the unique colours of Great Love.[99]

The colorful giving, or givenness, of the things we behold *is* their way of blossoming, flowering before our very eyes. Their enchanting colorfulness is an ontological disclosure of the fact that they presence, or come forth, as presents for our visual delight. *Thus, not to be able to accept and receive things as the presents (presentations) they are is to be unable, correspondingly, to behold things non-re-presentationally in their colorful presence.* (Consider the beauty of a spread of fresh vegetables: home-grown red peppers, white onions, eggplant, carrots, beets: these colorful things present a beauty with infinitely unfolding dimensions of meaning, both sacred and profane, and as vast as the reach and range of Being itself.)

That worldly things should lend themselves, by nature, to this colorful and pleasing and yet, in fact, profoundly meaningful mode of dis-play is, I think, the manifest "proof" of their presence, not as mere "sense-data," but as the *gifts of Being*. The colors of things immediately please us; they attract the attention of our sensuously responsive eyes somewhat like the way that the scent and color of flowers, which are the sexual organs of the plant, are attractive to bees and butterflies. But our everyday seeing is ego-logical. What would it be like to see our colorful world without the prism of Ego? What if our eyes were to become less hostile and reductive, more open and responsive to the mystery of Being? What if they were to become more ontologically thoughtful, so embodying our meditation on Being that they became exceptionally capable of thankfully receiving and accepting, as gifts from Being, what it is granted them to behold? Perhaps these things we see would cor-respondingly dis-play themselves in, and come forth to us as, a colorful *mandala* of Being.

Describing what he means when he tells us that his visual experience feels like the presencing of Being in the splendor of a *mandala*, Klong-chen rab-'byams-pa says: "It means to surround any prominent facet of reality with [unsurpassable] beauty."[100] Wouldn't it be wonderful to dwell that way in the world our eyes behold? What do we *need* for our visual experience to be different — more existentially deep and meaningful, more spiritually satisfying? If Ego colors the world we see with our everyday eyes, how much more beautiful and refreshing this world would be, could we but see it in its pristine warmth and radiance, without the Ego's defensive shroud!

In regard, then, for *our visual relationship with Nature*, crying acquaints us, though still obscurely, with the experiential possibility of a more wholesome way of seeing, whose sensuous rootedness in Nature may yet so touch and bestir us that we not only learn how to be *with* Nature in a peaceful and harmonious communion, but even come to know, from the depths of our pain and suffering — depths which our crying eyes opened up for us — a new way to abstract, idealize, and axiomatize what we observe, *without* having to objectify the being of Nature in destructive dualities that are painful and ultimately not fulfilling.[101] "The earth as the home of man," writes Dewey, "is humanizing and unified; the earth viewed as a miscellany of facts is scattering and imaginatively inert."[102] The point is: "When nature is treated as a whole, like the earth in its relations, its phenomena fall into their natural relations of sympathy and association with human life . . . ."[103]

Who knows? Perhaps, by grace of the opening which the cry begins, we may be able to *hear*, for the first time, and by a sort of sympathetic co-respondence, the crying sighs of the disappearing forests and the crying whisperings of the dying species, and *behold*, with a pain sharp enough to arouse some still slumbering visionary wisdom, the rape and plunder, and the mindless acts of profanation, by which we steadily change this patient, fertile Earth, our home from times immemorial, into a lunar wasteland too barren for any life. Who knows? The experience of crying may yet bestir us, may yet *open* our eyes, so we really see, *clearly and feelingly see*, not only the desecration we have wrought, but also the opportunities and prospects, the "auspicious occasions," which, even now, Nature graciously still makes visible, for a new way to be with her: a new way for human beings to build on the Earth and dwell under the canopy of the sky.[104]

(iii) Finally, *in regard for the social nature of vision*, crying is the disclosure of the compassionate truth, or trust, which is immanent in seeing. *For it avows, between the being who cries and the being who is beheld, a primordial and indestructible kinship of flesh and blood* — and it does so, moreover, with *an immediate*, sensuously felt evidence that unquestionably refutes the philosophers' crazy attempts to convince us that solipsism is true. Crying expresses, and indeed renews, our on-going communion with every sentient being we may see. Crying can teach us that seeing is much more than be-holding; it is always also to be be-held and be-holden, since every sentient being we be-hold can give itself to us only by virtue of its own enthralling hold, its own primordial existential *claim*, on our eyes. *What the eyes cry out for, then, is a new way to see with compassion: a way to see with our eyes, as we never have before, the kindred beauty and mystery of all sentient beings; a way to see these beings openly and acceptingly, without dualities* (including sexual polarizations) *which are painful and not fulfilling.*

Such transparently com-passionate seeing is not so easy: it involves an openness toward others, and a certain ease and composure, which can be, when pushed beyond a certain comfortable point, very frightening. It may readily arouse intense feelings of paranoia, vulnerability, and even confused identity. But compassion may become especially problematic when it reaches the point where it requires the opening up of our eyes' inherently *androgynous* (i.e., non-dualistic, polymorphous sexual) nature. And yet, without such an opening, how can we hope to be able to *see*, with true compassion, the full range of pain and suffering in others? And how can we hope really to *see* the innumerable ways by which we *cause* unnecessary pain and suffering in others?

Speaking more generally, now, crying is our openness to being touched and moved by our essential need, as human beings, to experience and deepen our understanding of what Heidegger calls "the innermost indestructible belongingness of man within granting."[105] And he makes it clear that we need to see the granting of our belongingness "come to light."[106] Crying helps to open our eyes to their healing belongingness, that we may behold, and "not [simply] block off,"[107] nor completely hide and veil from our eyes, "the opening of Being,"[108] "which first brings to its radiance what is present."[109] To see this granting opening "come to light" is to behold "the saving power begin to shine."[110]

In this part of the essay, we have been questioning our experience of the nature of crying, stirred by the hope that we may yet learn how to see, through the veil of tears, the shining of this healing presence. We still do not know how to see in a whole-some and non-dualistic way; but perhaps we have, at least, been moved to stake our thinking in the nearness of Being. "For questioning," says Heidegger, "is the piety of thought."[111]

According to Buddhism, "where an attitude is developed in which *shunyata* [openness] and *karuna* [compassion] are indivisible, there is the message of the Buddha, the Dharma and the Sangha."[112] There is a crying need for the compassionate, opening teachings of crying. Can we *hear* this need? Can our eyes really *see* this need and respond with compassion? Can we teach and learn from one another *how to see* with clarity, beyond the vale of tears, into "the quiet heart of the opening"?[113] Can we, by grace of our vision, compassionately relate with one another — no matter who we are, what we may be doing, and where we may be — as participants in the communal construction of reality as a Great Mandala of Being? Can we see others through eyes which communicate in what Merleau-Ponty calls a "consecratory gesture"?[114]

If, as Heidegger says, "that which frees — the mystery — is concealed and always concealing itself," then the healing freedom, or liberation, of our eyes must be seen in, and also as, "that which *conceals* in a way that *opens* to light, in whose lighting there shimmers that veil which hides the essential occurrence of all truth [*das Wesende aller Wahrheit*] and lets the veil appear as what veils."[115]

NOTES.

1 Five friends have helped me, in one way or another, to write this paper: Roger Levin, Francis Lassiter, Eugene Gendlin, Herbert Guenther, and Samuel Todes. I want to thank them here.

2 Martin Heidegger, "The Question Concerning Technology" in David Farrell Krell (ed.), *Basic Writings of Martin Heidegger* (New York: Harper & Row, 1977), p. 300.

3 "Letter on Humanism," in *Basic Writings of Martin Heidegger*, p. 230.

4 "Letter on Humanism," *op. cit.*, p. 237. See also June Singer's superlative Jungian study of the non-dual archetypes, in *Androgyny* (New York: Doubleday, Anchor, 1977).

5 John Dewey, *Democracy and Education* (New York: Macmillan, The Free Press, 1966), p. 123.

6 See the Introduction, p. xi, to Martin Heidegger, *The End of Philosophy* (New York: Harper and Row, 1973).

7 See *The End of Philosophy*, pp. 12-14.

8 "Metaphysics as History of Being," *The End of Philosophy*, pp. 12-14.

9 "Metaphysics as History of Being," *op. cit.*, p. 4.

10 *Op. cit.*, p. 30.

David Michael Levin

11 *Op. cit.*, pp. 52-53.

12 *Op. cit.*, p. 39.

13 *Ibid.*

14 *Op. cit.*, p. 76. See also p. 60, where Heidegger ponders the possibility of understanding reflexion as "the shining back of what shows itself."

15 *Ibid.*

16 *Op. cit.*, p. 77.

17 See, especially, Eugene Gendlin, *Focusing* (New York: Everest House Publishing, 1978).

18 Heidegger, "Recollection in Metaphysics," in *The End of Philosophy*, p. 78.

19 *Op. cit.*, p. 79.

20 The phrase I use for the third moment is to be found in "The Question Concerning Technology," in *Basic Writings*, p. 315.

21 See Heidegger's "Letter on Humanism," in *Basic Writings*, p. 208. He speaks, there, of "the fundamental experience of the oblivion of Being."

22 See James Hillman, *The Myth of Analysis* (New York: Harper & Row, 1978), p. 45: "The Ego steals its light from the lumen naturale, and the ego expands, not at the expense of primordial darkness . . ., but at the cost of childhood's godlike, dimmer light of wonder."

23 "The End of Philosophy and the Task of Thinking," in *Basic Writings*, p. 386.

24 Martin Heidegger, *Sein und Zeit* (Tubingen: Max Niemeyer, 1960), p. 145.

25 "Letter on Humanism," *Basic Writings*, p. 204. Italics added. There is a curious feature of this embodiment, which I discuss more fully in a paper concerned with the essential nature (and essential potentialities) of bodily movement. See "The Bodhisattva's Power to Fly," in *Gesar* (Berkeley: The Tibetan Buddhist Nyingma Institute), vol. V, no. 3 (Fall, 1978). Also see "The Embodiment of Compassion: How We Are Visibly Moved," in *Soundings* (December, 1978).

26 "Letter on Humanism," *Basic Writings*, p. 205.

27 Martin Heidegger, *Sein und Zeit*, p. 199. I have lifted Heidegger's phrase from Part I, ch. 6, #41, entitled "Das Sein des Daseins als Sorge." Concerning Heidegger's understanding of "Openness," see *Vom Wesen der Wahrheit* (Frankfurt: Klostermann, 1943), p. 18, where Heidegger says, incisively interpreting our relationship with Being in the concrete terms of our incarnation, that "the posture [*Verhalten*] of man is pervasively tuned by the openness of being as the whole."

28 Martin Heidegger, "The Turning," in *The Question Concerning Technology and Other Essays* (New York: Harper & Row, 1977), p. 48.

29 "The End of Philosophy," *Basic Writings*, p. 374.

30 See Hans Jonas, "The Nobility of Sight: A Study in the Phenomenology of the Senses," in Stuart Spicker (ed.), *Philosophy of the Body* (New York: Quadrangle, 1970). There is no point in repeating the superlative analysis Jonas makes in this paper. That is why I feel comfortable with such a brief discussion of these themes.

31 See Edmund Husserl, *The Crisis of European Sciences and Transcendental Phenomenology* (Evanston: Northwestern, 1970).

32 Martin Heidegger, "The Age of the World Picture," in *The Question Concerning Technology and Other Essays*, p. 119.

33 *Ibid.*

34 Martin Heidegger, "Science and Reflection," *op. cit.*, p. 179.

35 "Science and Reflection," *op. cit.*, p. 163.

36 *Ibid.*

37 *Ibid.*

38 *Op. cit.*, p. 164.

39 *Ibid.*

40 *Op. cit.*, p. 166.

41 *Op. cit.*, p. 167.

42 *Ibid.*

43 *Op. cit.*, p. 172. See also "The Question Concerning Technology," *Basic Writings*, p. 304, where Heidegger argues the same basic point.

44 "Science and Reflection," in *The Question Concerning Technology and Other Essays*, p. 173.

45 Merleau-Ponty, *Phenomenology of Perception* (London: Routledge & Kegan Paul, 1962), p. 216. See also *op. cit.*, p. 219: "The unity of either the subject or the object *is not a real unity, but a presumptive unity* on the horizon of experience. We must rediscover, *as anterior to the ideas of subject and object*, the fact of my subjectivity and the *nascent* object, that primordial *layer* at which both things and ideas *come into being*" (Italics added.) Although this understanding *approaches* the Tibetan Buddhist notion of *kun-gzhi rnam-shes* (Sanskrit: *alaya-vijñana*), it still is not free of a certain tendency to reify primordial experience. On this topic, see Longchenpa, *Kindly Bent to Ease Us*. Translated with commentary by Herbert V. Guenther. (Emeryville: Dharma Publishing, 1975). The notion in question is indexed in vol. I on p. 307.

46 Martin Heidegger, "The Age of the World Picture," in *The Question Concerning Technology and Other Essays*, p. 150. Italics added.

47 See "Letter on Humanism," *Basic Writings*, pp. 214-216; "The Question Concerning Technology," *op. cit.*, pp. 291-293; and "The Thing," in Albert Hofstadter (transl. and ed.) *Poetry, Language, Thought* (New York: Harper & Row, 1971), pp. 172-173.

48 This moving utterance is told in a legend about Indrabhuti, king of Uddiyana (Odiyan), who wanted, out of gratitude, to give his "Precious Guru" the Wish-fulfilling Gem he had gotten from the ocean divinities. See *Crystal Mirror*. Annual Journal of the Tibetan Nyingma Meditation Center (Emeryville, California: Dharma Publishing, 1975), vol. IV, p. 7.

49 Quoted by Tarthang Tulku in "The Life and Liberation of Padmasambhava," *Crystal Mirror*, vol. IV, p. 26.

50 "The Age of the World Picture," in *The Question Concerning Technology and Other Essays*, p. 154. I also recommend some relevant Tibetan books, especially: Tarthang Tulku, *Gesture of Balance* (Emeryville: Dharma Publishing, 1977), and Chogyam Trungpa, *The Myth of Freedom* (Boulder: Shambhala, 1975) and *Cutting Through Spiritual Materialism* (Berkeley: Shambhala, 1973).

51 Martin Heidegger, "The Thing," in *Poetry, Language, Thought*, p. 181.

52 See Gershom G. Scholem (ed.), *Zohar* (New York: Schocken, 1963). Also see Scholem's pioneer work, *On The Kabbalah and Its Symbolism* (New York: Schocken, 1969), p. 110 ff. The breaking open of the vessels (*shevirah*) occurred, according to *Kabbalah*, because they were not capable of containing the light of the emanations (*sefiroth*) which were sent forth from the Body of the Holy One.

53 See Philip Wheelwright, *The Presocratics* (New York: Odyssey, 1966), p. 32.

54 "The Word of Nietzsche," in *The Question Concerning Technology and Other Essays*, p. 112.

55 See Herbert V. Guenther's commentary on the *Rig-pa rang-shar chen-po'i rgyud* and other texts by Klong-chen rab-'byams-pa, in his edition of *Kindly Bent to Ease Us*, Part II, p. 16. For Buddhists, the heart is the center, the heart, of the mind.

56 I highly recommend the writings of Eugene Gendlin, especially the following: "Focusing," in *Psychotherapy: Theory, Research and Practice*, vol. VI, no. 1 (Winter, 1969), 4-15; "Experiential Phenomenology," in Maurice Natanson (ed.), *Phenomenology and the Social Sciences* (Evanston: Northwestern, 1973); and "Experiential Psychotherapy," in Raymond Corsini (ed.), *Current Psychotherapies* (Itasca, Illinois: E. F. Peacock, 1973).

57 Martin Heidegger, "On the Essence of Truth," *Basic Writings*, p. 128.

58 *Op. cit.*, 134.

59 Herbert V. Guenther, *The Tantric View of Life* (Boulder: Shambhala, 1976), p. 93.

60 Martin Heidegger, "Language," in *Poetry, Language, Thought*, p. 204. In *Freedom to Learn* (Columbus, Ohio: Charles E. Merrill Publishing, 1969), Carl Rogers writes, wisely: "any significant learning involves a certain amount of pain, either pain connected with the

learning itself or distress connected with giving up certain previous learnings" (pp. 157-158).

61 See Merleau-Ponty, *op. cit.*, pp. 278-79.

62 *Ibid.*, pp. 346-365.

63 Martin Heidegger, "What is Metaphysics?" in *Basic Writings*, p. 102. See also "On the Essence of Truth," *op cit.*, p. 132: "as a whole" does *not* describe a "mere" feeling or "mere" (i.e., subjective) experience, though it certainly *can* be felt and otherwise experienced. This is crucial because, as he says, "From the point of view of everyday calculations and preoccupations, this 'as a whole' *appears to be* incalculable and incomprehensible." Precisely this uncontrollable incalculability is what makes the wholesome spontaneity and involuntariness of crying *seem*, contrary to what it really and essentially is, so shamefully irrational and *unworthy* of philosophical thought.

64 Merleau-Ponty, *Phenomenology of Perception*, p. 430.

65 "The Essence of Truth," *Basic Writings*, p. 141.

66 Merleau-Ponty, *Phenomenology of Perception*, p. 225.

67 *Op. cit.*, p. 229.

68 *Op. cit.*, p. 223. Italics added.

69 *Op. cit.*, p. 241.

70 Martin Heidegger, "What Are Poets For?" in *Poetry, Language, Thought*, p. 140.

71 "What Are Poets For?" *Poetry, Language, Thought*, p. 120.

72 See "What Are Poets For?" *op. cit.*, p. 121.

73 Merleau-Ponty, *Phenomenology of Perception*, p. 291.

74 See Longchenpa, *Kindly Bent to Ease Us* (3 vols.). My first-hand experience with psychotropic mushrooms in Colombia, Mexico, and British Columbia has shown me very convincingly that our everyday visual perception is needlessly dull, impoverished and restricted, and that there *is* an alternative way of seeing which can be enjoyed *without* the immediate influence of the mushrooms.

75 Martin Heidegger, "Conversation on a Country Path," in *Discourse on Thinking* (New York: Harper & Row, 1966), p. 78.

76 *Ibid.*

77 In *The Principle of Ground*, Heidegger writes: "The foundation, the ground of the judgment, is that which, as the unifying unity of subject and predicate, bears their connection." See *Der Satz vom Grund* (Pfüllingen: Neske, 1957), p. 193. This is a very resonant truth, one of whose innumerable echoes I hear in an interpretation which reads as follows: *The underlying nature, the ground of vision, is that which, as the unifying unity of the "subject" and its "object," bears their mortal's embrace.* See Herbert V. Guenther, *Buddhist Philosophy in Theory and Practice* (Boulder; Shambhala, 1976), pp. 196-198. In the visionary *Mahayoga* experience of "unsurpassable realization," which is the heart of the *Anuttarayogatantra* practice, it is reported, as a phenomenological fact, that the so-called "subject" and the so-called "object" become co-responsive "partners" in an existential dance and embrace of love. June Singer echoes this possibility for our sight in her exciting book, already cited: *Androgyny: Towards a New Theory of Sexuality.*

78 Tarthang Tulku, "The Life and Liberation of Padmasambhava," in *Crystal Mirror*, vol. IV, p. 27.

79 Merleau-Ponty, *Phenomenology of Perception*, p. 288.

80 *Op. cit.*, p. 320. See also *op. cit.*, p. 156. Also relevant, here, are his "Notes," published at the end of *The Visible and the Invisible* (Evanston: Northwestern University Press, 1968). According to Gerardo Reichel-Dolmatoff, the Indians of Colombia's rain forest believe that, "To drink yahé [a potion made with a local psychotropic plant] is [to undergo an experience of] a spiritual coitus; it is, as the priests say, a spiritual communion." Thus, it is fitting that, according to traditional belief, "when one drinks yahé, one dies." See *The Shaman and the Jaguar: A Study of Narcotic Drugs Among the Indians of Colombia* (Philadelphia: Temple University Press, 1975), p. 181.

81 Merleau-Ponty, *Phenomenology of Perception*, p. 156.

82 *Op. cit.*, p. 154.

83 See *The Royal Song of Saraha*, p. 46. Translated with commentary by Herbert V. Guenther (Berkeley: Shambhala, 1973). Also see my paper, "Freud's Divided Heart and Saraha's Cure," *Inquiry*, vol. 20, nos. 2-3 (Summer, 1977).

84 *The Royal Song of Saraha*, p. 46.

85 Heidegger, "Memorial Address," in *Discourse on Thinking*, p. 54.

86 "Conversation on a Country Path," *Discourse on Thinking*, p. 61.

87 "Memorial Address," *op. cit.*, p. 55.

88 See three very valuable Jungian studies: June Singer, *Androgyny* (New York: Doubleday, Anchor, 1977); James Hillman, *The Myth of Analysis* (Evanston: Northwestern University Press, 1972); and John Weir Perry, *The Far Side of Madness* (New York: Prentice Hall, 1974).

89 "The Age of the World Picture," in *The Question Concerning Technology and Other Essays*, p. 174. Italics added.

90 *Op cit.*, p. 176.

91 "Memorial Address," *Discourse on Thinking*, p. 54.

92 "Letter on Humanism," *Basic Writings*, p. 221.

93 *Ibid.*

94 "The Thing," *Poetry, Language, Thought*, p. 181.

95 "The Turning," *The Question Concerning Technology and Other Essays*, p. 48.

96 *Ibid.* Italics added.

97 *Ibid.*

98 See Heidegger's intriguing remark on color in *Early Greek Thinking* (New York: Harper & Row, 1975), p. 100. Also consider Merleau-Ponty's discussion of color in *Phenomenology of Perception*, pp. 209-214, 227-229, and 304-305.

99 Herbert V. Guenther, *The Tantric View of Life*, p. 75. Concerning color and meditation practice, see also his *Philosophy and Psychology of the Abhidharma* (Boulder: Shambhala, 1976), pp. 137-141. Another relevant source of wisdom concerning the role of colors in therapy is Gerardo Reichel-Dolmatoff, *Amazonian Cosmos: The Sexual and Religious Symbolism of the Tukano Indians* (Chicago: University of Chicago, 1971), esp., pp. 104-108, 122-127, and 137-138.

100 Herbert V. Guenther, *The Tantric View of Life*, p. 198.

101 See Edmund Husserl, *The Crisis of European Sciences and Transcendental Phenomenology*, for the foundation of a radical critique of the processes of abstraction, idealization, and axiomatic formalization in contemporary science. This critique enables us to glimpse the possibility of an *alternative* scientific approach to these basic processes.

102 John Dewey, *Democracy and Education*, p. 212.

103 *Op. cit.*, p. 213.

104 See Heidegger, "Building, Dwelling, Thinking," in *Poetry, Language, Thought*. Also see Vincent Scully, *The Earth, The Temple and The Gods: Greek Sacred Architecture* (New York: Praeger, 1969), for a fastidiously researched, and well-documented, phenomenological evocation of the experience of building and dwelling in the ancient Greek *Lebenswelt*. "The Question Concerning Technology," *Basic Writings*, p. 314.

105 *Ibid.*

106 Martin Heidegger, "The Origin of the Work of Art," in *Poetry, Language, Thought*, p. 83.

107 "The End of Philosophy," *Basic Writings*, p. 386.

108 "The Origin of the Work of Art," in *Poetry, Language, Thought*, p. 83.

109 "The Question Concerning Technology," *Basic Writings*, p. 317.

110 *Ibid.*

111 *Ibid.*

112 Chogyam Trungpa and Herbert V. Guenther, *The Dawn of Tantra* (Berkeley: Shambhala, 1975), p. 32.

113 "The End of Philosophy," *Basic Writings*, p. 387. Italics added.
114 Merleau-Ponty, *Phenomenology of Perception*, p. 146.
115 "The Question Concerning Technology," *Basic Writings*, p. 306. Italics added. The German original appears on p. 33 of *Vorträge und Aufsätze* (Pfüllingen: Verlag Günther Neske, 1954).

Phenomenology, Psychology, and Science

Keith Hoeller

With our question, we want neither to replace the sciences nor to reform them. On the other hand, we want to participate in the preparation of a decision; the decision: Is science the measure of knowledge, or is there a knowledge in which the ground and limit of science and thus its genuine effectiveness are determined? Is this authentic knowledge necessary for a historical people, or is it dispensable or replaceable by something else? . . . However, with our question we stand outside the sciences, and the knowledge for which our question strives is neither better nor worse but totally different.[1]

In this essay we would like to raise the question of the relation between three subject-matters: phenomenology, psychology, and science. While this question has been raised before by numerous people seeking to employ phenomenology as a basis for psychology, it has not yet been raised in the manner in which we wish to do so here. In the past, this issue has been addressed solely as a critique of *natural* science, with the idea of a somewhat Husserlian notion of a *human* science being offered as a solution for psychology. The most notable elucidation of this idea is Amedeo Giorgi's *Psychology as a Human Science*, which sees phenomenological psychology in light of Kuhn's outline of science, that is, as a competing paradigm during the revolutionary stage of science.[2] Should phenomenological psychology win out in this competition, it would then become the dominant paradigm, and psychology would enter its normal science stage.

While we see this view as a forward step in psychology's history, and while we are in agreement with Giorgi's critique of psychology as a natural science, our own approach seeks to take a different look at the idea of phenomenological psychology as a human *science*. In order to do this, we will have to return to the original question of the relation of phenomenology, psychology, and science. Our task will be distinguished from Giorgi's in two ways: First, we will concern ourselves with Heidegger's critique of science, and not Husserl's. For although Husserl wanted to found psychology — and, indeed, philosophy itself — as a "rigorous science," Heidegger, who initially agreed with Husserl, later chose not to pursue a scientific enterprise, and this holds true for all of his published writings after his "turning," until his death. We feel that this development in the history of phenomenology may also imply a necessary and useful step for phenomenological psychology itself. And this places us in the midst of our second distinguishing feature: We wish to question whether or not phenomenology should be used as a basis for psychology as a human *science*, that is to say, whether it can be utilized appropriately as a "paradigm" which would lead to the development of "normal science." In other words, not only do we question the idea of psychology as a natural *science*, but we also question the idea of psychology as a human *science*. Our ultimate question, then, is this: Insofar as we wish to have a phenomenological psychology, does phenomenology, as it has developed in Heidegger, lend itself to being appropriated as a paradigm for an ultimately "normal" *science*, or does phenomenology in some revolutionary way transcend the notions of paradigm and normal science? That is the question whose answer will decide whether or not we as phenomenological psychologists want to have a *science*, or something else which, like the title of this essay suggests, might lie somewhere between phenomenology and science.

I. HEIDEGGER AND THE QUESTION OF SCIENCE

A. THE EARLY HEIDEGGER

In a recent article on Heidegger and science, Theodore Kisiel writes:

> And *Being and Time* is manifestly a philosophy of being and existence and not a philosophy of science. But the examination of existential phenomena in this *magnum opus* also includes reflections on an existential conception of science, distinct from his earlier logical conception, with a promise of a thoroughgoing interpretation of science as a positive mode of existence to be incorporated in the as-yet-unpublished Third Division of the First Part of the project. Instead, science appears in a less positive light in the Second Part of the Heideggerian project, the part entitled "the phenomenological destruction of the history of ontology," and later elaborated under the rubric of "overcoming metaphysics" or "epochal" conception of science. . . .[3]

And although Kisiel adds in a footnote, "This is no longer quite accurate in view of the recent publication of the lecture course of 1927, in which philosophy itself is taken as the "science of being," we think that an even stronger case can be made for the difference between the early and the later Heidegger on the question of science. For while it may be true that *Being and Time* is not explicitly a "philosophy of science," it is nevertheless still tied to Husserl's task of "philosophy as a rigorous science," and it does in fact aim to be a science, in both its published and unpublished parts. It certainly is Heidegger's most "scientific" work. The later Heidegger, on the other hand, aspires precisely not to be a science, and this will be shown to be an important development for our subject here.

Being and Time (1927)

In *Being and Time*, which clearly represents a fundamental break with Husserl, to whom the book is nevertheless dedicated, we find a Husserlian conception of science. As Kisiel points out,

PHENOMENOLOGY, PSYCHOLOGY, AND SCIENCE

The Husserlian approach to science is strikingly evident in the early pages of *Being and Time*. In terms of characteristics of the *Logical Investigations*, science is tentatively described as "the coherent totality of proofs which ground true propositions."[4]

Now Heidegger's own enterprise is foundational and of course not a positive science; rather, it seeks to ground the positive sciences: "Ontological inquiry is indeed more primordial, as over against the ontical inquiry of the positive sciences."[5] Nevertheless, in the famous Section 7 of *Being and Time*, where Heidegger describes "The Phenomenological Method of Investigation," he constantly uses the word "science." "The Preliminary Conception of Phenomenology," is described as the "science of phenomena." We are told that, "With regard to its subject-matter, phenomenology is the science of the Being of entities—ontology,"[6] and that, "Ontology and phenomenology are not two distinct philosophical disciplines among others. These terms characterize philosophy itself with regard to its object and its way of treating that object. Philosophy is universal phenomenological ontology."[7] And finally, Heidegger invokes Husserl himself, while at the same time suggesting that he is also going to go beyond him:

> The following investigation would not have been possible if the ground had not been prepared by Edmund Husserl, with whose *Logical Investigations* phenomenology first emerged. Our comments on the preliminary conception of phenomenology have shown what is essential in it does not lie in its *actuality* as a philosophical "movement." Higher than actuality stands *possibility*. We can understand phenomenology only by seizing upon it as a possibility.[8]

However, except for these early pages, *Being and Time* contains little talk of science and proceeds directly to the *Daseinsanalytik*. Does this mean that Heidegger has seized upon phenomenology as a possibility and left behind its actuality as a science? Not at all. For the *Daseinsanalytik* is *preparatory*, and later on in *Being and Time*, he reminds us that he will explicitly get to the authentic idea of science, not merely of beings, but of Being, in the promised Third Part of the First Division, which remained unpublished:

> The existential conception understands science as a way of existence and thus as a mode of Being-in-the-world, which discovers or discloses either entities or Being. Yet a fully adequate existential Interpretation of science cannot be carried out until the *meaning of Being and the "connection" between Being and truth* have been *clarified* in terms of the temporality of existence.[9]

And in case there is any doubt that Heidegger intended *Being and Time* as a "science," we now have at our disposal that portion of the work mentioned above.

Fundamental Problems of Phenomenology (1927; 1975)

With the publication of this lecture course which Heidegger gave at the University of Marburg during the summer semester of 1927, the year that *Being and Time* was published, we have what Heidegger labels in the margin of the manuscript: New Working Out of the Third Division of the First Part of *Being and Time*.[10] In this course it is made even clearer that *Being and Time*, far from being a break with Husserl on the issue of science, was intended to display "*Philosophy as the science of Being*":

> Being is the genuine and single theme of philosophy .... Philosophy is not the *science of beings*, but rather of *Being* or, as the Greek expression reads, ontology.[11]

Heidegger even goes on to say that the discussion of the fundamental problems of phenomenology is founded on nothing other than proving and demonstrating, "the possibility and necessity of the absolute science of Being."[12] With the word "absolute" it is clear that Heidegger meant to continue Husserl's enterprise of "philosophy as a rigorous science."

Clearly, at this stage, while Heidegger is embarking on his own project, there is still a crucial tie to Husserl in what we are justified in calling Heidegger's most "scientific" work. But *Being and Time* failed and the Third Division of the First Part was not published. Oddly enough, in the closing paragraph of the section on the phenomenological method, Heidegger gives us a premonition of what the problem will become:

> With regard to the awkwardness and "inelegance" of expression in the analyses to come, we may remark that it is one thing to give a report in which we tell about *entities*, but another to grasp entities in their *Being*. For the latter rask we lack not only most of the words, but, above all, the "grammar."[13]

In the "Letter on Humanism," Heidegger tells us that indeed the reason that *Being and Time* did not succeed and the remaining portion was not published was due to the failure of language:

> The section in question was held back because thinking failed in the adequate saying of this turning and did not succeed with the help of the language of metaphysics. ... This language is still faulty insofar as it does not yet succeed in retaining the essential help of phenomenological seeing and in dispensing with the inappropriate concern with "science" and "research." But in order to make the attempt at thinking recognizable and at the same time understandable for existing philosophy, it could at first be expressed only within the horizon of that existing philosophy and its use of current terms. In the meantime I have learned to see that these very terms were bound to lead immediately and inevitably into error. For the terms and the conceptual language corresponding to them were not rethought by readers from the matter particularly to be thought; rather, the matter was conceived according to the established terminology in its customary meaning.[14]

Thus, after his "turning" in the 1930's, Heidegger no longer characterizes his work as "science," and ceases to use such "metaphysical" terms, for they "inevitably lead to error." He begins to look more closely at what science is, and sees it in distinction to "philosophy." We would like to turn to Heidegger's later view of science, in order to lead up to the question of whether or not such a "turning" may not also be necessary for psychology, which has also attempted to use phenomenology as its method.

B. The Later Heidegger

Until recently, most psychologists who have turned to Heidegger have concentrated primarily on *Being and Time*. This occurred in part because of the detailed working out of the *Daseinsanalytik* in *Being and Time*; however, this was also the case, at least in America, because translations of Heidegger's later works did not begin to appear until the later sixties and early seventies. In fact, two of Heidegger's major essays on science and technology only appeared in English last year. Nevertheless, as the later Heidegger has become more available and, with time, better understood, a few psychologists have begun to focus on his later works. And one of the areas of concentration has been Heidegger's conception of science and technology.[15]

In this part of our essay, then, we would like to give an explication of the later Heidegger's conception of science and technology in order to give us a foundation for raising our ultimate question concerning the nature of psychology with respect to science. For it is after Heidegger's famous turning that he begins his critique of science and begins to focus on the radical difference between philosophy and science.[16]

What is a Thing? (1935-36; 1962)

While our question is of course not about the thing, in Heidegger's lectures at the University of Freiburg in 1935-36, we find an important section entitled "The Modern Mathematical Science of Nature and the Origin of a Critique of Pure Reason."[17] This section is of interest because in it Heidegger links the transformation of science to the transformation of western thinking, and he characterizes the kind of thinking from which it developed:

> It is very clear only that the transformation of science basically took place through centuries of discussion about the fundamental concepts and principles of thought, i.e., the basic attitude toward things and toward what is at all. . . . All this presupposed a unique passion for an authoritative knowledge, which finds its like only among the Greeks, a knowledge which first and constantly questions its own presuppositions and thereby seeks their basis. To hold out in this constant questioning appears as the only human way to preserve things in their inexhaustibility, i.e., without distortion.[18]

151

Thus, unlike Husserl, who wanted a presuppositionless philosophy, Heidegger posits a *constant* questioning, But does science in fact do this? Heidegger's well worked out answer is "no." For science has a twofold foundation: (1) "work experiences, i.e., the direction and the mode of mastering and using what is; (2) metaphysics, i.e., the projection of the fundamental knowledge of being, out of which what is knowledgeably develops."[19] For our purposes it is interesting to note that what Heidegger calls "work experience," seems quite like what Kuhn, writing several decades later, calls "normal science," i.e., the everyday activities of the scientist whereby the method is applied. And in addition what Heidegger calls "metaphysics" appears to be almost identical to Kuhn's "paradigm."

Heidegger then proceeds to ask: How is modern science different from ancient and medieval science? He examines three common beliefs. First, there is the notion that modern science deals with facts, while ancient and medieval science dealt with concepts. But modern science also deals with concepts and presuppositions, and the ancients were also concerned with facts, that is, observable events. Heidegger writes:

> The greatness and superiority of natural science during the sixteenth and seventeenth centuries is because all the scientists were philosophers. They understood that there are no mere facts, but that a fact is only what it is in the light of the fundamental conception and always depends upon how far that conception reaches. . . . Where genuine and discovering research is done, the situation is no different from that of three hundred years ago . . . the present leaders of atomic physics, Niels Bohr and Heisenberg, think in a thoroughly philosophical way, and only therefore create new ways of posing questions and, above all, hold out in the questionable.[20]

Thus, the false dichotomy of facts and concepts collapses because of the "fact" that the great scientists are always philosophers who understand that there are no mere "facts," but that facts can only be understood within a conceptual framework.

The second common belief is that modern science is experimental, while ancient and medieval science were not. But ancient and medieval science were also experimental, as can be readily seen in Aristotle. How then is modern science different?

The answer lies in the third common assumption concerning modern science: it is mathematical. But we are cautioned that we must not think of calculation and the mathematical merely in the sense of numbers, for it originally means that which we know prior to our acquaintance with things:

> The *mathemata*, the mathematical, is that "about" things which we really already know. Therefore we do not first get it out of things, but, in a certain way, we bring it already with us. From this we can now understand why, for instance, number is something mathematical.[21]

For example, when we grasp the number three while looking at three apples, we can do so only if we already have some notion of "three." In this sense we grasp what we already knew beforehand.

Heidegger examines Newton's First Law of Physics in order to exhibit how mathematical modern science really is. The Law says that every body, if left to itself, moves uniformly in a straight line. But is this a fact, an experimentally proven given? No, for there does not exist anywhere such a body left to itself and no experiment could ever bring such a body to direct perception. And what about Galileo's experiment at the Tower of Pisa? The two bodies did not arrive at precisely the same time at the bottom of the tower, although the difference was slight. But in spite of the difference, Galileo believed this proved his experiment. He and his opponents saw the same "fact," and yet interpreted it differently, according to their own preconceptions.[22]

The mathematical project of modern science is precisely this framework, ground-plan, or blueprint of presuppositions. It lays out *in advance* a blueprint for nature. It is this blueprint which makes the results and the very experimentation itself understandable. And yet this plan laid out over nature in advance, precisely skips over direct observation for it limits and delimits nature in advance and indeed, already knows what nature is, that is, a precalculable nexus of forces. This is quite different from how Aristotle saw nature. Modern science is mathematical in the narrow sense insofar as numbers are what we most clearly and distinctly already know in advance. But in addition numbers give us certainty, which became the criteria for all knowledge with Descartes, who would accept only that which was clear and distinct, which means the mathematical in both senses. And what could be more certain than that which we already know.

But the mathematical, which is a fundamental trait of modern thought, is grounded in something deeper. Until the emergence of the mathematical, all knowledge was based on the Church and faith. This was the framework within which knowledge appeared and was grounded. Natural knowledge, that not based upon divine revelation, had no ground. The new mathematical project thus brought with it a new freedom, and with this new freedom, "the mathematical strives out of itself to establish its own essence as the ground for itself and thus of all knowledge."[23] And in a hint of what is to come in his later writings, Heidegger tells us that modern science, modern technology, and modern metaphysics all have the same ground.[24]

This ground arises in Descartes. Descartes sought to ground all knowledge in the knowing subject (*cogito ergo sum*). This meant that there could not be any other knowledge except the mathematical kind. With Descartes, too, comes the priority of the method, for method determines in advance what shall be deemed true, how, in general, we are to pursue things. This method is laid out in the form of general principles or axioms. These axioms are purely metaphysical in nature for they decide in advance the nature of the world, this is to say, these axioms are ontological. The mathematical is thus set up as the ground of all knowledge, everything that is not secured in a mathematical way is therefore groundless, and thus is not knowledge for Descartes. (Thus, in one fell swoop, the everyday world, with its own kind of knowledge, is wiped out).

This attempt to ground all knowledge in the knowing subject is called subjectivism. The subject (not God, as in the past) is to be the ground of all knowledge, all being. This Heidegger calls the attempt at self-grounding, and we will later see how technology and science are seen to be simply human activity.

With this grounding in pure reason itself (the I think), we also have posited the principle of non-contradiction and the principle of sufficient reason. These become the guiding axioms of modern thinking, and pave the way for the necessity of Kant's *Critique of Pure Reason*.[25]

Let us now summarize Heidegger's exposition of science in *What is a Thing?* A fact, commonly believed to be self-evident, i.e., directly observable, is dependent upon the framework within which this "fact" is viewed. For Kuhn this framework is called a paradigm. Second, while modern science is believed to prove facts through experimentation, the experiment itself is dependent upon the framework in which it is seen, e.g., Galileo's experiment (which Kuhn tells us never took place). Third, modern science is mathematical in the sense that it lays out nature in advance as already known. The method of experimentation follows from the ground-plan.

We also discovered that modern science attempts to found the world in the knowing subject, and this is done by affirming only that which is certain, i.e., that which is calculable or known in advance: axioms. The very ground of science lies in Descartes and his efforts to ground all knowledge in the human subject, or rather, we might say that, for Descartes, man is the supreme measure of all things.

But before leaving *What is a Thing?* we must make one last comment. Phenomenology, like the human sciences, does not appear here. The term is one which he has abandoned after his turning. But the fundamental goal of phenomenology is not abandoned. For in *Being and Time* phenomenology is characterized as letting the things show themselves, and there he even adopts Husserl's dictum: To the things themselves. By mentioning this we hope to make it clear that this attitude is in direct opposition to the project of modern science which determines things in advance and lets them appear only within a certain framework. At this point, science and phenomenology are radically opposed.

PHENOMENOLOGY, PSYCHOLOGY, AND SCIENCE

"The Age of the World Picture" (1950)

In this essay Heidegger reflects upon what Kuhn would call "normal science," that is to say, the everyday application of a fixed paradigm. Heidegger writes:

> The essence of what we today call science is research. In what does the essence of research consist? In the fact that knowing establishes itself as a procedure within some realm of what is, in nature or in history. . . . This is accomplished through the projection within some realm of what is—in nature, for example—of a fixed ground plan of natural events. The projection sketches out in advance the manner in which the knowing procedure must bind itself and adhere to the sphere opened up. This binding adherence is the rigor of research.[26]

Heidegger then characterizes three aspects of modern scientific research: (1) the procedure of mathematical projection, (2) methodology, (3) ongoing activity, i.e., specialization, and institutionalization. What is of importance here is that he does not merely believe that these are characteristic of the natural sciences, but also the human sciences. For while there are differences, for example, the necessary inexactness of the human sciences, Heidegger believes that in their fundamentals, that is, in their very natures as modern sciences, they are the same, and this regardless of their methods.

The first feature of modern research, its essentially mathematical character, has already been discussed in *What is a Thing?* We also need spend no time on the importance of methodology. However, let us now look briefly at the third one for it constitutes the progress of all sciences: ongoing activity, i.e., specialization and institutionalization. It is the very specialization and institutionalization that allow the ongoing activity to proceed in a progressive manner. Thus, Heidegger says: "Specialization is not the consequence but the foundation of all research."[27] And it is science's institutionalization that allows the ongoing activity to occur:

> By this (ongoing activity) is to be understood first of all the phenomenon that a science today, whether physical or humanistic, attains to the respect due a science only when it has become capable of being institutionalized. However, research is not ongoing activity because its work is accomplished in institutions, but rather institutions are necessary because science, intrinsically as research, has the character of ongoing activity.[28]

With all of this, Heidegger of course is conjuring up the image of the modern university researcher, government and independent grant foundations, professional conferences, and the publication of research. In other words, the business, or "busyness," of modern academic life. And there is something qualitatively different about this, regardless of whatever romantic ideals about university life linger on:

> Hence the decisive development of the modern character of science as ongoing activity also forms men of a different stamp. The scholar

155

disappears. He is succeeded by the research man who is engaged in research projects. These, rather than the cultivating of erudition, lend to his work its atmosphere of incisiveness.[29]

All of this activity, however, is grounded in the very essence of the modern age, which, as we saw earlier, is an attempt to ground all knowledge in the self:

> Science as research is an absolutely necessary form of this establishing of self in the world; it is one of the pathways upon which the modern age rages toward fulfillment of its essence, with a velocity unknown to the participants. With this struggle of world views the modern age first enters into the part of its history that is the most decisive and probably the most capable of enduring.[30]

We can have such things as world views, and conflicts of world views, because the world itself has become a view, a picture for man to look at from his central vantage point.

And after all this analysis of the essence of science, Heidegger posits the fact that there is always something in science that, in spite of all its calculations remains incalculable. Can science help us to fathom the incalculable? As Heidegger did in *What is a Thing?* he rather suggests that for that we need something quite different:

> Man will know, i.e., carefully safeguard into its truth, that which is incalculable, only in creative questioning and shaping of the power of genuine meditation. Meditation transports the man of the future into that "between" in which he belongs to Being and yet remains a stranger amid that which is.[31]

"The Question of Technology" and "The Turning" (1954 & 1962)

It will be clear that at this point Heidegger has left Husserl far behind. For ultimately Husserl remained a Cartesian in his search for an absolute certainty. Husserl's quest for a "rigorous science," was a part of that Cartesianism. Heidegger's critique of science, and of the modern age, leads him far away from science, even far away from philosophy. For Heidegger the questions go back to the very beginning of western history, where reason first came to prominence over against nature. Reason has developed from the Greeks into its present almost god-like state. Nowhere is the reverence for reason greater than in the sciences, where reason has come to mean calculation. And calculation has come to mean instruments, that is, technology. Science and technology go hand in hand. This takes place because the essence of science, the essence of technology, and the essence of the modern age are all the same. Thus, we are led to asking: what is the essence of technology?

The essence of technology is itself nothing technological, anymore than the essence of a tree is a tree.[32] For Heidegger the essence of technology is an all-pervasive *framework* (*Gestell*) under which we stand in the modern era. This framework provokes man to approach nature in a predetermined way and to allow it to come forth only in a certain manner. Modern science, particularly modern physics, is the herald of this framework:

> The modern physical theory of nature prepares the way first not simply for technology but for the essence of modern technology. For already in physics the challenging gathering-together into ordering revealing holds sway. But in it that gathering does not yet come expressly to appearance. Modern physics is the herald of the framework, a herald whose origin is still unknown.[33]

The essence of technology is a way of revealing that does not let things come forth as they are, but literally *provokes* them and demands that they come forth only within a planned context. This is quite different from poetry or art, which brings forth in a manner that does not provoke. But the danger is that this way of revealing will become the only one, and thus the other ways will be threatened with extinction:

> The coming to presence of technology threatens revealing, threatens it with the possibility that all revealing will be consumed in ordering and that everything will present itself only in the unconcealedness of standing-reserve.[34]

This standing-reserve, like a stockpile of energy, renders everything in terms of its usefulness for man. Thus, nature itself comes to be seen as an energy fund or storehouse and is provoked by man through strip mining and dams.

But with the arrival of the essence of technology, the danger of dangers, there is the possibility that we will see it for what it is and that we will cultivate the other ways of revealing and thus prepare for a "turning." This turning will not involve a new science, but rather it will require that we become more thoughtful:

> The closer we come to the danger, the more brightly do the ways into the saving power begin to shine and the more questioning we become. For questioning is the piety of thought.[35]

"Science and Meditation" (1954)

In this essay Heidegger continues to pursue the *essence* of science, not just of one particular science, but of all of modern science. This essence is itself nothing scientific, and this is Heidegger's clue in tracking it down. But to do this he must pursue his way through science and ask what it is. What is interesting here is that again science is distinct from thinking, as is apparent already in the title.

We must still be clear that modern science is something distinguished from the "science" of the ancient and medieval world. In the Greeks we find, for example, that the highest kind of life was the *bios theoretikos*, the viewed life, in contrast to the *bios praktikos*, the handling and producing of things. This distinction also exists for the Romans in the words *vita contemplativa*, the contemplative life. and the *vita activa*, the active life. But the kind of *theorein* and *contemplatio* that occur in scientific *observation* is much different than earlier times, for it not only looks at reality in a new way, but it also encroaches upon it in an uncanny manner. *Science is the theory of the real*:

> And yet the "theory" that modern science shows itself to be is something essentially different from the Greek *theoria*[36]. . . . Theory makes secure at any given time a region of the real as its object-area. The area-character of objectness is shown in the fact that it specifically maps out in advance the possibilities for the posing of questions. Every new phenomenon emerging within an area of science is refined to such a point that it fits into the normative objective coherence of the theory. That normative objective coherence itself is thereby changed from time to time. But objectness as such remains unchanged in its fundamental characteristics. . . . Were objectness to be surrendered, the essence of science would be denied.[37]

Because of this notion of theory, which seeks to secure the real in its objectness, the method has priority, and the best method for this is a mathematical measurability, or, as Max Planck says, "That is real which can be measured." Heidegger believes this is true for science:

> The statement of Max Planck is true, however, only because it articulates something that belongs to the essence of modern science, not merely to physical science.[38]

What it articulates of course is its mathematical character, which necessarily leads to a mapping out of a domain in which the real may appear. Thus, compartmentalized sciences and specialization are needed. But in spite of all of this mapping out and determining the real itself, there is always something which escapes science itself. For science is only *one* way in which an inexhaustible reality comes to appearance. And at the basis of that reality is always something inconspicuous, indispensable, and inaccessible to the sciences. For in the sciences of physics, psychiatry, history, and philology, their very subject-matter remains inaccessible to them via their own methods:

> Nature, man, history, language, all remain for the aforementioned sciences that which is not to be gotten around, already holding sway from within the objectness belonging to them—remain that toward which at any given time those sciences are directed. but that which, in the fullness of its coming to presence, they can never *encompass* by means of their representing. The impotence of the sciences then is not grounded in the fact that their entrapping securing never comes to an end; it is grounded rather in the fact that in principle the objectness in which at any given time nature, man, history, language, exhibit themselves always itself remains only *one* kind of presencing, in which indeed that which presences can appear, but never absolutely must appear.[39]

Thus physics, as physics, can never make any assertions about itself. There is no experiment that physics can undertake to reach and fathom its own ground. And even psychiatry itself can never reach, through its own methods, its object of study:

> Psychiatry strives to observe the life of the human soul in its sick—and that also means in its healthy—manifestations. It represents these in terms of the objectness of the bodily-psychical-spiritual unity of the whole man. At any given time human existence, which is already presencing, displays itself in the objectness belonging to psychiatry. The openness-for-Being (*Da-sein*) in which man as man ek-sists, remains that which for psychiatry cannot be gotten around.[40]

However, the fact that the sciences cannot reach and know their own essence is disquieting:

> If it is entirely denied to science scientifically to arrive at its own essence, then the sciences are utterly incapable of gaining access to that which is not to be gotten around holding sway in their essence. Here something disturbing manifests itself. That which in the sciences is not at any given time to be gotten around—nature, man, history, language—is, *as* that which is not to be gotten around, intractable and inaccessible for the sciences and through the sciences.[41]

That all this has gone unnoticed is an amazing state of affairs, especially considering all the attention to the history and philosophy of science and to the so-called "foundational crisis" of the sciences, to which Husserl and even the early Heidegger addressed themselves. In this essay, on the contrary, Heidegger sees a peculiar "restiveness" in the sciences, and this amidst the noise:

> The passionate and incessant troubling over this is therefore above all a fundamental characteristic of modern times. How, then, could that state of affairs remain unheeded? Today we speak of "the crisis at the foundations" of the sciences. That crisis, in fact, touches only the fundamental concepts of the individual sciences. It is in no way a crisis of science as such. Today science goes its way more securely than ever before.[42]

But in spite of all this, in spite of the fact that science threatens to become the only kind of revealing, and thus eclipse the very thing it is trying to reveal, there is something else which can be done, and which is fitting, but which is not science. This Heidegger calls *meditation*, which is much more than merely making something conscious:

> Meditation is more. It is calm, self-possessed surrender to that which is worthy of questioning. . . . Meditation is of a different essence from the making conscious and the knowing that belong to science; it is also of a different essence from intellectual cultivation . . . (which is) based upon a belief in the invincible power of an immutable reason and its principles.[43]

Heidegger's view of history sees that the present scientific age is coming to its end and that "the signs are appearing of a world-age in which that which is worthy of questioning will someday again open the door that leads to what is essential in all things and in all destinings."[44]

But even though access to the inaccessible is closed to science, the individual scientist is another matter:

> Even if the sciences, precisely in following their ways and using their means, can never press forward to the essence of science, still every researcher and teacher of the sciences, every man pursuing a way through a science, can move, as a thinking being, on various levels of meditation and can keep meditation vigilant.[45]

We might add that this is exactly what the great scientists do, they become philosophical. Such thinking is necessary:

> Meditation is needed as a responding that forgets itself in the clarity of ceaseless questioning away at the inexhaustibleness of That which is worthy of questioning—of That from out of which, in the moment properly its own, responding loses the character of questioning and becomes simply saying.[46]

What is Called Thinking? (1954)

Heidegger has come a long way from the saying, "Phenomenology is the science of Being."[47] And we must note that even that sentence was held back and never published. Instead, he underwent a turning, and found better words for his thinking. The word "science" is left behind entirely as an adjective for his own work. For science came to be seen as too bound up with the essence of the modern age. It remained essentially a part of our modern Cartesianism. Husserl, who forever remained a Cartesian, could seek an absolute, apodictic, objective, rational science. Heidegger, however, even in the published part of *Being and Time*, began a path that allowed for a meditation quite distinct from Husserl's *Cartesian Meditations*. This path not only led to Heidegger's later abandonment of the word "science," but also to his ceasing to use the word "philosophy" to describe his task. For even "philosophy" remained within a tradition he sought to stand outside of, at its end, and to look at critically. Thus, we should not be surprised that he should ask "What is Called Thinking?"

And again Heidegger is quick to point out the difference between science and his thinking:

> For it is true that what was said so far, and the entire discussion that is to follow, have nothing to do with scientific knowledge, especially not if the discussion itself is to be a thinking. This situation is grounded in the fact that science itself does not think, and can not think—which is its good fortune, here meaning the assurance of its own appointed course.[48]

Heidegger then points out that the chasm that separates the sciences and thinking is unbridgeable:

160

> There is no bridge here—only the leap. Hence there is nothing but mischief
> in all the makeshift ties and asses' bridges by which men today would set up
> a commerce between thinking and the sciences. Hence we, those of us who
> come from the sciences, must endure what is shocking and strange about
> thinking—assuming we are ready to learn thinking.[49]

Science does not think, Heidegger says. Thinking and science lie across an unbridgeable gulf which can be leaped over, but not bridged. And this leap requires that those of us coming from the sciences must begin to think. For we do not think the way that thinkers think, as has already been seen in the different viewing of science and meditation.[50]

This thinking does not wish to speak against the sciences, but rather for their clarity of essence. This essence lies in the realm of the essence of modern technology. And it is only thinking that can lead the way into this essence.[51]

Since the sciences parted from philosophy they cannot find their way back. Only thinking can find them.[52] They remain apart, on one side, and one-sided. This one-sidedness accounts for the greatness of science, but cuts it off from what is inaccessible to it. But by delineating a certain sphere to themselves, they thus make progress and attain knowledge.[53]

Heidegger points out psychology as an example of a science that chose to break away from the confusion and conflict of philosophical ideas in order to establish itself as a science:

> Given this discord among philosophers concerning what the forming of
> ideas is in essence, there is patently just one way out into the open. We leave
> the field of philosophical speculation behind us, and first of all investigate
> carefully and scientifically how matters really stand with the ideas that
> occur in living beings, especially in men and animals. Such investigations
> are among the concerns of psychology. Psychology is today a well-
> established and already extensive science, and its importance is growing
> year by year. But we here leave to one side the findings of psychology
> concerning what it calls "ideas"; not because these findings are incorrect,
> let alone unimportant, but because they are scientific findings. For, being
> scientific statements, they are already operating in a realm which for
> psychology, too, must remain on that other side of which we spoke before.
> It is no cause for wonder, then, that within psychology it never becomes
> clear in any way what it is to which ideas are attributed and referred—to
> wit, the organism of living things, consciousness, the soul, the unconscious
> and all the depths and strata in which the realm of psychology is
> articulated. Here everything remains in question; and yet, the scientific
> findings are correct.[54]

The consequence of all this is that science, which is merely "correct," but not in fact "true," is able to make statements about the nature of reality, without its really knowing what that reality is as such. And with the progress that science makes by carving out an area of research and concentrating on it scientifically, we tend to be in awe of its results. But it is only one kind of knowledge and the danger is that it will become the only kind. Nowhere is this seen more clearly than in our attempts to simply experience a tree in bloom, in which we almost immediately yield ourselves and look to the sciences for an interpretation of the experience. Our eagerness to look to science poses a problem:

> It will not do to admit, just for the scientifically unguarded moments, so to speak, that, naturally, we are standing face to face with a tree in bloom, only to affirm the very next moment as equally obvious that this view, naturally, typifies only the naive, because pre-scientific, comprehension of things. For with that affirmation we have conceded something whose consequences we have hardly considered, and that is: that those sciences do in fact decide what of the tree in bloom may or may not be considered valid reality. Whence do the sciences—which necessarily are always in the dark about the origin of their own nature—derive the authority to pronounce such verdicts? Whence do the sciences derive the right to decide what man's place is, and to offer themselves as the standard that justifies such decisions? And they will do so just as soon as we tolerate, if only by our silence, that our standing face-to-face with the tree is no more than a pre-scientifically intended relation to something that we still happen to call "tree." In truth, we are today rather inclined to favor a supposedly superior physical and physiological knowledge, and to drop the blooming tree. When we think through what this is, that a tree in bloom presents itself to us so that we can come and stand face-to-face with it, the thing that matters first and foremost, and finally, is not to drop the tree in bloom, but for once let it stand where it stands. Why do we say "finally"? Because to this day, thought has never let the tree stand where it stands.[55]

This priority of the everyday world, what phenomenology has come to call the "life-world," is just what phenomenology has always sought to preserve over against the derived and authoritative knowledge of science. That this knowledge is more primary and closer to the things themselves, and thus not scientific, is just what Heidegger has sought to show throughout his critique of science. But the question which we will have to think about later in this paper is whether or not, once having begun to think, we wish to return to an unthinking posture, or whether or not even science itself, like philosophy, is coming to an end and needs to be overcome in its essence.

Releasement (1959)

In this short book, which is translated as *Discourse on Thinking* but whose proper title is *Releasement (Gelassenheit)*, Heidegger further develops the notion of the difference between the scientific and the meditative ways of thinking. Here he calls them calculative and meditative thinking. Calculative thinking is described as:

> the mark of all thinking that plans and investigates. Such thinking remains calculation even if it neither works with numbers nor uses an adding machine or computer. Calculative thinking computes. . . . Calculative thinking is not meditative thinking, not thinking which contemplates the meaning which reigns in everything that is.[56]

On the other hand, meditative thinking tends to things as they are and can be undertaken by anyone. "Why? Because man is a *thinking*, that is, a *meditating* being."[57] Nevertheless,

> meditative thinking does not just happen by itself any more than does calculative thinking. At times it requires a greater effort. It demands more practice. It is in need of even more delicate care than other genuine craft. But it must also abide its time. . . .[58]

Both calculative and meditative thinking are necessary and justifiable in their own ways. However, *man is in flight from thinking* and by this, Heidegger means that man is in *flight from meditative thinking*.[59] And in this there lies the greatest of dangers such that,

> the approaching tide of technological revolution in the atomic age could so captivate, bewitch, dazzle, and beguile man that calculative thinking may someday come to be accepted and practiced *as the only* way of thinking. What great danger then might move upon us? Then there might go hand and hand with the greatest ingenuity in calculative planning and inventing indifference toward meditative thinking, total thoughtlessness. And then? Then man would have denied and thrown away his own special nature— that he is a meditative being. Therefore, the issue is the saving of man's essential nature. Therefore the issue is keeping meditative thinking alive.[60]

And how do we keep meditative thinking alive? We do this through a *releasement toward things* and an *openness to the mystery*. A releasement toward things means that we say "yes" to technological contrivances and allow them into our daily life, while at the same time saying "no, " by letting them alone and not allowing them to rule our lives and consume us. An openness to the mystery means that we are open to the "hidden meaning in technology."[61] Both of these two attitudes offer us a radical alternative to the present domination of technology:

> Releasement toward things and openness to the mystery belong together. They grant us the possibility of dwelling in the world in a totally different way. They promise us a new ground and foundation upon which we can stand and endure in the world of technology without being imperiled by it.[62]

Nevertheless, we must always keep in mind that the essence of technology, that is, the essence of modern science and the modern age, is precisely not something man-made or man-dependent, but is dependent on something higher: the unfolding of the destiny of Being in the history of western thinking.

II. PHENOMENOLOGICAL PSYCHOLOGY AND THE QUESTION OF SCIENCE

In this part of the essay we would like to use what we have learned from Heidegger's critique of science in order to ask the question: Is the idea of a *phenomenological* psychology compatible with the idea of a human *science*? Having traveled this far, we feel that with Heidegger's new conception of science we might now be able to ask this question in a more direct way.

We would like to summarize Heidegger's notion of the essence of science and at the same time compare it more directly with Thomas Kuhn's analysis of science as given in his *The Structure of Scientific Revolutions*. We have chosen Kuhn's book not merely because of its importance to the history of science, but because it has been used as the basis for most attempts to found phenomenological psychology as a human science. Thus, the idea of what a science does, and should do, is very much dependent on Kuhn's analysis, and for our purposes here, we do not wish to debate Kuhn's merits and demerits. For if, for example, Giorgi, who has used Kuhn's model of science to argue why phenomenological psychology should be a science, would now wish to argue that Kuhn's model is not appropriate, this could not be considered an argument in favor of a psychology as a human science for we would have even less reason than before for understanding why psychology should be a science and what kind of a science it should be.[63]

In looking at Heidegger, Kuhn, and Giorgi what we shall unveil is that they are in surprising agreement about what science is. The difference will be that while Kuhn and Giorgi want to further the scientific enterprise, Heidegger chooses to further something else which is quite unscientific and unparadigmatic. It is the latter path that we feel will be more fruitful for phenomenological psychology.

A. HEIDEGGER AND KUHN ON THE ESSENCE OF SCIENCE

Throughout our discussion of Heidegger's critique of science, we have been trying to discover the essence of science. This essence is something different and broader than any single definition of science, and would ultimately encompass any definition of science that would still contain some resemblance to what we today call "science." Heidegger himself has made this quite clear when he points out that although the framework changes, the essence of science still remains throughout its history. And he further states that, were this essence denied, "the essence of science would be denied."[64] Kuhn also sees that the issue is broader than definitions:

> Can very much depend upon a *definition* of "science"? Can a definition tell a man whether he is a scientist or not? . . . Inevitably one suspects that the issue is more fundamental.[65]

Indeed, the *real* questions "are not, however, questions that could respond to an agreement on definition.[66]

It would also follow that such an essence would apply not only to the natural sciences, but also to the human sciences. While it is true that both Heidegger and Kuhn devote the bulk of their interpretation to the natural sciences, both do in fact apply it to the human sciences and feel that the application is equally justifiable. This is because regardless of the content, or the method in each science, if the approach is to be scientific, it will partake of the essence of science, which is the same in both the natural and the human sciences.

And what is the essence of science? What is it that most characteristically distinguishes science from other kinds of endeavors? For Heidegger the essence of science can be phrased in the following way: science is the application of a framework that is applied to a special object domain in order to do research. Heidegger has put this in a way that bears repeating:

> The essence of what we today call science is research. In what does the essence of research consist? In the fact that knowing establishes itself as a procedure within some realm of what is. . . . This is accomplished through the projection within some realm of what is . . . of a fixed ground plan of natural events. The projection sketches out in advance the manner in which the knowing procedure must bind itself and adhere to the sphere opened up. This binding adherence is the rigor of research.[67]

As we have noted, this is Kuhn's idea of "normal science," the everyday research activity of the scientist:

> In this essay, "normal science" means research firmly based upon one or more past scientific achievements, achievements that some particular scientific community acknowledges for a time as supplying the foundation for its further practice. . . . Achievements [of this sort] . . . I shall henceforth refer to as "paradigms," a term that relates closely to "normal science." By choosing it, I mean to suggest that some accepted examples of actual scientific practice . . . provide models from which spring particular coherent traditions of scientific research.[68]

It is clear to Kuhn that this is what characterizes *modern* science, for it does not refer to science before Newton.[69]

Now this "normal science" consists in the acceptance of a model by a scientific community which uses the model to "solve puzzles." And this normal science is precisely that which distinguishes science as science:

> . . . a careful look at the scientific enterprise suggests that it is normal science . . . rather than extraordinary science which most nearly distinguishes science from other enterpirses.[70]

"Extraordinary science" is the revolutionary stage which marks out the transition from one paradigm to another in a science. It is a philosophical period that offers competing paradigms to explain a significant "anomaly" that normal science can neither explain or do away with. But, in spite of these revolutionary periods when scientists turned to philosophy, it is still normal science which characterizes science:

> In a sense . . . it is precisely the abandonment of critical discourse that marks the transition to a science. Once a field has made that transition, critical discourse recurs only at moments of crisis when the bases of the field are again in jeopardy. Only when they must choose between competing theories do scientists behave like philosophers.[71]

Indeed, scientists do not really want to be philosophers:

> It is, I think, particularly in periods of acknowledged crisis that scientists have turned to philosophical analysis as a device for unlocking the riddles of their field. Scientists have not generally needed or wanted to be philosophers. Indeed, normal science usually holds creative philosophy at arm's length, and probably for good reasons. To the extent that normal research work can be conducted by using the paradigm as a model, rules and assumptions need not be made explicit.[72]

Thus, for Kuhn, too, there is a radical difference between philosophy and science. Science does not think, does not wish to think, and does so only when forced to. Nowhere is this more apparent than in Kuhn's description of normal science and the characteristics he attributes to it. *Normal science is dogmatic,*[73] *exclusive,*[74] *close-minded,*[75] *authoritarian,*[76] *and intolerant.*[77] *It is committed to only one way,*[78] *secure in its drastically restricted vision,*[79] *and as narrow and rigid as systematic theology.*[80] But it is precisely these characteristics that give science its stamp, so that in agreement on the basics the group can press forward and progress in an efficient manner, for

> . . . once the reception of a common paradigm has freed the scientific community from the need constantly to re-examine its first principles, the members of that community can concentrate exclusively upon the subtlest and most esoteric of the phenomena that concern it. Inevitably, that does increase both the effectiveness and the efficiency with which the group as a whole solves new problems.[81]

This efficient progress through the dogmatism of normal science is science itself. For once the essentials are agreed upon, the group can proceed to successfully solving puzzles, whose outcome is already known in advance:

> Whether his work is predominantly theoretical or experimental, he usually seems to know, before his research project is even well under way, all but the most intimate details of the result which that project will achieve. If the result is quickly forthcoming, well and good. If not, he will struggle with his apparatus and with his equations until, if at all possible, they yeild results which conform to the sort of pattern which he has foreseen from the start.[82]

Thus, Kuhn acknowledges what Heidegger calls the mathematical element of modern science, whereby everything is known in advance, or as Kuhn puts it, "everything but the detail of the outcome was known in advance."[83]

But the dogmatism of science also explains why revolutions are necessary. Nothing else would work once a paradigm begins to break down. But because the science has become rigidified, younger people, or people new to the field, i.e., people who have escaped the indoctrination methods of the science, are necessary in order to think of a new way of looking at things.[84] The traditional practitioners of the science can be counted upon only as opponents, who will regard anything new as "intrinsically subversive."[85] This struggle is then basically a *political* struggle between the old and the new, for as Max Planck has said: "A new scientific truth is not usually presented in a way that convinces its opponents . . . ; rather they gradually die off, and a rising generation is familiarized with the truth from the start."[86]

Thus, the new generation wins out, a new paradigm is adopted and normal science begins once again, efficiently progressing from its dogmatic adherence to group norms. This is science, for Kuhn and for Heidegger. Science *aims* at an unthinking, unquestioning, authoritarian acceptance of a common set of beliefs. Occasionally, though, science is forced to question, to become philosophical, to think. And between the two (normal and revolutionary science), there lies an abyss. However, for Kuhn the ultimate end goal is normal science, whereas for Heidegger it is revolutionary science, i.e., philosophy. Why is this so?

We think we can understand Heidegger's own preference for thinking over science if we ask ourselves just what it is that Kuhn's distinction between normal and revolutionary science, between uncritical acceptance and a thoroughgoing questioning attitude, really describes. For in fact the distinction is not merely peculiar to science; it has parallels in other areas of life, indeed, in life itself, in the relation between the individual and the group. Heidegger himself has described this distinction in *Being and Time* where he speaks of the everyday, unquestioning attitude of the they, the very "dictatorship of the they," and the authentic questioning of the individual who seeks to appropriate what is his or her own. Thus, what Kuhn is really describing is the inauthentic and the authentic modes of science, that is to say, normal science is inauthentic and revolutionary science is authentic, and, like human existence itself, primarily and for the most part, science is characterized by the inauthentic mode, i.e., normal science. Heidegger of course is interested not so much in doing away with the inauthentic, which is a necessary part of life, but rather in emphasizing and seeking the authentic and wresting it from its lostness in the inauthentic mode. Thus, his *aim*, unlike Kuhn's, is toward the authentic element of science, that is, its thoughtful, philosophical attitude which can be taken up by the individual scientist and is taken up by the great scientists who become philosophical. And this becomes relevant to our discussion when we ask just what it might mean if we were to shift our own attention in psychology from the goal of a normal science to that of an authentic, revolutionary science, and whether this would still be science. That it would be revolutionary is we hope beginning to become quite clear.

B. GIORGI AND KUHN: PHENOMENOLOGY AS THE PARADIGM FOR PSYCHOLOGY AS A HUMAN SCIENCE

Now, after having discussed Heidegger and Kuhn's views of science, we feel we are ready to take a look at Giorgi's *Psychology as a Human Science: A Phenomenologically Based Approach*.[87] We would like to show how Giorgi adopts Kuhn's conception of science in order to found phenomenology as the paradigm for psychology conceived as a human science. We would then like to ask whether or not phenomenology does in fact lend itself to being used as a paradigm for an ultimately normal science or whether it is possible that there is something unparadigmatic about phenomenology that might preclude its being used in such a way.

In his Preface Giorgi begins by placing his work within the humanistic or Third Force tradition in psychology. His major goal is to show that psychology can be *both* humanistic and scientific. He therefore wishes to dispel the notion that, a humanistic psychology cannot be a science:

> Moreover, it is precisely the prejudice that Third Force psychology must be either antiscientific or nonscientific that we would like to challenge. Consequently, both the term "human" and the term "science" are important to us. We would insist upon the relevance of the term *human* to those who want to build a psychology of the human person according to the conception of science as developed by the natural sciences and who adhere rigidly to that concept despite changes in subject matter. We would insist upon the relevance of *science* for those who want to study the humanistic aspects of man without any concern for method or rigor whatsoever.[88]

But in order to do this, Giorgi has to seek a solution by "... extending and deepening the very concept of science itself so that science is not committed to only one set of philosophical presuppositions."[89] And while Giorgi says, "I feel no special commitment to the expression 'human science' itself,"[90] it is clear that he does have something scientific in mind:

> However, what I mean to communicate by the term "human science" is that psychology has the responsibility to investigate the full range of behavior and experience of man as a person in such a way that the *aims* of science are fulfilled. . . .[91]

Thus, while he does not want psychology to be a natural science, he does want it to be a human science, taking its place between the natural sciences and art.[92] But it is still a science, although with an approach and method much more appropriate for its subject matter.

But what is science, even a human science? For that answer Giorgi turns directly to Kuhn's understanding of science and its development through alternating stages of normal and revolutionary science. Consequently, psychology is presently in a revolutionary stage, searching to find its paradigm:

> Perhaps the clearest way of communicating our intention is to state that, in Kuhn's terms, psychology needs another paradigm. We feel that the paradigm within which psychology has been laboring has reached the limits of its usefulness, and that it is time to find a new paradigm.[93]
>
> In any event, we would assert that with respect to peculiarly human phenomena, psychology is definitely in its preparadigmatic phase. There is as yet no science that has fully articulated and expressed paradigms for the systematic and disciplined study of peculiarly human phenomena.[94]

Thus, Giorgi sees phenomenological psychology, understood by him as a human science, as a competing paradigm during a revolutionary or preparadigmatic stage of a science. And while he is aware of the fact that science is a "dialectical process" between normal and revolutionary stages,[95] he is also aware that, in order to be science at all, science must adopt a paradigm and therefore attain to the status of normal science:

> A revolution occurs any time that a particular scientific community agrees that the existing paradigm can no longer be accepted, and they turn to a new paradigm, and when they do so, they begin to act within the perspective of normal science once again.[96]

He also says, "We have been using the term 'paradigm' as employed by Kuhn, meaning the set of rules, theories, facts, problems, etc., that guide the research activities of scientists in the pursuit of normal science."[97] And when he describes the characteristics of science that a human science would have to have in order to be a science, he turns to ". . . descriptions of the characteristics that Kuhn observed in the pursuit of normal science."[98] He concludes that phenomenological psychology as an ultimately normal science is indeed quite possible.

But this again throws us back upon the same question that we have raised from the outset of this paper. Are phenomenology and science compatible to the extent that phenomenology can be appropriated as a paradigm for a normal science?

C. CAN PHENOMENOLOGY BE APPROPRIATED AS A PARADIGM FOR PSYCHOLOGY AS A HUMAN SCIENCE?

Let us summarize our path thus far: We have followed Heidegger and Kuhn's paths and have discovered an essential difference between an open, critical attitude on the one hand (thinking for Heidegger, revolutionary science for Kuhn), and a closed, uncritical attitude on the other hand (science for Heidegger, normal science for Kuhn). Now, science, in order to be science at all, must agree on a paradigm and become normal science;

169

otherwise, it remains at a revolutionary or prescientific stage, somewhat like philosophy or art, and does not progress like science does. But normal science, while it is efficient and occasionally produces recognizable results, is also dogmatic, exclusive, close-minded, authoritarian, intolerant, narrow, and rigid.[99] And these traits are not just something extrinsic to science, but form its very essence, or as Feyerabend, following Kuhn on this point, puts it: "The massive dogmatism I have described is not just a *fact*, it has also a most important *function. Science would be impossible without it*."[100] Thus, since phenomenology is characterized by a constant questioning and a dedication to let the phenomena appear as they are (and not merely within the confines of a fixed paradigm), the *aims* of phenomenology and science are in fact *opposed*. How, then, could phenomenology be used as a paradigm for psychology as a human science? Is not the very idea of a "human science" a contradiction in terms?

First, it should be clear that if the phenomenological approach were to be adopted by psychology as a paradigm and were to be used as the model for a *normal* science, it would have ceased to have the essence of phenomenology, for it would have become all of the things it presently *aims against*. That is to say, a formerly open, critical, presuppositionless attitude would have become a fixed paradigm and method for doing research. In other words, it would have ceased to be phenomenological or "human."

Second, if the phenomenological approach were truly to be appropriated by psychology, then, in keeping with the spirit of phenomenology, we would not have a *normal* science, but rather a permanently revolutionary science, which is to say, according to Heidegger and Kuhn, it would have ceased to be "science."

Concluding a recent article on the topic of phenomenology, psychology, and science, Romanyshyn has also recognized that psychology stands before two possibilities:

> Understood in this light, I would say that at least two options are open for psychology. Either psychology can understand itself as a science with a different and broader interpretation of this (scientific) attitude. Or it can understand itself as another kind of discipline, that is, as a discipline which organizes its knowledge in another way.[101]

Given these two options, and thus having to choose between science and phenomenology, we would suggest that psychology choose the second one. What would this mean?

In very brief terms, it would mean pursuing phenomenological psychology while leaving science to itself. If we are indeed, as Heidegger says, at the end of philosophy, and the essence of modern philosophy is the same as the essence of modern science, then we are also at the end of science, and even science itself must be overcome. This would mean that our task would be to develop "a thinking which can be neither metaphysics nor science."[102]

PHENOMENOLOGY, PSYCHOLOGY, AND SCIENCE

For phenomenology has always sought to develop a knowledge that is more appropriate for the everyday lifeworld in which we all exist. Science is only one kind of knowledge, and even its knowledge is derived from the concrete world of human experience. To study that lifeworld, to do it justice, we need a different kind of knowledge which is faithful to the subject matter.

The first American phenomenological psychologist, or radical empiricist, was William James. In concluding his book on James, John Wild addresses himself to the questions that occupy us here. Concerning James' radical empiricism, Wild writes:

> First of all, is it a science? Are his empirical investigations to be construed as would-be contributions to the science of psychology? James often speaks this way in his *Principles*. But as his thought matured, he came to recognize that he was doing something different at a more fundamental level where not only objective factors, but also "subjective" factors are at work. The sciences may have to begin with what is known by direct acquaintance. But then each of them leaves this behind, in order to turn to the special objects of its field, and to deal with them in as objective a way as is possible. James' method, on the other hand, requires him to dwell on this direct knowledge, vague and subjective though it be, and then to use concepts for the sake of clarifying and expressing the implicit meanings that are present in it. He is concerned with experience as we live it, and with the world in which we exist. *But there is no science of being, no science of the world.* These are taken for granted and presupposed by the sciences . . . however, they are the chief objects of James' concern.[103]

But while "there is no science of being, no science of the world," there is another kind of knowledge. This is what we need to develop in order to have a phenomenological psychology.

This knowledge is not science, but something more originary, more appropriate to human beings and to Being. As Heidegger says, it is, like art, a kind of truth:

> Still another way in which truth becomes is the thinker's questioning, which, as the thinking of Being, names Being in its question-worthiness. By contrast, science is not an original happening of truth, but always the cultivation of a domain of truth already opened, specifically by apprehending and confirming that which shows itself to be possibly and necessarily correct within that field. When and insofar as a science passes beyond correctness and goes on to a truth, which means that it arrives at the essential disclosure of what is as such, it is philosophy.[104]

In order to arrive at the truth of human being, and not merely what is correct, we psychologists may have to linger awhile longer with phenomenological philosophy. And if we truly wish to borrow its insights and its essence, we may have to discover that what we will end up with will not be science, in its essence. But it will have everything in common with authentic, revolutionary science, i.e., philosophy. The reason for that lies in the very matter of thinking itself:

171

Keith Hoeller

> Historically, only one Saying belongs to the matter of thinking, the one
> that is in each case appropriate to its matter. Its material relevance is
> essentially higher than the validity of the sciences, because it is freer. For it
> lets Being—be.[105]

If we as psychologists are to let Being, and beings, be, it will no longer do to read about the difference between phenomenology and science, and then turn around and attempt to use phenomenology to further our "scientific" endeavors. It has been "correct" for us, coming as we do from the sciences, to begin with familiar terms. But it is not yet "true," for we can do so only by overlooking the difference, not only between phenomenology and science, but also between Being and beings. And it is that "ontological difference," as Heidegger says, which first makes human beings *human*.

NOTES

1 Martin Heidegger, *What is a Thing?* trans. W. B. Barton and Vera Deutsch (Chicago: Regnery, 1967), p. 10. In general, all translations are taken directly from the English. However, I have occasionally made very minor changes.

2 Amedeo Giorgi, *Psychology as a Human Science: A Phenomenologically Based Approach* (New York: Harper & Row, 1970); and Thomas Kuhn, *The Structure of Scientific Revolutions* (Chicago: University of Chicago Press, 1962, second, enlarged edition, 1970). In addition to his book, I am grateful to Professor Giorgi for a very cordial and helpful exchange of letters which enabled me to further clarify my own position and to better understand his view with respect to the matters discussed in this paper.

3 Theodore Kisiel, "Heidegger and the New Images of Science," *Research in Phenomenology*, vol. VII (1977), p. 163. For further explications of Heidegger's view of science, *see* Joseph J. Kockelmans and Theodore J. Kisiel, *Phenomenology and the Natural Sciences: Essays and Translations* (Evanston: Northwestern University Press, 1970), pp. 147-201. *See also* William J. Richardson, "Heidegger's Critique of Science," *The New Scholasticism*, vol. XLII (1968), pp. 511-36.

4 Theodore J. Kisiel, "Science, Phenomenology, and the Thinking of Being," in Kockelmans and Kisiel, *Phenomenology and the Natural Sciences*, p. 168. *See also* Martin Heidegger, *Being and Time*, trans. John Macquarrie and Edward Robinson (New York: Harper & Row, 1962), p. 32.

5 Heidegger, *Being and Time*, p. 31.

6 *Ibid.*, p. 61.

7 *Ibid.*, p. 62.

8 *Ibid.*, pp. 62-63.

9 *Ibid.*, p. 408.

10 Heidegger, *Gesamtausgabe*, vol. 24: *Die Grundprobleme der Phänomenologie* (Frankfurt am Main: Vittorio Klostermann, 1975), p. 1.

11 *Ibid.*, p. 15.

12 *Ibid.*

13 Heidegger, *Being and Time*, p. 63.

14 Heidegger, "Letter on Humanism," trans. Frank A. Capuzzi, with the collaboration of J. Glenn Gray, in *Basic Writings*, ed. David Farrell Krell (New York: Harper & Row, 1977), pp. 208 and 235.

15 *See* Heidegger, *The Question Concerning Technology and Other Essays*, trans. William Lovitt (New York: Harper & Row, 1977). *See also* Robert D. Romanyshyn, "The Attitude of Science and the Crisis of Psychology," in *Duquesne Studies in*

Phenomenological Psychology, vol. II, ed. A. Giorgi, C. Fischer, and E. Murray (Pittsburgh: Duquesne University Press, 1975), pp. 6-18; and Paul F. Colaizzi, "Technology in Psychology and Science," in *Duquesne Studies*, vol. II, ed. Giorgi *et al.*, pp. 19-37.

16 *See* Joseph J. Kockelmans, "Heidegger on the Essential Difference and Necessary Relationship Between Philosophy and Science," in Kockelmans and Kisiel, *Phenomenology and the Natural Sciences*, pp. 147-66.

17 Heidegger, *What is a Thing?* pp. 65-108.

18 *Ibid.*, p. 65.

19 *Ibid.*, p. 66.

20 *Ibid.*, p. 67.

21 *Ibid.*, p. 74.

22 *Ibid.*, pp. 89-90.

23 *Ibid.*, p. 97.

24 *Ibid.*

25 *Ibid.*, pp. 107-08.

26 Heidegger, "The Age of the World Picture," in *The Question Concerning Technology and Other Essays*, p. 118.

27 *Ibid.*, p. 123.

28 *Ibid.*, p. 124.

29 *Ibid.*, p. 125.

30 *Ibid.*, p. 134.

31 *Ibid.*, p. 136.

32 Heidegger, "The Question Concerning Technology," in *The Question Concerning Technology and Other Essays*, p. 12.

33 *Ibid.*, p. 22.

34 *Ibid.*, p. 33.

35 *Ibid.*, p. 35.

36 Heidegger, "Science and Meditation," in *The Question Concerning Technology and Other Essays*, p. 166.

37 *Ibid.*, p. 169.

38 *Ibid.*, pp. 169-70.

39 *Ibid.*, pp. 175-76.

40 *Ibid.*, pp. 174-75.

41 *Ibid.*, p. 177.

42 *Ibid.*, p. 178. *Compare* Heidegger, *Being and Time*, p. 29.

43 *Ibid.*, p. 180.

44 *Ibid.*, p. 181.

45 *Ibid.*, pp. 181-82.

46 *Ibid.*, p. 182.

47 Heidegger, *Die Grundprobleme der Phänomenologie*, p. 15.

48 Heidegger, *What is Called Thinking?* trans. Fred D. Wieck and J. Glenn Gray (New York: Harper & Row, 1968), pp. 7-8.

49 *Ibid.*, p. 8.

50 *Ibid.*

51 *Ibid.*, p. 14.

52 *Ibid.*, p. 18.

53 *Ibid.*, pp. 32-33.

54 *Ibid.*, pp. 40-41.

55 *Ibid.*, pp. 44-45.

56 Heidegger, *Discourse on Thinking*, trans. John M. Anderson and E. Hans Freund (New York: Harper & Row, 1966), p. 46.

57 *Ibid.*, p. 47.

58 *Ibid.*, pp. 46-47.

59 *Ibid.*, pp. 45-46.

60 *Ibid.*, p. 56.

61 *Ibid.*, pp. 54-55.

62 *Ibid.*, p. 55.

63 In a personal communication, Professor Giorgi has informally indicated that he may not be as tied to Kuhn's conception of science as I have inferred from his book that he really is.

64 Heidegger, *The Question Concerning Technology and Other Essays,* p. 169.

65 Kuhn, *The Structure of Scientific Revolutions*, p. 160.

66 *Ibid.*

67 Heidegger, *The Question Concerning Technology and Other Essays*, p. 118.

68 Kuhn, *The Structure of Scientific Revolutions*, p. 10.

69 *Ibid.*, p. 12.

70 Kuhn, "Logic of Discovery or Psychology of Research?" in *Criticism and the Growth of Knowledge*, ed. Imre Lakatos and Alan Musgrave (Cambridge: Cambridge University Press, 1970), p. 6.

71 *Ibid.*, pp. 6-7.

72 Kuhn, *The Structure of Scientific Revolutions*, p. 88.

73 Kuhn, "The Function of Dogma in Scientific Research," in *Scientific Change: Historical Studies in the Intellectual, Social and Technical Conditions for Scientific Discovery and Technical Invention, from Antiquity to the Present*, ed. A. C. Crombie (London: Heinemann, 1963), p. 349. *See also* Paul K. Feyerabend, "Consolations for the Specialist," in *Criticism and the Growth of Knowledge*, ed. Lakatos and Musgrave, pp. 205-06, who originally made this point.

74 Kuhn, *Ibid.*, p. 352.

75 *Ibid.*, p. 393.

76 *Ibid.*

77 Kuhn, *The Structure of Scientific Revolutions*, p. 24.

78 Kuhn, "The Function of Dogma in Scientific Research," p. 349.

79 *Ibid.*, p. 363, and *The Structure of Scientific Revolutions*, p. 24.

80 *Ibid.*, p. 350, and *The Structure of Scientific Revolutions*, p. 166.

81 Kuhn, *The Structure of Scientific Revolutions*, pp. 163-64.

82 Kuhn, "The Function of Dogma in Scientific Research," p. 348.

83 *Ibid.*, p. 362.

84 Kuhn, *The Structure of Scientific Revolutions*, p. 90.

85 Kuhn, "The Function of Dogma in Scientific Research," p. 364.

86 *Ibid.*, p. 348.

87 Giorgi, *Psychology as a Human Science* (New York: Harper & Row, 1970).

88 *Ibid.*, p. xi.

89 *Ibid.*, pp. xi-xii.

90 *Ibid.*, p. xii.

91 *Ibid.*

92 *Ibid.*, p. 24.

93 *Ibid.*, p. 174.

94 *Ibid.*, p. 175.

95 *Ibid.*, p. 107.

96 *Ibid.*

97 *Ibid.*, p. 176.

98 *Ibid.*, p. 111.

99 See notes 73-80.

100 Paul K. Feyerabend, *Against Method* (London: NLB, 1975), p. 298.

101 Robert Romanyshyn, "Psychology and the Attitude of Science," in *Existential-Phenomenological Alternatives for Psychology*, ed. Ronald S. Valle and Mark King (Oxford: Oxford University Press, 1978), p. 46.

102 Heidegger, *On Time and Being*, trans. Joan Stambaugh (New York: Harper & Row, 1972), p. 59.

103 John Wild, *The Radical Empiricism of William James* (Garden City & New York: Doubleday-Anchor, 1970), pp. 406-07.

104 Heidegger, *Poetry, Language, Thought,* trans. Albert Hofstadter (New York: Harper & Row, 1971), p. 62.

105 Heidegger, *Basic Writings*, p. 236.

The Place of the Unconscious in Heidegger*

WILLIAM J. RICHARDSON

In 1953, Martin Heidegger published in the German magazine *Merkur* a short study of the poet Georg Trakl, entitled, "Eine Erörterung seines Gedichtes."[1] He begins by explaining what he means in this context by the word *Erörterung,* which one would be inclined to translate as "discourse" or "discussion" or something of the kind. But, true to form, he gives to *Erörterung* a meaning all his own. The stem of the word is *Ort* ("place"), and so he begins by saying: *erörtern* here means first of all *weisen in* [i.e., "to point toward," in the sense of "showing"] a place. Secondly it means *beachten* [i.e., "to regard," in the sense of "heeding" or "respecting"] a place . . . ."[2] If our task is to discuss (i.e., *erörtern*) the unconscious in terms of Heidegger's thought, we will be most faithful to him, I think, if we content ourselves with the double function that he himself finds suggested by that word, namely to show (first find) that place and to regard that place where the unconscious may be found in his thought. In this sense, let us make our own the remainder of Heidegger's opening paragraph. ". . . Both of these senses, 'showing' the place and 'respecting' the place, are the preparatory steps to any *Erörterung.* But we are already ambitious enough if we content ourselves in these remarks with preparatory steps. The *Erörterung* ends, as becomes a way of thought, with a question. . . ."[3]

For the task of trying to discern the place of the unconscious in the work of a difficult thinker who never considers the problem is itself so difficult that the most we can hope to do in a short space is to point out that place and regard it, as it were, from a distance. We can hardly hope to enter into the place and dwell there. By that I mean that in a brief treatment we can hardly become sufficiently at home there to be able to spell out any detailed applications for the practice of psychotherapy. But psychotherapy, after all, is the prerogative of psychotherapists. To restrict the scope of our work, let us confine our purpose to the simple task of letting a philosopher be a philosopher, resting in the tranquil hope that nothing can be more enlightening to those who are dedicated to the healing of man than a deeper understanding—if such it be—of what man really is.

Let us take as the axis of this discussion two citations from very different contexts, which, when juxtaposed, show a remarkable consonance. The first comes from a commonplace of psychoanalysis: that passage in *The Interpretation of Dreams* (1900) where Freud speaks at length about the Oedipus myth. After recounting the original story, he adds the following:

* This article originally appeared in the *Review of Existential Psychology & Psychiatry,* Vol. V, no. 3, (1965), pp. 265-90.

THE PLACE OF THE UNCONSCIOUS IN HEIDEGGER

> . . . The action of the play consists in nothing other than the process of revealing, with cunning delays and ever-mounting excitement—a process that can be likened to the work of psychoanalysis—that Oedipus himself is the murderer of Laius, but further that he is the son of the murdered man and of Jocasta. Appalled at the abomination which he has unwittingly perpetrated, Oedipus blinds himself and forsakes his home. The oracle has been fulfilled.[4]

This passage invites three remarks: In the first place, the Oedipus myth, according to Freud, holds a perennial fascination for man (this becomes clear in the paragraphs that follow) not merely because it had the good fortune to be dramatized by the towering genius of a Sophocles, but rather because it presents in theatrical form a drama that takes place (in one way or another) within the interior of every man. Let us take it, then, even at the risk of oversimplification, to suggest (at least in symbolic form) the entire dimension of the unconscious as Freud conceived it, together with that particular characteristic which Freud considered most proper to the unconscious—for that matter to man in his totality—namely, the primacy of sex. Secondly, let us remark that the action of the play is fundamentally a process of revelation (*Enthüllung*) to Oedipus. This says two things: *Eine Hülle,* as noun, is a covering of some kind, like a cloak, or a veil. To *ent-hüllen,* means to tear off that cloak, to pull aside that veil, to un-veil, to re-veal. Furthermore, this re-vealing, is not a single, definitive, once-and-for-all act, but a process that takes place over a period of time, a temporal process, a process in which Oedipus himself must collaborate but of which he is not the unique source, a process by which is revealed to Oedipus who he *is*. Finally this process of self-revelation, i.e., of the revelation of Oedipus of his true self, is by Freud's own testimony comparable to the work of a psycho-analysis.

The text I should like to juxtapose to this one of Freud in order to form the axis for these reflections comes from Heidegger's university lecture course of 1935, entitled *Introduction to Metaphysics.* There he writes as follows:

> . . . Consider the Oedipus Rex of Sophocles. At the beginning Oedipus is the savior and lord of the State, living in an aura of glory and divine favor. He is driven out of this seeming-to-be, which is not a merely subjective view of himself but the manner in which his *Dasein* happens to shine forth, up to the [moment] when his Being as murderer of his father and desecrator of his mother comes to non-concealment. The way from that radiant beginning to the gruesome end is a struggle between seeming-to-be (concealment and distortion) and non-concealment (Being). About the city lies the hidden truth about the murderer of Laius, the former king. With the passion of a man who stands in the refulgence of glory and is a Greek, Oedipus sets out to reveal this hidden truth. Step by step, he must bring himself to non-concealment, and in the end he can bear it only by putting out his own eyes, i.e., he deprives himself of all light, lets the darkness of night fall around him, and in his blindness cries out for all doors to be thrown open so that a man may be revealed to the people as who he *is*.[5]

The similarity of Heidegger's use of the Oedipus myth and that of Freud is, I think, striking. As in Freud, so in Heidegger the personal tragedy of Oedipus may be taken to represent in symbolic form the entire drama of the human condition itself. As for Freud, so for Heidegger, the drama unfolds as a process of revelation in which Heidegger collaborates but of which he is not the source. As with Freud, so with Heidegger, the self-revelation of Oedipus is comparable to that process which seems to be central to each one's proper enterprise: for Freud, it is the process of psychoanalysis, for Heidegger (it would seem), it is the achievement of authenticity.

I would like to suggest, then, that if we could comprehend with some fidelity the sense in which Heidegger intends his allusion to the Oedipus story we might find some way of access to the place of the unconscious in his thought. I propose, then, to let this working hypothesis serve as the axis about which the present discussion (*Erörterung*) revolves. It divides itself naturally into two: in the first part I shall try to show (first find) the place where the question of the unconscious in Heidegger may arise; in the second part I shall try to look upon that place with proper regard and appreciate its meaning.

SHOWING (FINDING) THE PLACE

To point out the place where the unconscious may be found in Heidegger's thought is a difficult task and a perilous one. It is difficult because he never thematizes the problem as such. On the contrary, it would seem that if we were to ask him about it directly, he would repudiate the question as foreign to the only question he wants to raise. For the question about unconscious psychic processes is clearly a question about man. Heidegger's question is not about man but about Being (*Sein*). In a letter written in 1962 in which he describes the beginnings of his thought, he recalls how it happened that when he was in his final year of the *Gymnasium* in Constance (the date was 1907 and Heidegger was 18 years old) a priest-friend gave him a copy of the doctoral dissertation of the neo-scholastic thinker, Franz Brentano, entitled *The Manifold Sense of Being in Aristotle,* where "Being" translates the German *Seiendes* and the Greek *on.* He writes:

> . . . On the title page of his work, Brentano quotes Aristotle's phrase: *to on legetai pollachos.* I translate: "A being becomes manifest (i.e., with regard to its Being) in many ways." Latent in this phrase is the *question* that determined the way of my thought: what is the pervasive, simple, unified determination of Being that permeates all of its multiple meanings? . . .[6]

In a private conversation in 1959, Heidegger expanded this a little further. He explained how with this question in mind he had read through the relevant passages in Aristotle to find the answer, only to discover that Aristotle had never even raised the question about Being. For the question to be raised in what he called "first philosophy" (we call it now "metaphysics") was: *ti to on hêi on*; what are beings as beings? In Aristotle, then, the question of Being was forgotten. In like fashion, Heidegger discovered that the Being-question was ignored in all the philosophers whose works he could lay his hands on. So it happened that the first experience of the Being-question was followed quickly by the experience of the forgottenness of Being. Yet even this was a paradox, for the philosophers, as indeed all ordinary men, used the word "is," and only man can say "is" for only man can use language. The paradox lies in the fact that, despite man's forgetfulness of Being in ordinary everyday life (and even in the speculation of the philosophers), man nonetheless retains some kind of comprehension of Being, otherwise he could not say "is." For by Being is meant the very is-ness of what is or, as Professor William Barrett writes it, the Is of what is.[7]

If, then, Heidegger's own task was to interrogate the meaning of Being, the best way—in fact the only way—to start was to examine his comprehension of Being in man as such, even though he is normally forgetful, i.e., unconscious, of it. So it was that from the beginning Heidegger conceived of man only in terms of this comprehension of Being. That is why he designates man by a word that suggests this openness toward Being: he calls himself *Dasein,* later the *Da des Seins,* the "There" of Being among beings.

It is clear, then, that for Heidegger himself man is interesting only to the extent that he is a means of access to the meaning of Being. That is why he is so selective in his choice of data for the analysis in *Sein und Zeit.* And among the data that he does not select is the evidence for the existence of unconscious psychic processes. If we, for our part, try to find the place that the unconscious would occupy if he had treated it, we are forced to argue by way of inference, of analogy, or simply of surmise. I say this is difficult. It is not only difficult, it is dangerous, too. We have no explicit texts to guide us, so for the most part we must speak in our own name and proceed at our own risk.

Let us proceed in the following manner. Let us begin by admitting quite frankly that the problem is in itself so amorphous that no one way of approaching it is imposed by *die Sache Selbst.* We must, then, make an option, and I make that option in terms of the general background that the readers of this *Review* may be presumed to share, namely a general acquaintance with the notion of phenomenology.

Now the problem of the unconscious in Heidegger (and I am thinking especially of the Heidegger who chose phenemenology as his method of predilection, namely the so-called "early Oedipus" of *Sein und Zeit)*—the problem of the unconscious in Heidegger, I say, is intimately connected with the more general problem of the place of the unconscious in phenomenology as such. If we could locate the unconscious in the more general perspectives of phenomenology, and afterward could see how Heidegger conceives phenomenology for himself, we might have a valid way of discerning what place the unconscious may have in Heidegger's own problematic.

With the most general sense of the word "phenomenology" there is no need to delay: it is the "study" of "phenomena"; a *phainomenon,* according to its

179

Greek etymology, is "that which appears." Appears to what? To some type of awareness, to consciousness. Phenomenology in this general sense then, would seem to imply that the study of appearances is to be accomplished somehow through the analysis of the data of consciousness.

Now if we can accept this very unrefined—almost banal—description of what phenomenology is all about, there arises an equally banal difficulty about using it as a manner of coming to grips with the unconscious. For how can a method whose only scope is the study of the conscious processes in man discover anything about what is by definition not conscious, *un*conscious, in him? The students of phenomenology—and in particular the interpreters of Edmund Husserl, who in our time is taken to be the father of phenomenological method—are of course perfectly aware of the difficulty. We shall come to them immediately, but before we do, it might be worth recalling that although Husserl's importance for contemporary phenomenology is beyond question, it was not Husserl who invented the term or who for the first time gave it a central place in philosophical thought. The progenitor of phenomenology in any thematic, philosophical sense was Hegel, for the first of his major works bore the title *Phenomenology of the Spirit* (1807).[8]

It would be a distraction for us to go into Hegel's conception of phenomenology in detail. But he is worth mentioning for two reasons: 1. Heidegger gives us a detailed analysis of the introduction to Hegel's *Phenomenology* which, when we are ready for it, may throw some light on Heidegger himself. 2. One of the most authoritative interpreters of Hegel in our day, Jean Hyppolite, lectured a few years ago to the Psychoanalytic Society of France on the subject "The Phenomenology of Hegel and Psychoanalysis," and, in introducing his subject, he alludes (curiously enough) to the Oedipus myth in Freud, as also to Freud's comparison of Oedipus' self-discovery with the process of psychoanalysis. He remarks: ". . . to read once more [Hegel's] *Phenomenology [of the Spirit]* in this context would consist in envisioning the whole of this work [that is] so difficult and sinuous as the true Oedipus tragedy of the entire human spirit. . . ."[9] What he has in mind, I think, is how Hegel would explain the whole of "reality" in terms of a single, all encompassing, dynamic principle, conceived as an Absolute Subject, which in and through human consciousness moves in dialectic fashion through the course of history toward a full awareness of itself. The *Phenomenology of the Spirit* describes the process by which the Absolute comes to appearance through successive stages in the dialectic. It is this movement toward self-discovery that Hyppolite describes as the "true Oedipus tragedy [i.e., psychoanalytic process] of the entire human spirit."

For our purposes, we may be content to recall simply Hegel's starting point, namely normal everyday human consciousness, the consciousness of the man on the street as well as those who engage in psychotherapy. Hegel calls it "natural consciousness" (*das natüraliche Bewusstsein*) and it is interior to this consciousness of the normal man that there resides for Hegel a principle that is radically unconscious, namely the Absolute Spirit itself, as yet unaware of itself as Absolute. Hyppolite speaks of it as the "ontological unconscious of consciousness." "Perhaps here," he says, "there is a key to the problem of the unconscious: it is not [one] thing situated behind [another] thing but fundamentally the soul of consciousness, a certain inevitable fashion by which natural consciousness is itself."[10]

Precisely how Heidegger, in interpreting Hegel, will describe this duality of an ontological unconscious interior to the "natural" consciousness of man will be, perhaps, illuminating. But we won't be able to understand what Heidegger means until we have sketched briefly the place of the unconscious in Husserl.

For Husserl's interpreters make it clear that there is a place for the unconscious in Husserl's thought, despite the fact that his unique concern was to analyze what he called the "intentionality of consciousness." By that he meant that every act of a conscious subject (whether it be an act of knowing or of affectivity) tends toward, i.e., "intends," some object. It is through this act of intending (i.e., through the "intentionality" of the conscious act) that an object is present to, and meaningful for, consciousness. It was Husserl's purpose, and he pursued it indefatigably, to examine closely all the implications of this fact. In effect, that meant that his task was initially to search for the intentional meaning of the different conscious acts (like thinking, wishing, desiring, regretting, etc.) that make up the day-in day-out experiences of our ordinary life in the world. It was a search for the "essences" of these acts. As Paul Ricoeur puts it:

> . . . These essences [are not Platonic Ideas that belong to another World but] the *a priori* structures of every lived experience; they are the ideal contents that language presupposes every time we say "I wish," "I desire," "I regret," and every time we understand a situation, or comportment, to signify a wish, a desire, a regret. . . .[11]

The method of disengaging these meaning-structures was descriptive and narrative. That is, one would select a few well-chosen examples, or even envision a few fictional ones, and manipulate them imaginatively in such a manner as to strip away the matter-of-fact circumstances that embodied these examples in any given concrete human situation, and slowly, by careful comparison and conscientious description, disengage from all of the variable matter-of-fact circumstances in each example the invariable signification (meaning) that through the variations remains constant in all. To describe how this process developed and deepened into an analysis of the world itself (as sum total of meaning objects), and still more of consciousness as "constituting" its intentional objects and its world, would take us to the very heart of what Husserl called "transcendental subjectivity." But such a digression is out of the question here.

As the the relationship between phenomenology, whose self-appointed task is to analyze the intentionality of consciousness, and psychoanalysis, whose first principle is that there are beyond doubt unconscious psychic processes, no less an authority than Eugen Fink, Husserl's last assistant, offers a commentary on Section 46 of Husserl's last major work, *The Crisis of European Science and Transcendental Phenomenology* (1936), to the effect that the true disciple of Husserl has every right to speak of an intentionality of the unconscious.[12] For every explicit analysis of a given conscious intention presupposes that before it can be taken as theme for explication, it must be a merely implicit intention of consciousness, i.e., it is wrapped up in a type of non-thematic, functional intentionality that is identical with the complex totality of lived experience as such. This non-thematic, functional, lived intentionality may be called "unconscious," i.e., the intentionality of unconscious processes.

Perhaps one will object to this argumentation on the grounds that it violates the very notion of the unconscious. For it gratuitously imputes to the unconscious the structure of consciousness itself, namely intentionality; it thereby reduces the unconscious to simply an inferior form of consciousness; and the actual experience of psychoanalysis (at least as described by Freud) tells us that the unconscious is precisely what the word implies; a dynamic process which is the seat of all active, primitive, brutish, infantile, aggressive and sexual drives, directed by the pleasure principle and ignoring time, death, logic, values and morality—all of which runs counter to the experience of conscious life.[13] Fink foresees the difficulty and replies that it springs from a certain naïveté. To insist obstinately upon the irreducibility of the unconscious to consciousness and to define it by simply the negation of everything conscious implies that we know exactly what consciousness is. But this is what phenomenology is designed to examine. That is why Professor Alphonse De Waelhens can remark:

> . . . If it is *really* true that the phenomenology of Husserl is the philosophy which undertakes at long last the task of interrogating to the fullest extent what consciousness *is* . . . , *then* a genuine explicitation of what the unconscious is will not be accomplished except by beginning with phenomenology and [simply] extending it.[14]

How this proposal works out in the concrete we can see in one of Ricoeur's most recent studies on volition. He argues for a reciprocal dependence between psychoanalysis and phenomenology. He concedes, for example, that Freud is clearly a determinist, but then shows how, in theorizing about the non-volitional character of the psychic economy and also in applying this theory to practice, Freud actually presupposes some conception of volition which he should depend upon phenomenology to discern. On the other hand, phenomenology should respect the findings of psychoanalysis as legitimate data for its analyses. If the phenomenologist really wishes to extend the notion of intentionality so that it can be satisfactorily applied to the theory of unconscious processes, then he must learn in practice to disassociate the conception of intentional meaning from its normal affiliation with the evidence of immediate consciousness. He must learn, then, to read the meanings of unconscious intentionality not simply through the explication of the data of implicit conscious meanings but through the language of signs by which the unconscious reveals itself in consciousness. (I take him to mean the normal signs by which psychoanalysis itself discerns the unconscious: dreams, parapraxias, symptomatic actions, etc.). But this is not done by analyzing the immediate data of consciousness. Rather it is the work of interpretation, of exegesis, of "hermeneutic"—that austere asceticism of penetrating through what seems-to-be in order to discover what is.[15]

All this will seem hasty and probably superficial. My only excuse is that it pretends to be no more than a propaedeutic to Heidegger. If for the sake of form we should draw a tentative conclusion at this point, let it be simply this: that Freud's own conception of unconscious psychic processes was articulated according to the conceptual structures of nineteenth century physical science, according to which man was conceived fundamentally as an energized machine. If a philosophy such as phenomenology (of whatever stripe) has a place in it for what is valid in Freud's insight, but incorporates this valid insight into a conception of man that is slightly more human, then perhaps psychoanalysis may profit from its help.

· · ·

For all that *Sein und Zeit* was dedicated to Edmund Husserl, the phenomenology that is found within it is certainly of a different stripe from that of Husserl. And yet it is but seldom that Heidegger explicitly repudiates Husserl's conception of phenomenology. There are, of course, insinuations galore, but to the best of my knowledge, there are only two texts that clearly and decisively show his distance from Husserl and neither one is in *Sein and Zeit*.

We shall consider here only one of these texts.[16] It comes from the essay *On Essence of Ground* (1929)—brief, dense and more than ordinarily difficult.[17] The argument of the essay itself is not sufficiently important for our purposes to warrant the time necessary for its exposition. It will suffice simply to say that Leibniz was the first to formulate the "principle of ground" (*der Satz vom Grund*), which we know better (from Leibniz's Latin formula: *principium rationis sufficientis*) as the "principle of sufficient reason." Ever since Leibniz, philosophers have talked about "ground" as if they knew what it meant, but actually no one has ever analyzed it. What then does "ground" in this formula mean? With that question, Heidegger is off and running. The rest of the essay is in large part a condensed résumé of the basic analysis of *Sein und Zeit*. In particular, this involves restating the analysis of *Dasein* as a being whose nature it is to-be-in-the-World. But the language here is slightly different from what is found in the earlier work. Here *Dasein* is called "transcendence." In the original Latin sense, "to transcend" means "to climb," or "to step" (*-scendere*) "across,"

183

or "beyond" (*trans-*). "Transcendence," then, means a passage over or beyond something.

"Transcendence" is not a characteristically Heideggerean word. It may well have become thematic for him by reason of his study of Kant. For as Heidegger reads Kant, the principle task of *The Critique of Pure Reason* was to solve the problem of transcendence. The word as it stands here is not Kant's, but Heidegger feels justified in attributing it to him because of Kant's use of the world "transcendental": ". . . I call that knowledge transcendental which concerns itself in general not so much with objects *as with our manner of knowing objects insofar as this must be a priori possible.*"[18]

How Kant's transcendental reflection proceeds is now a commonplace. What Heidegger underlines is Kant's insistence on the *finite* character of "our manner of knowing objects." Before all else, this finitude consists in the fact that we do not and cannot *create* the objects that we know but rather we receive them as given to us (i.e., insofar as they give themselves to us as beings-to-be-known). Kant's question, then, concerns the conditions of possibility of *finite* knowing. Now one of these conditions, the most fundamental, is that these beings-to-be-known are somehow accessible to the knower. And since these conditions of possibility are *a priori,* i.e., are built into the knower prior to all contact with these beings through his experience, then the accessibility of the beings-to-be-known must be accounted for somehow by the structure of the knower. In other words, the knower is built with such a structure that he establishes a certain domain, or opens up a certain horizon around him, within which these beings can be encountered and can become known. This domain (horizon) of knowability must consist, Heidegger argues, in what might be called the pre-knowledge of these beings-to-become-known, a sort of antecedent seizure of what makes them be(knowable), i.e., of their structure *as* beings, of their Being-structure itself. Such an horizon of possible encounter, projected by the knower, is what in Kant's name Heidegger calls "transcendence." The matter can hardly be put more clearly than Heidegger puts it himself:

> A finite knowing essence can enter into comportment with a being other than itself which it has not created, only when this already existing being is in itself such that it can come to the encounter. However, in order that such a being as it is can come to an encounter [with the knower] it must be "known" already by an antecedent knowledge simply as a being, i.e., with regard to its Being-structure. A finite [knower] needs [a] fundamental power of orientation which permits this being to stand over in opposition to it. In this original orientation, the finite [knower] extends before him an open domain within which something can "correspond" to him. To dwell from the beginning in such a domain, to institute it in its origin, is nothing else than the transcendence which characterizes comportment with beings. . . .[19]

Heidegger's entire exposition of Kant consists in analyzing the nature of transcendence. Basing his exposition on the first edition of *The Critique of Pure*

Reason (1781), Heidegger sees that transcendence is not established by the *a priori* (where *a priori* always means prior to experience, or "pure") structure of sense intuition (i.e., space and time) nor by the *a priori* structure of the understanding (i.e., the categories) that are unified by the conscious ego, but by an *a priori* synthesis of the two that is accomplished by the so-called "schemata" of the transcendental imagination.[20] The words *die transzendentale Einbildungskraft* tells us exactly how Heidegger understands Kant to intend it. It is a *Kraft,* because it is a "power" within the knower. Power to do what? To *bilden,* i.e., to build, establish, or institute a domain within which beings-to-be-known may be encountered. Why *transzendentale?* Because this domain is the horizon of transcendence.

So much for Kant. Now the only place where Heidegger thematizes transcendence in his own name (outside of the essay *On the Essence of Ground*) is in the closing section of the Kant-book. There the term comes naturally to him, for it arises out of the whole preceding analysis. He seems to use it in concluding his study, then, as a convenient way to situate his own problematic with regard to Kant's. Kant, he maintains, saw the awesome consequences of conceiving the transcendental imagination as radically as we described it, and drew back as from a yawning abyss. That is why he changed his analysis in the second edition of the *Critique* (1789).[21] Heidegger wants to accept these consequences and explore them to the full. He would elaborate the implications of what it means to say that the horizon in which an encounter between man and beings-to-be-known takes place is an antecedent seizure—com-prehension—of the Being structure of beings. Soon he expresses this fact in language proper to himself: ". . . Man is a being who is immersed among other beings in such a way that the beings that he is not as well as the being that he is himself have already constantly become manifested to him. This manner of being [proper to] man we call existence. . . ."[22] A few lines later he explains his own meaning more fully. "By the existence of man comes to pass an irruption in the totality of beings of such a sort that . . . beings *as* beings become manifest. . . ."[23] And why? Because from the very beginning of his philosophical way Heidegger had realized that although man "first of all and for the most part" forgets Being, he nonetheless has built into his very structure a privileged comprehension of Being by reason of which he can say "is." "Comprehension" here must not be understood as a mere intellectual understanding, but as a -*prehendere*, i.e., a "seizure" of Being, *cum-*, i.e., "with" and in and as its very structure as a being among the rest. That is why man is called *Dasein*. The word "existence" adds nothing to this but a nuance. In the essay *On the Essence of Truth* (1930), Heidegger writes it "ek-sistence." The nuance, then, is that by reason of *Dasein*'s privileged access to Being, it has an ecstatic structure, it -*sistit* ("stands") *ek-* ("outside of") itself and toward Being. By the same token, *Dasein* may be called "transcendence," too, because, standing outside of itself and toward Being it passes beyond all beings (including itself) to the Being-process that lets them be what they are. Finally, all through *Sein und Zeit,* it is called "Being-in-the-World" as well. For when one proceeds by a phenomenological analysis, beginning with the experience of everyday life, Being as horizon of transcendence discloses itself as World, and *Dasein* as the process of transcendence is nothing else but the disclosure of the World. Briefly, then: Being-in-the-World, transcendence, existence—all these are one, namely, *Dasein,* which, as comprehension of Being, designates the essence of man.

One more remark, and we return to the critique of Husserl. It will be noticed that in all these formulae there is implied a double dimension in *Dasein*: that dimension according to which *Dasein* is a being among the rest and like the rest, simply because it is; that dimension according to which *Dasein* differs from all other beings, because it has a privileged com-prehension of Being. Heidegger characterizes this double dimension by two sets of formulae. One set is geared to the word "existence." That dimension according to which *Dasein* is a being like others is called "existentiell," and that according to which its structure is open to Being is called "existential." The second set of formulae comes from the Greek word for a being: *on.* Accordingly, the existentiell dimension is called "ontic," the existential dimension is called "ontological." These two dimensions (levels) of *Dasein* are distinct but not separate. The ontic-existentiell level cannot be at all unless it is structured; reciprocally, unless there is a being for which the existential-ontological may serve as structure, it cannot be a structure.

Let us come now to Heidegger's criticism of Husserl. At a given point in the argument of the essay *On the Essence of Ground,* he remarks, almost unobstrusively, "If we characterize all comportment with Being as intentional, then intentionality is possible only on the basis of transcendence . . . ."[24] The remark, innocuous as it appears, yields the following inferences: First of all, the intentionality of consciousness as Husserl describes it (whether this intentionality be explicitly thematized, or remain unthematic and functional) is a relationship between *beings,* i.e., between a being as intentional consciousness and a being as intended as the immanent term of the conscious act. In other words, it is a comportment on the ontic-existentiell level. Secondly, the text suggests that this ontic-existentiell comportment with beings is first made possible by the ontological dimension of *Dasein,* by reason of which *Dasein* is open to the Being of these beings and thus can comport itself with them *as* beings. Thirdly, the text suggests that to conceive man in Husserlian fashion as merely a being who is the subject of conscious (or, for that matter, unconscious) acts is to forget the true dimension that gives man his primacy among beings, namely, his comprehension of Being itself (in other words, it is another sign of the forgetfulness of Being). Fourthly, the text suggests that this com-prehension of Being characterizes *Dasein*'s structure as a being, and when, as a being, *Dasein* enters into comportment with other beings, thus becoming a conscious subject, it is *Dasein*'s ontological structure that lets it be a subject and lets it be conscious, but as structure is not conscious at all. Finally the text suggests that *Dasein,* as Heidegger conceives it, is a *self,* to be sure, but *not a conscious subject.* It is a pre-subjective, onto-conscious self.[25] Let us formulate then, the following hypothesis: the place where unconscious processes may be situated in Heidegger's thought seems to be in the existential-ontological dimension of this *onto*-conscious self.

REGARDING THE PLACE

The formulation of an hypothesis absolves the first part of this *Erörterung,* i.e., the "pointing out" of the place where the unconscious may be located in Heidegger's thought. It remains simply "to regard" this place briefly in order to comprehend its meaning. What remains to be said may be polarized around two questions: What role does phenomenology play in this conception of the unconcious? What indeed, is to be understood by an onto-conscious self? We begin with the second question, for that is where the preceding exposé has left us.

It will be perfectly clear to Heideggerean scholars that the term "onto-conscious" has no textual foundation in Heidegger to recommend it. What it is intended to express, however, is quite simple. *Dasein* as a self that is *not a* (conscious) *subject* is very Heideggerean. It is one of the important themes in *Sein und Zeit,* but to call it simply "non-subjective" is more misleading than to call it "pre-subjective," for it is a self that can *become* conscious as an ego. If by the same reasoning process we call it "pre-conscious," we run immediately into difficulty, for "pre-conscious" (after Freud) has a consecrated meaning that is not at all what is intended here. We say "onto-conscious" for want of something better, to suggest that the self in question is the ontological dimension of the conscious subject *as* conscious, the Being-dimension of *Dasein* by reason of which it is the "There" (*Da*) of Being among beings. This dimension is not conscious, therefore may be called "*un*conscious," for the same reason that Being is not *a* being—in other words, because of the "not" that *diffentiates* Being from beings and constitutes what Heidegger calls the "ontological difference."[26]

To understand this notion of *Dasein* as a pre-subjective, onto-conscious (*un*conscious) self, let us recall for a moment Heidegger's polemic against subjectivism. He engages in it in two ways: in *Sein und Zeit* by the conception of *Dasein* as transcendence (Being-in-the-World); in the later works by his effort to overcome metaphysics, which, he maintains, since Descartes has been profoundly subject-ist. In *Sein und Zeit,* he admits that *Dasein* is essentially human and therefore belongs to someone who can say "ego." As long as we remain on the ontic level, i.e., on the level of consciousness, the self-hood of *Dasein* appears as a principle of stable unity that abides among the changes and multiplicity of experience. As we saw in Husserl's conception on intentionality, the conscious ego is referred to these experiences and they to it. It "lies under" these experiences, it is their *hypo-keimenon, subjectum,* "subject." The traditional ontologies, Heidegger claims, interpreted the Being of such a subject in terms of substance, which meant that it was a being so different than the rest, a "mere entity" (*Vorhandenes*). But *Dasein* is different from other beings—not in its ontic but in its ontological dimension—because it is open to Being. It is not therefore, a substance but a process—a process of transcendence,and if, as onto-conscious, it may legitimately be called "unconscious," then as unconscious it is profoundly *dynamic*. It is *Dasein*'s transcendence to Being that makes all encounter with beings as beings possible. Let us take, for example, the encounter that takes place in an act of knowledge. Husserl would explain it in terms of an intentional act of consciousness. Heidegger would say that when we examine all the conditions of knowledge, we discover that they include a pre-cognitional intimacy of *Dasein* with their Being-structure, out of which arises the subject-object relationship of knowledge as a derivative and deficient mode.[27]

The second mode of Heidegger's polemic against subject-ism appears with its history. The simplest example is his analysis of Descartes. We are all familiar with what Descartes tried to do. Coming upon the scene in seventeenth-century Europe when, on the one hand, a wide-spread scepticism would tempt man to doubt his own power to arrive at truth, and, on the other hand, burgeoning scientific discovery tempted man to exalt his powers for arriving at truth—at least scientific truth, *Dasein* conceived his task as establishing some "unshakable foundation of truth" (*fundamentum inconcussum veritatis*): foundation, because it would be the ground upon which all truths would ultimately rest; unshakable, because man himself would be the final arbiter of it.

The "unshakable foundation of truth" was, of course, the Cartesian *cogito ergo sum:* "I, in thinking, am [while thinking]." The statement itself, was true, for it corresponded to the situation of fact. Moreover, the statement was not only true but certain, for in making it the thinker not only knew the situation of fact but knew that he knew it and was thinking it accurately (for even to doubt it was itself a type of thinking that implied the existence of the one who thought). Because of its certitude, this truth was unshakable. It was, besides, the foundation of all other truths, for any other truth would be formulated by a type of thinking that rested on the basic truth consisting in the thinker's certainty of his own existence.

All this, of course, is quite classical. But one consequence of Descartes' starting point is significant. The ego, whose existence for Descartes is certified in the act of thinking, is for the first time in the history of thought conceived as a subject, something that "lies under" everything else—in this case, that under-lies all truth. In other words, the ego that is aware of its own existence is a "subject" for the very same reason that it is a "foundation" of truth. But if we go one step further, we see that everything that is not the thinking subject becomes something about which the subject thinks, i.e., an "object" of thought. As a result, everything that is becomes either a subject or an object of thought. As a matter of fact, the world itself is nothing more than the sum total of the objects of thought, a sort of Collective Object. In a word, the first consequence of Descartes' discovery of the unshakable foundation of truth in the self-awareness of a thinking ego is that all reality becomes divided into subjects and objects.

What follows from this? When everything that is is jammed into the categories of subject and object, then the wondrous depth, beauty and deep down freshness of beings is overlooked. The marvelous mystery of presence— i.e., of Being— is forgotten. All beings become pawns that man can control, the way he controls a scientific experiment. But this is not the worst of it. Not only have other beings become so many empty shells because their Being-dimension is forgotten, but man, when he makes himself the object of his own objectifying thought, loses all appreciation of his own dignity, for the unique prerogative of man lies in his transcendence, in his com-prehension of Being.

Once Descartes conceived of "reality" in terms of subjects and objects, this polarity would characterize the thought of all the major thinkers down to our own time. To be sure, Heidegger never formally dialogues with Freud, but it seems easy to surmise the gist of what he would say if he did. Because of Freud's own remarkable gift for clinical analysis, plus the fact that his conceptual categories were drawn from his background in physical science, Freud could not help but conceive man as an object of clinical investigation, like any other scientific object. Furthermore, since he described the unconscious in terms of what he knew about ontic-consciousness, then no matter how profoundly the unconscious might lie in the depths of man, it, too, remained ontic to the last. In any case, one might argue in Heidegger's name, I think, that of all the major figures that have influenced contemporary man's conception of himself, Freud perhaps more than anyone else (because of his stature) was oblivious to the Being-dimension in man, i.e., of Being itself.

One word more before we return to the problem of phenomenology. It concerns Hegel. For Heidegger, he, too, was caught in the vice of subject-ism though in an extremely subtle way. In the last analysis, then, Heidegger separates himself from Hegel. Yet there is much in Hegel he can accept, in particular the distinction at the beginning of the *Phenomenology of the Spirit* between "natural" consciousness and what Hegel calls "real" consciousness, but which Hyppolite interprets as the "ontological unconscious of consciousness"—i.e., Absolute Spirit, present in human consciousness, but still unaware of itself. In interpreting this passage, Heidegger translates the distinction into a language proper to himself: what Hegel calls "natural" knowing, Heidegger calls "ontic"; what Hegel calls "real" knowing and Hyppolite the "ontological unconscious," Heidegger calls simply "ontological." Now it would be utterly absurd, of course, to suggest that the ontological dimension of *Dasein* for Heidegger is the equivalent of Hegel's Absolute, still unaware of itself. But it does seem that we may argue by analogy (an analogy, scholastics would probably say, of "proper proportionality"): as the "ontological uncon-sciousness" of Absolute Spirit at the beginning of Hegel's *Phenomenology* is to "natural" consciousness, so the "ontological" dimension of Heidegger's *Dasein* in *Sein und Zeit* is to "ontic" consciousness. In other words, with the help of Hyppolite's authority we may find in Heidegger's interpretation of Hegel a confirmation of the hypothesis that the place of the unconscious in Heidegger is to be found in the ontological dimension of a pre-subjective, onto-conscious self.

And now, a brief word about phenomenology. In Heidegger's letter de-scribing his own beginnings, two important remarks follow one another: the first pertains to the phenomenological method, the second to the notion of Being itself. After explaining how the Being-question was first posed for him, he writes:

> Dialogues with Husserl provided the immediate experience of the phe-nomenological method that prepared the concept of phenomenology explained in the Introduction to *Sein und Zeit* (Section 7). In this evolution a normative role was played by the reference back to fundamental words of Greek thought which I interpreted accordingly: *logos* (to make manifest) and *phainesthai* (to show oneself).[28]

In other words, phenomenology for Heidegger means the process of letting appear, as what it is, that whose nature it is to appear.

The second remark reads as follows:

> A renewed study of the Aristotelian treatise (especially Book IX of the *Metaphysics* and Book VI of the *Nicomachean Ethics*) resulted in the insight into *alētheuein* as a process of revealment, and in the characterization of truth as non-concealment, to which all self-manifestation of beings pertains.[29]

I take Heidegger to mean here: The process that lets beings manifest themselves as what they are is Being itself. This manifestation of beings by Beings is a process of revelation, i.e., of pulling aside some veil of darkness ("-velation") that conceals beings and letting them become un-concealed ("*re*-velation") as what they are. Such a process of non-concealment is what the Greeks under-stood by *alētheuein,* the coming-to-pass of *alētheia: lēthē* was their word for "concealment," the alpha-prefix a sign of privation; hence, *a-lētheia* meant the privation of concealment (non-concealment). Now the normal translation of *a-lētheia* is "truth," so that the Being-process as *alētheuein* must be conceived as the coming-to-pass of truth.

But this is not as simple as it sounds. If we take the two passages together, it is very clear that for Heidegger the function of phenomenology is the process of letting that be manifest (revealed) whose nature it is to become manifest (revealed)—in other words, to let beings be revealed in their Being, their non-concealment, their truth. But if it is the very nature of beings that they be revealed, why do they need any help from phenomenology? Because the revelation in them is so finite, so limited by a "not" (let us call it "negativity"), that the Being-dimension of them is concealed as much as it is revealed, with the result that "first of all and for the most part" they seem to be what they are not. In *Sein und Zeit*, Heidegger himself asks the question: what must phenomenology let-be-manifest? He answers:

> . . . Obviously that which first of all and for the most part does *not* show itself, that which alongside of what first of all and for the most part does show itself is *concealed*, yet at the same time is something that essentially belongs to what first of all and for the most part does show itself, in such a way, indeed, as to constitute its sense and ground [namely, its Being.][30]

A case in point: *Dasein* itself in its normal everyday condition appears to be what it is not, namely a being in all respects like the rest, simply because it is. The task of a phenomenological analysis of *Dasein*, then, is to penetrate through what *Dasein* "first of all and for the most part" seems-to-be on the existentiell level of everyday intercourse and let it appear as what it is, existential as well as existentiell. The whole phenomenological analysis of *Dasein* is therefore an "existential" analysis, which slowly discerns what it means to say that ". . . the ontic excellence of *Dasein* consists in the fact that it *is* ontologically."[31]

The analysis may also be called "hermeneutic." How Heidegger came by the word is at the moment not important. What is important is the meaning he gives it. It is derived from the Greek word *hermeneuein,* which bears affinity with the Greek deity Hermes, herald of the gods. The verb suggests, then, to "bear tidings," or more simply, to "make manifest." In other words, for Heidegger phenomenology and hermeneutic are one.

If it were feasible, our task now would be to put our hypothesis to the test by going slowly through *Sein und Zeit* to see if it is really true to say that the place of the unconscious in Heidegger is in the ontological dimension of *Dasein,* conceived as a pre-subjective, onto-conscious self. But to do that we would have to do more than simply "regard" the place, we would have to dwell there for a while, and obviously that is impossible here. In lieu of that, let us conclude by enumerating a few of the practical questions that should be kept in mind if we are to take this hypothesis seriously and see in it a genuine relevance for psychotherapy.

In order that these questions be pointed, it might be well to sketch in the most general fashion the broad lines of *Sein und Zeit,* so that they may be once more in focus. Heidegger wants to interrogate the meaning of Being by making a phenomenological analysis of *Dasein*'s structural com-prehension of Being. What does the analysis yield? That *Dasein* is finite transcendence, whose ultimate meaning is time.[32]

191

Dasein is transcendence. We know what that means. *Dasein* passes beyond all beings (including itself) to the Being of beings. Here Being reveals itself as the World, and *Dasein,* because transcendence, is the disclosure of the World. The ontological components of disclosure are three: com-prehension (*Verstehen*), which discloses the World as such; the ontological disposition (*Befindlichkeit*), which discloses *Dasein*'s relationship to other beings in its matter-of-fact situation (anxiety is but a mode, albeit an important one, of this disposition); logos (*Rede*), which enables man to articulate his relationship to beings (it is the ontological foundation of language). Add to this only that *Dasein* is never solitary—it must share its transcendence with other *Daseins*, which are always with it in the World.

This transcendence is finite, i.e., it is constricted, permeated by many kinds of "not": *Dasein* is not the master of its origin but finds itself as if "thrown" into a matter-of-fact situation determined by certain concrete possibilities—some bequeathed to it, some imposed by milieu, some that it has freely chosen. *Dasein* is not independent of other beings but referred to them, referentially dependent on them. As a matter of fact, it is so entangled with other beings that it is, as it were, "fallen" upon them, experiencing a certain drag toward them and the tendency to think of nothing but beings, thus becoming oblivious of the privilege by which it transcends them. *Dasein* is not capable of experiencing Being except in terms of beings, so that the most that can be said about Being is that it is not-a-being, it is Non-being (*Nichts*). Finally, *Dasein* is not destined to exist forever, it is Being-unto-an-end. In man, this end is death— *Dasein* is Being-unto-death. The sum total of these signs of finitude, *Dasein*'s cumulative negativity, is what Heidegger calls "guilt."

Now to achieve itself fully, i.e., to be authentic, *Dasein* must simply let itself be as transcendence that is finite. To let itself be as transcendence, *Dasein* must overcome the tendency of its fallen condition to lose itself among beings—it must re-collect its great prerogative of access to Being. To let itself be as finite is to acquiesce to its finitude, i.e., to its ontological guilt, not as if it were surrendering in despair to a tragic destiny but as consenting with tranquillity to be no more than it is. The voice that calls *Dasein* to authenticity is the voice of "conscience." *Dasein* responds to that voice by letting itself be as finite transcendence through "re-solve."

Dasein is finite trancendence, whose ultimate meaning—i.e., whose ultimate source of unity—is time. As transcending existence, *Dasein* is always coming to Being through beings, and it is thus that Being comes continually to *Dasein*. This coming is *Dasein*'s future. But Being comes to a *Dasein* that in the matter-of-fact condition of its throwness is already existing. This condition of already-having-been is *Dasein*'s past. Finally, Being as it comes to *Dasein* renders all beings (including itself) manifest as present to *Dasein*. This presence is *Dasein*'s present. What gives unity (therefore ultimate meaning) to *Dasein* is this unity of future, past and present, i.e., the unity of time itself.

Dasein, then, is essentially temporal. Because temporal, it is also historical, and this historicity is the foundation of history. And because *Dasein* is never solitary but shares transcendence with other *Daseins*, it also shares their common history.

Now to achieve authenticity precisely as temporal/historical, *Dasein* must accept the temporal/historical character of finite transcendence. It must continue to let Being come through its (single and collective) past and render beings present. As a temporal/historical process, *Dasein* achieves authenticity through "re-trieve." When resolve is seen in its temporal/historical character, then, it is nothing else but re-trieve: that process that lets Being come again (future) out of a possibility already exploited before (past) and give a fresh presence to what is (present).

Such, then, are the general perspectives of *Sein und Zeit.* But through them all there runs a particular theme that may not go unmentioned: the problem of truth. Ever since Aristotle, philosophers have assumed that truth consists in a conformity between a mind judging and a thing judged. It resides properly in the judgment that is expressed in a proposition. But what of this conformity? It is a relationship that can be expressed by saying that the mind *so* judges *as* a being in itself is. But what guarantees the validity of this so . . . as relationship? Is it not the discovery by *Dasein* that the being that is judged is (manifest) as it is judged to be? More fundamental than conformity, then, is the process in *Dasein* by which it discovers beings as they are—in their Being. But this is exactly what is meant by transcendence.

Let us see what follows from this. If truth in its origin, i.e., original truth, is identical with *Dasein*'s existence, then everything that the analysis has so far yielded concerning the structure of *Dasein* now characterizes the nature of truth. Insofar as *Dasein* is transcendence, it com-prehends the Beings of beings. That is why Heidegger can say that *Dasein* is "in the truth." But *Dasein*'s transcendence is finite, it is permeated by a multiple negativity. For that reason, the coming-to-pass of truth is likewise pervaded by a "not." Consider, for example, that aspect of *Dasein*'s negativity which is called "fallen-ness," i.e., *Dasein*'s built-in drag toward beings that propels it toward inauthenticity. The process of original truth, too, is fallen among beings. This means that the discovery of beings is always somehow askew. They are discovered, to be sure, but always inadequately, and drop back immediately into their previous hiddenness. For *Dasein* to apprehend a being (*ergreifen*) is simultaneously to misapprehend (*vergreifen*) it; to uncover (*entdecken*) is to cover-up (*verdecken*); to discover (*erschliessen*) is to cover-over (*verschliessen*). This condition of undulant obscurity Heidegger calls "untruth." ". . . The full . . . sense of the expression 'Dasein is in the truth' says simultaneously 'Dasein is in the untruth' . . ."[33] And why? Because transcendence is finite.

Clearly, then, the coming-to-pass of finite transcendence is the coming-to-pass of truth. Now if *Dasein* achieves authenticity through that gesture of self-acceptance that is called re-solve, then re-solve must be also the eminent mode of truth—but also of un-truth. In other words, if by re-solve *Dasein* accepts the finitude of transcendence, it simultaneously consents to the finitude of truth. ". . . [Dasein] is simultaneously in truth and un-truth. This applies in the most 'authentic' sense to re-solve as authentic truth. [Re-solve] authentically makes un-truth its very own. . . ."[34] i.e., accepts the inescapable finitude of existence.

"All this has been disengaged through the existential analysis of *Dasein,* i.e., by the effort to let-be-seen the ontological—i.e., onto-conscious (unconscious)—structure of man's ontic (conscious) activity. Can the analysis meet the demands of practical psychotherapy?[35]

Let us start with the phenomenological method itself. If a man of Paul Ricoeur's eminent stature, when faced with the unconscious, is forced to transform Husserl's description of the evidence of consciousness into an interpretation, i.e., a hermeneutic, of signs (such as dreams, parapraxias, etc.), is it possible that he might accomplish the task more easily if he started explicitly with a less Husserlean and more Heideggerean conception of phenomenology, which would ambition to be nothing else than a hermeneutic, and whose only task from the very beginning seeks only to let what seems-to-be reveal itself as what it is?

More practically, does Heidegger offer any help in understanding the structure of the therapeutic situation? If Heidegger insists that *Dasein* is never solitary but shares its transcendence with others, and if in each *Dasein* there is an existential component of logos that makes possible all language, does this help us to understand the necessarily dialogical character of therapy? I am thinking of the problem of transference and counter-transference, as well as of the revelatory character of the interview as such.

Does the perspective of Heidegger have a place for the importance of biographical data in therapy? I am thinking of the facticity of *Dasein*'s throwness into a situation of concrete possibilities—some bequeathed, some imposed by milieu, some chosen by *Dasein* itself.

Does Heidegger's perspective offer hope that if we could get deep enough into *Dasein*'s ontological structure, perhaps the essential of Freud's conception of the unconscious could be synthesized with the essential of Jung's? I am thinking of the fact that *Dasein* for Heidegger is not only singular but plural and therefore that its onto-conscious dimension is not only individual but collective.

Would Heidegger's conception of *Dasein* as Being-unto-death offer any satisfactory way to account in ontological fashion for the tendency in man that Freud describes as the "aggressive," or "death," instinct?

Can Heidegger's notion of Being itself be of help? In *The Introduction to Psychoanalysis,* Freud first argues to the existence of the unconscious from the small errors that everyone commits: slips of the tongue (*versprechen*), slips of the pen (*verschreiben*), misreading (*verlesen*), mishearing (*verhören*), etc. Heidegger speaks of a similar type of phenomena: every apprehension (*ergreifen*) is a misapprehension, every discovery (*entdecken*) a covering-over (*verdecken*), every disclosure (*erschliessen*) at once a closing-over (*verschliessen*), etc.[36] The difference is that for Heidegger these phenomena are due to the finitude of truth based on the fact that Being, revealing itself in finite fashion through finite *Dasein,* inevitably conceals itself too. Does the negativity of Being in finite self-revelation through *Dasein* offer a better account of the negativity of all finite comportment than Freud does? If so, this could go very far: for one might be able to find here an ontological ground, i.e., ground in an ontological unconscious, for such classic phenomena as illogicality, distortion, displacement, ambivalence, resistance, etc., and all that these imply.

Finally, can Heidegger offer a conception of freedom that even Freud might be persuaded to accept—freedom that does not exclude unconscious motivation (this would be part of the law of seeming-to-be in what is), at least in this sense: it would be a freedom that knows how to accept itself as finite transcendence, let itself be what it is with all its negativity of whatever kind. In any case, such is the freedom achieved in re-solve. If resolve is fundamentally reponse to the call of conscience, one might infer, too, that this response would ground all responsibility.

CONCLUSION

Let us come a full circle and end as we began. Both Freud and Heidegger write of Oedipus's tragic destiny in a manner proper to themselves. For Freud as well as Heidegger, it was achieved through a process of revelation. But Freud likened the revelation to psychoanalysis; Heidegger to the achievement of authenticity. Let us read Heidegger's remarks once more in the light of the preceding *Erörterung:*

> . . . At the beginning Oedipus is the savior and lord of the state, living in an aura of glory and divine favor. He is driven out of this seeming-to-be, which is not a merely subjective view of himself but the manner in which his *Dasein* happens to shine forth, up to the [moment] when his Being as murderer of his father and desecrator of his mother comes to non-concealment. The way from that radiant beginning to this gruesome end is a struggle between seeming-to-be (concealment and distortion) and non-concealment (Being). About the city lies the hidden [truth] about the murderer of Laius, the former king. With passion of a man who stands in refulgence of glory and is a Greek, Oedipus sets out to reveal this hidden [truth]. Step by step, he must bring himself to nonconcealment, and in the end he can bear it only by putting out his own eyes, i.e., he deprives himself of all light, lets the darkness of night fall around him, and in his blindness cries out for all doors to be thrown open so that a man may be revealed to the people as what he *is.*

What really *did* come-to-pass in Oedipus? This is the point where we must leave psychotherapy to psychotherapists.

William J. Richardson

NOTES

1 M. Heidegger, "Georg Trakl. Eine Erörterung seines Gedichtes," *Merkur,* VII (1953), 226-258. The study was subsequently republished under a different title ("Die Sprache im Gedicht," *Unterwegs zur Sprache* [Pfullingen: Neske, 1959], pp. 35-82). References are made to the latter version because of its greater accessibility. See Heidegger, *On the Way to Language,* trans. Peter Hertz and Joan Stambaugh (New York: Harper and Row, 1971), pp. 159-198.

2 "Erörtern meint hier zunächst: in den Ort weisen. Es heisst dann: den Ort beachten. . . ." (M. Heidegger, *Unterwegs zur Sprache,* p. 37).

3 ". . . Beides, das Weisen in den Ort und das Beachten des Ortes, sind die vorbereitenden Schritte einer Erörterung. Doch wagen wir schon genug, wenn wir uns im folgenden mit den vorbereitenden Schritten begnügen. Die Eröterung endet, wie es einem Denkweg entspricht, in eine Frage. . . ." (M. Heidegger, *Unterwegs zur Sprache,* p. 37).

4 S. Freud, *The Interpretation of Dreams,* trans. J. Stachey et. al. in *The Standard Edition of the Complete Psychological Works of Sigmund Freud* (London: Hogarth, 1958), IV, 262.

5 ". . . Denken wir an Sophokles' Oedipus Tyrannus. Oedipus, zu Anfang der Retter und Herr des Staates, im Glanz des Ruhmes und der Gnade der Götter, wird aus diesem Schein, der keine bloss subjektive Ansicht des Oedipus von sich selbst ist, sondern das, worin das Erscheinen seines Daseins geschieht, herausgeschleudert, bis die Unverborgenheit seines Seins als des Mörders des Vaters und des Schänders der Mutter geschehen ist. Der Weg von jenem Anfang des Glanzes bis zu diesem Ende des Grauens ist ein einziger Kampf zwischen dem Schein (Verborgenheit und Verstelltheit) und der Unverborgenheit (dem Sein). Um die Stadt lagert das Verborgene des Mörders des vormaligen Königs Laïos. Mit der Leidenschaft dessen, der in der Offenbarkeit des Glanzes steht und Grieche ist, geht Oedipus an die Enthüllung dieses Verborgenen. Schritt für Schritt muss er dabei sich selbst in die Unverborgenheit stellen, die er am Ende nur so erträgt, dass er sich selbst die Augen austicht, d.h. sich aus allem Licht herausstellt, verhüllende Nacht um sich schlagen lässt und als ein Geblendeter dann schreit, alle Türen aufzureissen, damit dem Volk ein solcher offenbar werde, als der, de er *ist*." (M. Heidegger, *Einführung in die Metaphysik* [Tübingen: Niemeyer, 1953], p. 81). Writer's translation, Heidegger's italics. For slightly different translation and full context of passage, see M. Heidegger, *Introduction of Metaphysics,* trans. R. Manheim (New Haven: Yale, 1959), pp. 106-107.

6 ". . . Brentano setzte auf das Titelblatt seiner Schrift den Satz des Aristoteles: *to on legetai pollachōs.* Ich übersetze: 'Das Seiende wird (nämlich hinsichtlich seines Seins) in vielfacher Wiese offenkundig.' In diesem Satz verbirgt sich die meinen Denkweg bestimmende *Frage:* Welches ist die alle mannigfachen Bedeutungen durchherrschende einfache, einheitliche Bestimmung von Sein? . . ." (M. Heidegger. "Preface" to W. J. Richardson, S. J., *Heidegger: Through Phenomenology to Thought* [The Hague: Nijhoff, 1963], pp. x-xi. Writer's translation, Heidegger's italics.

7 See William Barrett, *What is Existentialism?* (New York: Grove, 1964), p. 137. The details of the preceding paragraph are not based on any published statement of Heidegger but on remarks made to the present writer in a private conversation at Freiburg-Zähringen (Breisgau), February 24, 1960.

8 G. W. F. Hegel, *Phänomenologie des Geistes*[6] (Hamburg, Meiner, 1952).

9 ". . . Relire ainsi la Phénoménologie consisterait envisager la totalité de cette oeuvre si difficile et sinueuse comme la véritable tragédie d'Oedipe de l'esprit humain tout entier. . . ." (J. Hyppolite, "Phénoménologie de Hegel et psychanalyse," *La Psychanalyse.* Vol. III: Psychanalyse et sciences de l'homme [Paris: Presses Universitaires de France, 1957], 17-32, p. 19).

10 "Peut-être y a-til là une clé du problème de l'inconscient: il n'est pas une chose située derrière une chose, mais fondamentalement une certaine âme de la conscience, une certaine façon inévitable, pour la conscience naturelle, d'être ellememe." (J. Hyppolite, "Phénoménologie de Hegel . . . ," p. 19).

11 ". . . Pour Husserl ces essences seraient plutôt les structures, *a priori* de toute expérience vécue; ce sont des contentus idéaux que le langage présuppose toutes les fois que nous disons: je veux, je

196

désire, je regrette ou que nous comprenons une situation, un comportement comme signifiant voulouir, désir, regret. . . ." (P. Ricoeur, "Philosophie de la volonte et de l'action," Proceedings of Second Lexington Conference, *The Phenomenology of Will and Action, Ed. Erwin Straus and Richard Griffith (Pittsburgh: Duquesne University Press, 1967)*. Cited according to original French manuscript, p. 10. Writer's translation.

12 See E. Fink, Beilage XXI zu #46 of E. Husserl, *Die Krisis der europäischen Wissenschaften und die transzendentale Phaenomenologie* (The Hague: Nijhoff, 1954), p. 473.

13 See H. Ellenberger, "The Unconscious before Freud," *Bulletin of the Menninger Clinic*, XXI (1957), 3-15, p. 14.

14 ". . . Si, *vraiment*, la phénoménologie husserlienne est la philosophie qui accepte de s'interroger, enfin et jusqu'au bout, sur ce qu'*est* la conscience, . . . alors une véritable explicitation de ce qu'est l'inconscient ne peut s'effectuer qu'á partir de la phénoménologie et dans le prolongement de celle-ci." (A. D. Waelhens, "Réflexions sur une problématique Husserlienne de l'inconscient, Husserl et Hegel," in *Edmund Husserl, 1859-1959* (The Hague: Nijhoff, 1959), 221-237, p. 225.

15 See P. Ricoeur, "La philosophie . . . ," pp. 24-26.

16 We omit the second because an interpretation of it would suppose a more detailed exposition of Husserl's problematic than the preceding sketch supplies. Reference will be made to it in footnote form below (see note 25).

17 M. Heidegger, *Vom Wesen des Grundes*[4] (Frankfurt: Klostermann, 1955); see *The Essence of Reasons,* trans. Terence Malick (Evanston: Northwestern University Press, 1969).

18 ". . . Ich nenne alle Erkenntnis transzendental, die sich nicht sowohl mit Gegenständen, *sondern mit unserer Erkenninisart von Gegenständen, insofern diese a priori möglich sein soll,* überhaupt beschäftigt. . . ." (I. Kant, *Kritik der reinen Vernunft,* ed. R. Schmidt [Hamburg: Meiner, 1952], B 25).

19 "Ein endlich erkennendes Wesen vermag sich zum Seienden, das es selbst nicht ist und das es auch nicht geschaffen hat, nur dann zu verhalten, wenn dieses schon vorhandene Seiende von sich aus begegnen kann. Umjedoch als das Seiende, das es ist, begegnen zu konnen, muss es im vorhinein schon überhaupt als Seiendes, d.h. hinsichtlich seiner Seinsverfassung, 'erkannt' sein. . . . In dieser ursprünglichen Zuwendung hält sich das endliche Wesen überhaupt erst einen Spielraum vor, innerhalb dessen ihm etwas 'korrespondieren' kann. Sich im vorhinein in solchem Spielraum halten, ihn ursprünglich bilden, ist nichts anderes als die Transzendenz, die alles endlich Verhalten zu seiendem ausziechnet. . . ." (M. Heidegger, *Kant und das Problem der Metaphysik*[2] [Frankfurt: Klostermann, 1951], pp. 69-70). Writer's translation.

20 It is quite significant for the thesis that we are developing that Dr. Margetts situates the unconscious in Kant here in the transcendental imagination, precisely because it lies deeper than the conscious ego with its categories of the understanding. See E. L., Margetts, M.D., "The Unconscious in the History of Medical Psychology," *The Psychiatric Quarterly*, XXVII (1953), 115-138, p. 124-125.

21 See M. Heidegger, *Kant and the Problem of Metaphysics,* trans. J. Churchill (Bloomington: Indiana University Press, 1962), pp. 166-176.

22 ". . . Der Mensch ist ein Seiendes, das immitten von Seiendem ist, so zwar, dass ihm dabei das Seiende, das er nicht ist, und das Seiende, das er selbst ist, zumal immer schon offenbar geworden ist. Diese Seinsart des Menschen nennen wir Existenz. . . ." (M. Heidegger, *Kant und das Problem der Metaphysik,* p. 205). Writer's translation.

23 "Mit der Existenz des Menschen geschieht ein Einbruch in das Ganze des Seienden dergestalt, das jetzt erst das Seiende . . . an ihm selbst, d.h. *als* Seiendes offenbar wird. . . . (M. Heidegger, *Kant und das Problem der Metaphysik,* p. 206). Writer's translation, Heidegger's italics.

24 "Kennzeichnet man alles *Verhalten* zu Seiendem als intentionales, dann ist die Intentionalität nur möglich auf dem Grunde der Transzendenz . . . ." (M. Heidegger, *Vom Wesen des Grundes,* p. 16). Writer's translation, Heidegger's italics.

197

William J. Richardson

25 The second text, alluded to above (see note 16), in which Heidegger explicitly separates himself from Husserl, is found in his letter to Husserl concerning the latter's article on Phenomenology for the *Encyclopaedia Britannica* (1927). See W. Biemel. "Husserls Encyclopaedia Britannica Artikel und Heideggers anmerkungen dazu," *Tijdschrift voor Philosophie,* XII (1950), 246-280, n.b. pp. 274-280, especially p. 280. For a discussion of the issues involved, see Richardson, *Heidegger:* . . . , pp. 178-179.

26 See M. Heidegger, *Vom Wesen des Grundes,* p. 15. The import of the "ontological difference" for Heidegger's entire problematic is far too vast for any adequate treatment in footnote form. The interested reader will find a relatively simplified statement of it in the present writer's article, "Heidegger and God—and Professor Jonas," *Thought,* XL (Spring, 1965), 22-31.

27 The treatment here of this difficult problem is necessarily brief. For a fuller discussion of the matter, together with its textual foundation in Heidegger, see Richardson, *Heidegger:* . . . , pp. 97-103.

28 "Durch die unmittelbare Erfahrung der phänomenologischen Methode in Gesprächen mit Husserl bereitete sich der Begriff von Phänomenologie vor, der in der Einleitung zu "Sein und Zeit" (#7) dargestellt ist. Hierbei spielt die Rückbeziehung auf die entsprechend ausgelegten Grundworte des griechischen Denkens: *logos* (offenbar machen) und *phainesthai* (sich zeigen) eine massgebende Rolle." (M. Heidegger, "Preface" to Richardson, *Heidegger:* . . . , p. xi).

29 "Ein erneutes Studium der Aristotelischen Abhandlungen (im besonderen des neunten Buches der "Metaphysik" und des sechsten Buches der "Nikomachischen Ethik") ergab den Einblick in das *alētheuein* als entbergen und die Kennzeichnung der Wahrheit als Unverborgenheit, in die alles Sichzeigen des Seienden gehört . . . ." (M. Heidegger, "Preface" to Richardson, *Heidegger:* . . . , pp. xi-xiii.

30 ". . . Offenbar solches, was sich zunächst und zumeist gerade *nicht* zeigt, was gegenüber dem, was sich zunächst und zumeist zeigt, *vorborgen* ist, aber zugleich etwas ist, was wesenhaft zu dem, was sich zunächst und zumeist zeigt, gehört, so zwar, dass es seinen Sinn und Grund ausmacht." (M. Heidegger, *Sein und Zeit*[9] [Tubingen: Niemeyer, 1960], p. 35). Writer's translation, Heidegger's italics.

31 ". . . Die ontische Auszeichnung des Daseins liegt darin, dass es ontologisch *ist.*" (M. Heidegger, *Sein und Zeit,* p. 12). Writer's translation, Heidegger's italics.

32 The following résumé summarizes the writer's interpretation of *Sein und Zeit* as found in his longer study, *Heidegger:* . . . , pp. 27-105.

33 ". . . Der volle existenzial-ontologische Sinn des Satzes: 'Dasein ist in der Wahrheit' sagt gleichursprünglich mit: 'Dasein ist in der Unwahrheit'. . . ." (M. Heidegger, *Sein und Zeit,* p. 222).

34 ". . . Erschlossen in seinem 'Da', hält, es sich gleichursprünglich in der Wahrheit und Un-wahrheit. Das gilt 'eigentlich' gerade von der Entschlossenheit als der eigentlichen Wahrheit. Sie eignet sich die Unwahrheit eigentlich zu. . . ." (M. Heidegger, *Sein und Zeit,* pp. 298-299).

35 The questions that follow pretend to do nothing more than *suggest* in a most schematic way the type of question that might be raised in trying to determine the relevance of the preceding hypothesis for psychotherapy. The questions as formulated do not in any sense exhaust the problems involved, either intensively or extensively.

36 We deliberately restrict ourselves here to a few examples. The list could be prolonged extensively. For example, see: *Vom Wesen der Wahrheit*[3] (Frankfurt: Klostermann, 1954), p. 22; *Platons Lehre von der Wahrheit*[2] (Bern: Francke, 1954), p. 32.

A Bibliography on Martin Heidegger for the Behavioral Scientists*

This bibliography contains mostly English titles of books, articles, and dissertations dealing with Martin Heidegger and his impact on psychology and psychiatry. It is intended to give the researchers in the behavioral sciences an overview of the work which has already been done and it should serve as a useful tool for those wishing to undertake further research. The bibliography is divided into the following sections: I. Books. II. General Articles. III. Proper Names. IV. Subjects. V. Bibliographies.

I. BOOKS

Ballard, Edward G. & Scott, Charles E., eds. *Martin Heidegger in Europe and America*. The Hague: Martinus Nijhoff, 1974, xii-200pp.

Cousineau, Robert Henri. *Humanism and Ethics*. An introduction to Heidegger's letter on humanism with a critical bibliography. Louvain: Ed. Nauwelaerts; Paris: Beatrice-Nauwelaerts, 1972. 144pp.

Deely, John N. *The Tradition via Heidegger*. An essay on the meaning of being in the philosophy of Heidegger. The Hague: Martinus Nijhoff, 1971. xxviii-210pp.

Demske, James M. *Being, Man and Death*. A Key to Heidegger. Lexington: The University Press of Kentucky, 1970. 165pp.

Erickson, Stephen A. *Language and Being*. An analytical phenomenology. New Haven-London: Yale University Press, 1970. vii-234pp.

Frings, Manfred S., ed. *Heidegger and the Quest for Truth*. Chicago: Quadrangle Books, 1968. 205pp.

Gelven, Michael. *A Commentary on Heidegger's 'Being and Time'*. A section-by-section interpretation. New York: Harper & Row, 1970. xiv-234pp.

Grene, Marjorie. *Martin Heidegger* (Studies in modern European literature and thought). London-New York: Hillary House, 1957. 128pp.

Hoeller, Keith. *Heidegger and Psychology*. Studies in Existential Psychology & Psychiatry. Seattle: *Review of Existential Psychology & Psychiatry*, 1988, 232pp.

---

* This bibliography was originally published in 1979, and with Professor Lapointe's permission, I have updated it through 1988. [K. H., Editor]

Howey, Richard L. *Heidegger and Jaspers on Nietzsche*. A critical examination of Heidegger's and Jasper's interpretation of Nietzsche. The Hague: Martinus Nijhoff, 1973. 218pp.

King, Magda. *Heidegger's Philosophy*. A guide to his basic thought. New York: Macmillan, 1964. xx-193pp. Oxford: Basil Blackwell, 1965. Also New York: Dell Publishing Co., 1966.

Kockelmans, Joseph J., ed. *A Companion to Martin Heidegger's Being & Time*. University Press of America, 1986.

Kockelmans, Joseph J. *Martin Heidegger*. A first introduction to his philosophy. Pittsburgh, Pa: Duquesne University Press-Louvain: E. Nauwelaerts, 1965. vii-182pp.

Kockelmans, Joseph J. *On Heidegger and Language*. Ed. and transl. by Joseph J. Kockelmans (Northwestern University Studies in phenomenology and existential philosophy). Evanston, Ill: Northwestern University Press, 1972. 380pp.

Kockelmans, Joseph J. *On the Truth of Being: Reflections on Heidegger's Later Philosophy*. Studies in phenomenology & existential philosophy. Indiana University Press, 1985. 352pp.

Langan, Thomas D. *The Meaning of Heidegger*. A critical study of an existentialist phenomenology. New York: Columbia University Press, 1959. 246pp.

Macomber, William B. *The Anatomy of Disillusion*. Heidegger's notion of truth. Evanston, Ill: Northwestern University Press, 1967. 227pp.

Magnus, Bernd. *Heidegger's Metahistory of Philosophy: Amor fati*, being and truth. The Hague: Martinus Nijhoff, 1970. xiv-146pp.

Marx, Werner. *Heidegger and the Tradition*. Transl. by T. Kisiel and M. Greene. Introd. by T. Kisiel. Evanston, Ill.: Northwestern University Press, 1970. xxxii-275pp.

Mehta, J. L. *Martin Heidegger: The Way & the Vision*, rev. ed. University of Hawaii Press, 1967. 526pp.

Mehta, Jarava L. *The Philosophy of M. Heidegger*. Varanasi: Banares Hindu University Press, 1967. xxii-566pp. Rev. ed. includes chapters I, VIII, IX & X of the original ed., New York: Harper & Row, 1971. xx-279pp.

Richardson, William J. *Heidegger*. Through phenomenology to thought. Preface by M. Heidegger. The Hague: Martinus Nijhoff, 1963. xxxii-764pp.

Schmitt, Richard. *Martin Heidegger on Being Human*. An introduction to '*Sein und Zeit*'. New York: Random House, 1969. 274pp.

200

Shahan, Robert W. and Mohanty, J. N. *Thinking about Being: Aspects of Heidegger's Thought*. University of Okalahoma Press, 1985. 208pp.

Sheehan, Thomas, ed. *Heidegger: The Man & the Thinker*. Precedent Publishing, Inc., 1981. 367pp.

Sherover, Charles M. *Heidegger, Kant and Time*. With an introd. by W. Barrett, Bloomington-London: Indiana University Press, 1971. 322pp.

Tweedie, D. F. *The Significance of Dread in the Thought of Kierkegaard and Heidegger*. Boston, 1954.

II. GENERAL ARTICLES

1940-1949

Löwith, Karl. "Heidegger: Problem and background of existentialism." *Social Research*, Vol. 15, 1948, 345-369.

Stern, Anders G. "On the pseudo-concreteness of Heidegger's philosophy." *Philosophy and Phenomenological Research*, Vol. 8, 1947-1948, 337-371.

1950-1959

Barrett, William. *Irrational Man*. A study in existential philosophy. New York: Doubleday and Co., 1958, 184-212.

Blackham, H.J. "Heidegger," in *Six Existentialist Thinkers*. London: Routledge & Co., 1952, 86-109.

Collins, James. "Martin Heidegger," in *The Existentialists*. A critical study. Chicago: Henry Regnery, 1952, 150-187.

Grene, Marjorie. *Dreadful Freedom*. Chicago: University of Chicago Press, 41-94. Re-issued under the title of *Introduction to Existentialism*, Ibid. 1959.

Grimsley, Ronald. *Existential Thought*. Cardiff: Wales Univ. Press, 1955, 39-89.

Heinemann, F. H. *Existentialism and the Modern Predicament*. London, 1954, 84-108.

Roberts, David E. "Martin Heidegger," in *Existentialism and Religious Belief*. New York: Oxford University Press, 1959, 145-192.

Schrader, George A., Jr. "Heidegger's ontology of human existence." *Review of Metaphysics*, Vol. 10, 1956, 35-56.

Sonnemann, Ulrich. *Existence and Therapy*. New York: Grune & Stratton, 1954, 102-131 and passim.

1960-1969

Allers, Rudolf. "The meaning of Heidegger." *The New Scholasticism*, Vol. 36, 1962, 445-474.

Ballard, Edward G. "A brief introduction to the philosophy of M. Heidegger," in *Studies in Recent Philosophy*. Tulane Studies in Philosophy, 12. New Orleans: Tulane University, 1963, 106-151.

Bixler, Julius S. "The failure of Martin Heidegger." *The Harvard Theological Review*, Vol. 56, 1963, 121-143.

Camele, A. "M. Heidegger and meaning for man." *Listening*, Vol. 1, 1966, 140-149.

Harries, Karsten. "Heidegger: The search for meaning," in *Existential Philosophy*. Kierkegaard to Merleau-Ponty, ed. by G. Schrader. New York. McGraw-Hill, 1967, pp. 161-208.

Naess, Arne. "Martin Heidegger," in *Four Modern Philosophers*. Carnap, Wittgenstein, Heidegger, Sartre. Trans. by Alastair Hannay (Phoneix Books, 337). Chicago-London: The Univ. of Chicago Press, 1969.

Rosen, Stanley. "Philosophy and ideology: Reflections on Heidegger." *Social Research*, Vol. 35, 1968, 260-285.

Wahl, Jean. *Philosophies of Existence*. An introduction to the basic thought of Kierkegaard, Heidegger, Jaspers, Marcel, Sartre. Transl. from the French by F. M. Lory. New York-London: Schocken Books, Routledge & Kegan Paul, 1969.

1970 to date

Caputo, John D. "Time and being in Heidegger." *The Modern Schoolman*, Vol. 50, 1973, 325-349.

Caputo, John D. "Being, ground and play in Heidegger." *Man and World*, Vol. 3, 1970, 26-48.

Caputo, John D. "The rose is without why. An interpretation of the later Heidegger." *Philosophy Today*, Vol. 15, 1971, 3-16.

Lichtheim, George. "On the rim of the volcano," in *Collected Essays*. New York: Viking Press, 1973, 234-246.

Löwith, Karl. "The nature of man and the world of nature. For Heidegger's 80th birthday." *The Southern Journal of Philosophy*, Vol. 8, 1970, 309-318.

Maurer, Reinhart. "From Heidegger to practical philosophy." Transl. from the German by Walter E. Wright. *Idealistic Studies*, Vol. 3, 1973, 133-162.

Pöggeler, Otto. "Heidegger today." *The Southern Journal of Philosophy*, Vol. 8, 1970, 273-308.

Scharff, Robert C. "On existentialist' readings of Heidegger." *The Southern Journal of Philosophy*, Vol. 2, 1971, 7-20.

Seidel, George J. "Heidegger: Philosopher for ecologists?" *Man and World*, Vol. 4, 1971, 93-99.

Smith, F. J. "A critique of Martin Heidegger." *Southwestern Journal of Philosophy*, Vol. 6, 1975, 137-156.

Smith, F. J. "Two Heideggerian analyses." *The Southern Journal of Philosophy*, Vol. 8, 1970, 409-420.

Solomon, Robert C. "Martin Heidegger: Being and being human," in *From Rationalism to Existentialism*. Existentialists and their nineteenth-century backgrounds. New York: Harper & Row, 1972, 174-243.

Spiegelberg, Herbert. "Martin Heidegger as a phenomenologist," in *The Phenomenological Movement*. A historical introduction, Vol 1. The Hague: Martinus Nijhoff, 1960, 271-355.

Stambaugh, Joan. "A Heidegger primer." *Philosophy Today*, Vol 19, 1975, 79-86.

Stegmüller, Wolfgang. "Existentialist ontology: Martin Heidegger," in *Main Currents in Contemporary German, English and American Philosophy*. Bloomington, Indiana: Indiana University Press, 1970, 133-180.

Van de Water, Lambert. "Being and being human: An impasse in Heidegger's thought." *International Philosophical Quarterly*, Vol. 13, 1973, 391-402.

III. PROPER NAMES

ADLER, Alfred

Lyons, Joseph. "Heidegger, Adler, and the paradox of fame." *Journal of Individual Psychology*, Vol. 17, 1961, 149-161.

ARISTOTLE

Sheehan, Thomas. "Heidegger, Aristotle and phenomenology." *Philosophy Today*, Vol. 19, Summer 1975, 87-95.

BARTH, Karl

Oshima, Sueo. "The ontological structures of human existence in Barth and Heidegger. Toward a theology of fellowship." *Rice University Studies*, Vol. 60, 1974, 103-129.

BECKETT, Samuel

Dobrez, Livio. "Beckett and Heidegger." *Southern Review* (University of Adelaide), Vol. 7, 1974, 140-153.

BINSWANGER, Ludwig

Burstow, Bonnie. "A critique of Binswanger's existential analysis." *Review of Existential Psychology & Psychiatry*, Vol. XVII, 1980-81, 245-252.

O'Donnell, Patrick. "Ludwig Binswanger and the poetics of compromise." *Review of Existential Psychology & Psychiatry*, Vol. XVII, 1980-81, 235-244.

BOSS, Medard

Boss, Medard. "Martin Heidegger's Zollikon seminars." *Rev. Exist. Psych. Psychiatry*, Vol. 16, 1978-79, 7-20.

Marshall, John M. "Martin Heidegger and Medard Boss: Dialogue between philosophy and psychotherapy." University of Oklahoma, 1974. *Diss. Abs.*, Vol. 36/05-A, p.2869.

BUDDHISM

Umehara, T. "Heidegger and Buddhism." *Philosophy East and West*, Vol. 20, 1970, 271-281.

CAMUS, Albert

Bennett, David. "Creativity in Heidegger and Camus." *Dialogue* (PST), Vol. 23, 1981, 43-50.

Nicholson, G. "Camus and Heidegger: anarchists." *University of Toronto Quarterly*, Vol. 41, 1971, 14-23.

CASSIRER, Ernst

Hamburg, Carl H. "A Cassirer-Heidegger seminar." *Philosophy and Phenomenological Research*, Vol. 25, 1964-1965, 208-222.

DERRIDA, Jacques

Ferguson, Frances C. "Reading Heidegger: Jacques Derrida and Paul de Man." *Boundary 2*, Vol. 4, Winter 1976, 593-610.

Riddel, Joseph N. "From Heidegger to Derrida to Chance: Doubling and (poetic) language." *Boundary 2*, Vol. 4, Winter 1976, 571-592.

DEWEY, John

Kestenbaum, Victor. "Phenomenology and Dewey's empiricism: A response to Leroy Troutner." [see infra.] *Educational Theory*, Vol. 22, 1972, 99-108.

Troutner, Leroy F. "The Dewey-Heidegger comparison revisited: A perspectival partnership for education." *Educational Theory*, Vol. 22, 1972, 28-44.

Troutner, Leroy F. "The Dewey-Heidegger comparison revisited. A reply and a clarification." *Educational Theory*, Vol. 22, 1972, 212-220.

Troutner, Leroy F. "John Dewey and the existential phenomenologist," in D.E. Denton, ed., *Existentialism and Phenomenology in Education*: Collected Essays. New York: Teachers College Press, 1974, 9-50.

DILTHEY, Wilhelm

Scharff, Robert Caesar. "Erlebnis' and Existenz'" Dilthey and Heidegger on the approach to human experience." Boston College, 1971. *Diss. Abs.*, Vol. 31/07-A, p.3603.

FREUD, Sigmund

Bartels, Martin. *Selbstbewusstsein und Unbewusstes*. Studien zu Freud und Heidegger. Berlin-New York: Walter de Gruyter, 1976, 215pp.

Battaglia, Rosemarie Angela. "Presence and absence in Joyce: Heidegger, Derrida, Freud." State University of New York, 1985. *Diss. Abs.*, Vol. 46/02-A, p.428.

Groth, H. Miles. "Interpretation for Freud and Heidegger." *International Review of Psychoanalysis*, Vol. 9, 1982, 67-74.

Heaton, J. M. "Freud and Heidegger on the interpretation of slips of the tongue." *Journal of the British Society for Phenomenology*, Vol. 13, 1982, 129-142.

Kockelmans, Joseph J. "Daseinsanalysis and Freud's Unconscious." *Review of Existential Psychology & Psychiatry*, Vol. XVII, 1980-81, 21-42.

Pomedi, Michael M. "Heidegger and Freud: The power of death." Duquesne University, 1972. *Diss. Abs.*, Vol. 33/05-A, p.2430.

Sarro, R. "The interpretation of the Oedipus myth according to Freud and Heidegger." *Journal of Existential Psychiatry*, Vol. 1, 478-500.

Vonessen, Heinz. Die Angst und das menschliche Dasein. Dargestellt an den Interpretationen der Angst bei S. Kierkegaard, S. Freud und M. Heidegger. Unpublished Ph.D. dissertation, Heidelberg, 1960, 240pp.

HEGEL, G. W. F.

Werkmeister, W. H. "Hegel and Heidegger," in *New Studies in Hegel's Philosophy*, ed. by W.E. Steinkraus. New York-Toronto: Holt, 1971, 142-155.

HÖLDERLIN, Friedrich

Harries, Karsten. "Heidegger and Hölderlin: The limits of language." *The Personalist*, Vol. 44, 1963, 5-23.

Lazarin, Michael John. "Wonder and the ontological difference. Heidegger and Hölderlin: As on a Holiday." Duquesne University, 1980. *Diss. Abs.*, Vol. 41/04-A, p.1638.

Warminski, Andrzej. *Readings in Interpretation: Hölderlin, Hegel, Heidegger.* Fwd. by Gasche, Rudolphe. University of Minnesota Press, 1987. 261pp.

HUSSERL, Edmund

Dreyfus, Hubert. "The priority of *the* world to *my* world. Heidegger's answer to Husserl [and Sartre]." *Man and World*, Vol. 8, 1975, 121-130.

Maloney, Thomas. "Phenomenological reduction in Husserl and Heidegger." *Dialogue* (PST), Vol. 29, 1986, 13-21.

Merlan, Philip. "Time consciousness in Husserl and Heidegger." *Philosophy and Phenomenological Research*, Vol. 8, 1947-1948, 23-54.

Mohanty, J. N. "Consciousness and existence: Remarks on the relation between Husserl and Heidegger." *Man and World*, Vol. 11, 1978, 324-335.

Schacht, R. L. "Husserlian and Heideggerian phenomenology." *Philosophical Studies*, Vol. 23, 1972, 292-314.

Smith, F. J. "Being and subjectivity: Heidegger and Husserl," in *Phenomenology in Perspective*, ed. by F.J. Smith. The Hague: Martinus Nijhoff, 1970, 122-156.

Stapleton, Timothy J. "Husserlian themes in Heidegger: the basic problems of phenomenology." *Philosophy Today*, Vol. 27, 1983, 3-17.

Stewart, M. "The problem of logical psychologism for Husserl and the early Heidegger." *Journal of the British Society for Phenomenology*, Vol. 10, 1979, 184-193.

JASPERS, Karl

Gugel, Raymond E. "Jaspers' critique of Heidegger: The arrogance of thought." *International Philosophical Quarterly*, Vol. 27, 1987, 161-171.

Heenan, Michael Joseph. "A comparative analysis of the movement from existence to transcendence in the philosophies of Heidegger, Jaspers, and Marcel." St. John's University, 1985. *Diss. Abs.*, Vol. 46/02-A, p.441.

Krell, David F. "The Heidegger-Jaspers relationship." *Journal of the British Society for Phenomenology*, Vol. 9, 1978, 126-129.

JUNG, Carl G.

Avens, Robert S. "Heidegger and archetypal psychology." *International Philosophical Quarterly*, Vol. 22, 1982, 183-202.

Capobianco, Richard M. "A philosophical examinaton of C.G. Jung's notion of the self. Boston College, 1986. *Diss. Abs.*, Vol. 47/-5A, p.1748.

Parkes, Graham R. "Time and the soul: Heidegger's ontology as the ground for an archetypal psychology." University of California, Berkeley, 1978. *Diss. Abs.*, Vol. 39/09-A, p.5555.

Soleau, Jeffrey K. "The whole and the holy: Thing' and Symbol' as structures of integration in the thought of Martin Heidegger and Carl Jung." Duke University, 1985. *Diss. Abs.*, Vol. 46/08-A, p.2336.

KAFKA, Franz

Kuhr, A. "Neurotische Aspeckte bei Heidegger und Kafka." *Zeitschrift für psychosomatische Medizin*, Vol. 1, 1954-1955, 217-227.

KIERKEGAARD, Søren

Dreyfus, Hubert L. and Jane Rubin. "You can't get something for nothing: Kierkegaard and Heidegger on how not to overcome nihilism." *Inquiry*, Vol. 30, 1987, 33-75.

Stavrides, Maria M. "The concept of existence in Kierkegaard and Heidegger." Columbia University, 1952. *Diss. Abs.*, Vol. 12/05, p.641.

Wyschograd, Michael. "Kierkegaard and Heidegger—The ontology of existence." Columbia University, 1954. *Diss. Abs.*, Vol. W1954.

LACAN, Jacques

DeNeef, A. Leigh. *Traherne in Dialogue: Heidegger, Lacan & Derrida*. Duke University Press, 1988. 275pp.

Medina, Angel. "Heidegger, Lacan and the boundaries of existence: Whole and partial subjects in psychoanalysis." *Man and World*, Vol. 18, 1985, 389-403.

Richardson, William J. "The mirror inside: The problem of the self." *Review of Existential Psychology & Psychiatry*, Vol. XVI, 95-112.

Wilden, Anthony. "On Lacan: Psychoanalysis, language, and communication." Univ. of California, San Diego: *Contemporary Psychoanalysis*, Vol. 9, 1973, 445-470.

LEVINAS, Emmanuel

Keyes, C. D. "An Evaluation of Levinas' critique of Heidegger." *Research in Phenomenology*, Vol. 2, 1972, 121-142.

O'Connor, Noreen. "Being and the good: Heidegger and Levinas." *Philosophical Studies* (Ireland), Vol. 17, 1980, 212-220.

MARCEL, Gabriel

Snyder, Roger David. "An approach to some philosophical concepts of Marcel and Heidegger, using various psychological techniques." Graduate Theological Union, 1972. *Diss. Abs.*, Vol. 33/10-B, p.5040.

MARCUSE, Herbert

Ahlers, R. "Technologie und Wissenschaft bei Heidegger und Marcuse." *Zeitschrift für philosophische Forschung*, Vol. 25, 1971, 575-589.

MARX, Karl

De George, R. T. "Heidegger and the Marxists." *Studies in Soviet Thought*, Vol. 5, 1965, 289-298.

Zimmerman, Michael. "Marx and Heidegger on the technological domination of nature." *Philosophy Today*, Vol. 23, 1979, 99-112.

MASLOW, Abraham

Keogh, Andrew. "Authenticity and self-actualization: A rapprochement between the philosophy of Heidegger and the psychology of Maslow." University of Toronto (Canada), 1978. *Diss. Abs.*, Vol. 39/07-A, p.4323.

MERLEAU-PONTY, Maurice

Camele, Anthony. "Time in Merleau-Ponty and Heidegger." *Philosophy Today*, Vol. 19, Fall 1975, 256-268.

Hoeller, Keith (Ed.). *Merleau-Ponty and Psychology* (Studies in Existential Psychology & Psychiatry), Seattle: *Review of Existential Psychology and Psychiatry*, 1985, 262pp,

Kockelmans, Joseph J. "On the function of psychology in Merleau-Ponty's early works." *Review of Existential Psychology and Psychiatry*, Vol. 18, 1983, 119-142.

NIETZSCHE, Friedrich

Bales, Eugene F. "Beyond revenge: Paths in Heidegger and Nietzsche." *Philosophy Today*, Vol. 30, 1986, 137-150.

Gelven, Michael. "From Nietzsche to Heidegger." *Philosophy Today*, Vol. 25, 1981, 68-80.

Gray, J. Glenn. "Heidegger evaluates' Nietzsche." *Journal of the History of Ideas*, Vol. 14, 1953, 340-349.

Havas, Randall E. "Nietzsche, nihilism, and the autonomy of reason: Heidegger's interpretation of the will to power." Harvard University, 1986. *Diss. Abs.*, Vol. 47/11-A, p.4100.

Howey, Richard L. "A critical examination of Heidegger's and Jasper's interpretations of Nietzsche." University of Southern California, 1969. *Diss. Abs.*, Vol. 30/05-A, p.2076.

Krell, David F. "Art and truth in raging discord: Heidegger and Nietzsche on the will to power." *Boundary 2*, Vol. 4, Winter 1976, 379-392.

Krell, David F. "Nietzsche and the task of thinking: Martin Heidegger's reading of Nietzsche." Duquesne University, 1971. *Diss. Abs.*, Vol. 32/09-A, p.5288.

Lampert, Laurence A. "The views of history in Nietzsche and Heidegger." Northwestern Univerity, 1971. *Diss. Abs.*, Vol. 32/06-A, 3370.

Magnus, Bernd. "Heidegger and Nietzsche's doctrine of eternal recurrence." Columbia University, 1967. *Diss. Abs.*, Vol. 31/06-A, 2975.

Okhamafe, E. Imafedia. "Zarathustra and Heidegger's call of conscience." *Journal of the British Society for Phenomenology*, Vol. 14, 1983, 99-103.

Schutte, Ofelia. "The solitude of Nietzsche's Zarathustra." *Review of Existential Psychology & Psychiatry*, Vol. XVII, 1980-81, 209-222.

Smith, P. Christopher. "Heidegger's break with Nietzsche and the principle of subjectivity." *The Modern Schoolman*, Vol. 52, 1974-1975, 227-245.

Vincenzo, Joseph Pasqual. "Nietzsche and Heidegger: The truth of nihilism." Pennsylvania State University, 1984. *Diss. Abs.*, Vol. 45/06-A, 1781.

Zimmerman, Michael E. "A comparison of Nietzsche's overman and Heidegger's authentic self." *The Southern Journal of Philosophy*, Vol. 14, Summer 1976, 213-232.

RYLE, Gilbert

Murray, Michael. "Heidegger and Ryle: Two versions of phenomenology." *Review of Metaphysics*, Vol. 27, 1973-1974, 88-111.

SARTRE, Jean-Paul

Schroeder, William R. "Others: An examination of Sartre and his predecessors." University of Michigan, 1979. *Diss. Abs.*, Vol. 40/02-A, p.906.

SCHELER, Max

Frings, Manfred S. "Heidegger and Scheler." *Philosophy Today*, Vol. 12, 1968, 21-30.

TILLICH, Paul

O'Meara, Th. F. "Tillich and Heidegger: A structural relationship." *The Harvard Theological Review*, Vol. 61, 1968, 249-261.

TRAKL, Georg

Fóti, Véronique. "The path of the stranger: On Heidegger's interpretation of Georg Trakl." *Review of Existential Psychology & Psychiatry*, Vol. XVII, 1980-81, 223-234.

WITTGENSTEIN, Ludwig

Erickson, Stephen A. "Meaning and language in Heidegger and Wittgenstein." *Man and World*, Vol. 1, 1968, 563-586.

Harries, Karsten. "Wittgenstein and Heidegger: The relationship of the philosopher to language. " *Journal of Value Inquiry*, Vol. 2, 1968, 281-291.

IV. SUBJECTS

AESTHETICS

Bartky, S. L. "Heidegger's philosophy of art." *British Journal of Aesthetics*, Vol. 9, 1969, 353-371.

Bossart, W. H. "Heidegger's theory of art." *Journal of Aesthetics and Art Criticism*, Vol. 27, 1968-1969, 55-66.

Hall, R. L. "Heidegger and the space of art." *The Journal of Existentialism*, Vol. 8, 1967-1968, 91-108.

Hamrick, William S. "Heidegger and the objectivity of aesthetic truth." *The Journal of Value Inquiry*, Vol. 5, 1970-1971, 120-130.

Kaelin, Eugene F. "Notes toward an understanding of Heidegger's aesthetics," in *Phenomenology and Existentialism*, ed. by Lee & Mandelbaum. Baltimore: The Johns Hopkins University Press, 1967, 59-92.

Stack, George J. "The being of the work of art in Heidegger." *Philosophy Today*, Vol. 13, 1969, 159-173.

ANXIETY (Angst, Dread)

Gray, J. Glenn. "Homelessness and anxiety: Sources of the modern mode of being." *Virginia Quarterly Review*, Vol. 48, Winter 1972, 24-39.

Mood, John J. "Leadbelly on Angst, Heidegger on the blues." *Philosophy Today*, Vol. 14, 1970, 161-167.

Petot, Jean Michel. "Anxiety and existence." *Perspectives Psychiatriques*, Vol. 56, 1976, 97-109.

Rauhala, Lauri. "The existential analysis of anxiety and its implications for clinical psychology." *Psychiatria Fennica*, 1974, 191-200.

Rose, John Marcus. "Plotinus and Heidegger on anxiety and the nothing." Georgetown University. *Diss. Abs.*, Vol. 47/07-A, 1986, 2614.

Strasser, Stephan. "The concept of dread in the philosophy of Heidegger." *The Modern Schoolman*, Vol. 35, 1957-1958, 1-20.

Towse, Margaret S. "To be or not to be': Anxiety following bereavement." *British Journal of Medical Psychology*, Vol. 59, 1986, 149-156.

Tweedie, Donald F., Jr. "The significance of dread in the thought of Kierkegaard and Heidegger." Boston University Graduate School, 195. *Diss. Abs.*, Vol. W1954.

AUTHENTICITY

Ciaffa, Jay A. "Toward an understanding of Heidegger's conception of the inter-relation between authentic and inauthentic existence." *J. Brit. Soc. Phenomenol.*, Vol. 18, 1987, 49-50.

Grant, Grell V. "Heidegger on inauthenticity and authenticity." *Gnosis*, Vol. 1, 1979, 81-94.

Grene, Marjorie. "Authenticity: An existential virtue." *Ethics*, Vol. 62, July 1952, 266-274.

Kellner, Douglas Mackay. "Heidegger's concept of authenticity. . ." Columbia University. *Diss. Abs.*, Vol. 34/07-A, 1973, 4327.

BEING

Pöggeler, Otto. "Being as appropriation." *Philosophy Today*, Vol. 19, Summer 1975, 151-178.

Watson, James R. "Being-there: The neighborhood of being." *Philosophy Today*, Vol. 19, Summer 1975, 118-130.

BUDDHISM

Hellner, Timothy James. "Two kinds of thinking: As represented in the Buddhist tradition and the writings of Heidegger." University of Louisville. *Diss. Abs.*, Vol. 15/04, 1977, 233.

Steffney, John. "Heidegger and zen: A study of radicalization." Temple University. *Diss. Abs.*, Vol. 41/05-A, 1980, 2167.

CHOICE

Leyvraz, Jean-P. "Le moment du choix chez Heidegger." *Studia Philosophica Gandensia*, Vol. 26, 1966, 139-158.

CONCERN

Stack, George J. "Concern in Kierkegaard and Heidegger." *Philosophy Today*, Vol. 13, 1969, 26-35.

CONSCIOUSNESS AND INTENTIONALITY

Olafson, Frederick A. "Consciousness and intentionality in Heidegger's thought." *American Philosophical Quarterly*, Vol. 12, 1975, 91-103.

Scott, Charles E. "Heidegger and consciousness." *The Southern Journal of Philosophy*, Vol. 8, 1970, 355-372.

DASEIN & DASEINSANALYTIK

Biemel, Walter. "Heidegger's Begriff des Daseins." *Studia Catholica*, Vol. 24, 1949, 113, 129.

Binswanger, Ludwig, *Being-in-the-World*. Selected Papers of Ludwig Binswanger. Ed. by Jacob Needleman. New York: Basic Books, 1963.

Binswanger, Ludwig. "Existential Analysis and Psychotherapy." *Psychoanalytic Review*, Vol. 45, 1958-59, 79-83.

Binswanger, Ludwig. "The Existential Analysis School of Thought," in *Existence*. A new dimension in psychiatry and psychology. Ed. by Rollo May, Ernest Angel, and Henri F. Ellenberger. New York: Basic Books, 1958, 191-213.

Binswanger, Ludwig. "Heidegger's Analytic of Existence and Its Meaning for Psychiatry," in *Being-in-the-World*. By Ludwig Binswanger. Ed. and transl. by Jacob Needleman. New York: Basic Books, 1963, 206-222.

Boss, Medard. "Die Bedeutung der Daseinsanalyze für die Psychologie und Psychiatrie." *Psyche*, Vol. 6, 1952-1953, 178-186.

Boss, Medard. *Psychoanalysis and Daseinsanalysis*. Transl. by Ludwig B. Lefebvre. New York: Basic Books, 1963.

Khan, Mohammad A. "Daseinsanalyse or existential analysis." *Pakistan Philosophical Journal*, Vol. 12, July-Dec. 1973, 60-68.

Kunz, H. "Die Bedeutung der Daseinsanalytik Martin Heidegger für die Psychologie und die philosphische Anthropologie," in *Martin Heideggers*

Einfluss auf die Wissenschaften, ed. by C. Astrada et al. Bern: Francke-Verlag, 1949.

May, Rollo, Ernest Angel, and Henri F. Ellenberger (eds). *Existence* A new dimention in psychiatry and psychology. New York: Basic Books, 1958.

Taverna P. "Le basi della Daseinsanalyse': Da Heidegger a Binswanger [1]." *Neuropsichiatria*, Vol. 24, 37-49.

Weber, A. *"Daseinsanalyse* as an approach." *Zeitschrift für Kinder und Jugendpsychiatrie*, Vol. 4, 1976, 113-123.

DEATH

Bukala, C. R. "Heidegger plus: A dialectic of living-dying-living." *Philosophy Today*, Vol. 27, 1983, 154-168.

Canine, John David. "The educational implications of Heidegger's and Kierkegaard's concepts of death." Wayne State University. *Diss. Abs.*, Vol. 45/02-A, 1983, 449.

Choron, Jacques. *Death and Western Thought*. New York: Collier, 1967, 239-247.

Dauenhauer, Bernard P. "On death and birth." *The Personalist*, Vol. 57, Spring 1976, 162-170.

Edwards, Paul. "Heidegger and death as possibility'." *Mind*, Vol. 84, 1975, 548-566.

Edwards, Paul. "Existentialism and death: A survey of some confusions and absurdities," in *Philosophy, Science and Method*. Essays in honor of Ernest Nagel, ed. by S. Morgenbesser et al. New York: Columbia Univ. Press, 1969, 473-505.

Edwards, Paul. "Heidegger and death: A deflationary critique." *The Monist*, Vol. 59, April 1976, 161-186.

Gray, J. Glenn. "Martin Heidegger: On anticipating my own death." *The Personalist*, Vol. 46, 1965, 439-458.

Hammett, Jenny Lee Yates. "Existential conceptions of death: Heidegger, Tillich, Rilke." Syracuse University. *Diss. Abs.*, Vol. 34/10-A, 1973, 6699.

Hoeller, Keith. See SUICIDE.

Hoffman, Frederick J. *The Mortal No: Death and the modern imagination*. Princeton: Princeton University Press, 1964, 424-452.

213

Langfur, Stephen Joseph. "Death's second self: A response to Heidegger's question of being through the insights of Buber and the findings of Freud." Syracuse University. *Diss. Abs.*, Vol. 38/08-A, 1977, 4883.

Magurshak, Daniel John. "Death and freedom: A critical analysis of Heidegger's notion of Sein-zum-tode." Northwestern University. *Diss. Abs.*, Vol. 37/07-A, 1976, 4419.

May, William Francis. "Dread before death and revolt against death: A study of Heidegger and Camus." Yale University, 1962. *Diss. Abs.*, Vol. X1962.

O'Mahony, B. E. "Martin Heidegger's existential analysis of death." *Philosophical Studies (Maynooth)*, Vol. 18, 1969, 58-75.

Paskow, Alan. "What do I fear in facing my death?" *Man and World*, Vol. 8, May 1975, 146-156.

Pindle, Arthur Jackson, Jr. "A critical study of Heidegger's interpretation of death." Yale University. *Diss. Abs.*, Vol. 39/04-A, 1978, 2343.

Singh, R. Raj. "Death—contemplation and philosophy: Heidegger and the legacy of Socrates." *De Phil.*

Slote, Michael A. "Existentialism and the fear of dying." *American Quarterly*, Vol. 12, Jan. 1975, 17-28.

DECISION MAKING

Tripp, Charles James. "The comparative study of decision making methodologies: A look at the decision making framework and Heidegger's Being and Time'." Wayne State University. *Diss. Abs.*, Vol. 35/12-A, 1974, 7989.

DREAMS

Foucault, Michel and Binswanger, Ludwig. *Dream and existence*. Trans. by F. Williams and Jacob Needleman. Seattle: Review of Existential Psychology and Psychiatry, 1986, 112pp.

EASTERN PHILOSOPHY

Herman, Paul Edward. "The contributions of Ramana Maharshi and Heidegger to an East-West integral psychology." California Institute of Asian Studies. *Diss. Abs.*, Vol. 35/12-B, 1974, 6072.

EDUCATION

Khoobyar, Helen. "Educational import of Heidegger's notion of truth as letting-be." *Philosophy of Education*, Vol. 30, 1974, 47-58.

Mayer, A. "Martin Heideggers Beitrag zur Pädagogik." *Zeitschrift für Pädagogik*, Vol. 6, 1960, 138-148.

Rice, Irvin K. "Pedagogic theory and the search for being: Denton's direction in the epistemology of education," *Educational Theory*, Vol. 25, Fall 1975, 389-396.

ENCOUNTER

Uslar, D. von. "Vom Wesen der Gegegnung im Hinblick auf die Unterschedung von Selbstein und Sein Selbst bei Heidegger." *Zeitschrift für philosophische Forschung*, Vol. 13, 1959, 85-101.

ETHICS

Butkus, Robert G. J. "Heidegger's thought and ethics." University of Waterloo (Canada), 1976. *Diss. Abs.*, Vol. 37/06-A, 3688.

Caputo, John D. "Heidegger's original ethics." *The New Scholasticism*, Vol. 45, 1971, 127-138. [See Weber infra].

Gallagher, James. "The ontological contexts for the ethical elements in Being and Time' and Being and Nothingness' (Heidegger, Sartre)." New School for Social Research. *Diss. Abs.*, Vol. 44/12-A, 1983, 3712.

Nagami, Isamu. "Human existence and the Cartesian ego in the work of Heidegger and Watsuji: An inquiry on ethics and technological rationality. . ." University of Chicago, 1977. *Diss. Abs.*, Vol. X, 1978. 15/04, 1977, 233.

Tyman, Stephen Thomas. "Heidegger and the proto-ethical motive for overcoming the ambiguity in metaphysics." University of Toronto (Canada). *Diss. Abs.*, Vol. 42/01-A, 1980, 253.

Warnock, Mary. *Existentialist Ethics*. London: Macmillan New York: St. Martin's Press, 1967.

Weber, R. "A critique of Heidegger's concept of 'solicitude'." *The New Scholasticsm*, Vol. 42, 1968, 537-560. [See Caputo supra].

EVERYDAYNESS (Alltäglichkeit)

Schoenborn, A. von. "Heideggerian everydayness." *The Southwestern Journal of Philosophy*, Vol. 3, 1972, 103-110.

Zimmerman, Michael. "On discriminating everydayness, unownedness, and falling in *Being and Time*. *Research in Phenomenology*, Vol. 5, 1975, 109-128.

EXISTENCE

Acikgenc, Alparslan. "The concept of existence in Sadra and Heidegger." The University of Chicago. *Diss. Abs.*, Vol. X, 1983.

Hinners, Richard. "The freedom and finiteness of existence in Heidegger." *The New Scholasticism*, Vol. 33, 1959, 32-48.

Schrader, George A. "Heidegger's ontology of human existence." *Review of Metaphysics*, Vol. 10, 1956-1957, 35-56.

EXISTENTIALISM

Kelner, M. S. "The concept of existential phenomenology in foreign psychiatry." *Zhurnal Nevropatologii i Psikhiatrii*, Vol. 72, 1972, 463-469.

Tavrizyan, G. M. "The problem of the subject in French existentialism." *Voprosy Filosofii*, Vol. 3, 1975, 48-59.

Troutner, Leroy Franklin. "Educational implications of existentialism: An analysis and comparison of Martin Heidegger and John Dewey. . ." Stanford University, 1962. *Diss. Abs.*, Vol. 23/06, 2035.

Von Schoenborn, Alexander. "Being, man, and questioning: An ontological prolegomenon to Heidegger's existentialism." Tulane University. *Diss. Abs.*, Vol. 32/05-A, 1971, 2750.

Zimmerman, Michael. "Heidegger's "existentialism" revisited." *International Philosophical Quarterly*, Vol. 24, 1984, 219-236.

EXPERIENCE

Rather, L. J. "Existential experience in Whitehead and Heidegger." *Review of Existential Psychology and Psychiatry*, Vol. 1, 1961, 113-119.

FALL

Freud, E. H. "Man's fall in Heidegger's philosophy." *The Journal of Religion*, Vol. 24, 1944, 180-187.

Tropea, Gregory. *Religion, Ideology & Heidegger's Concept of Falling*. Scholars Press, 1987. 261pp.

FREEDOM

Davis, Harold A. D. "Freedom and the fourfold in the thought of Martin Heidegger." McMaster University (Canada), 1974. *Diss. Abs.*, Vol. X, 1974.

Lessing, Arthur. "Man is Freedom:' A critical study of the conception of human freedom in the philosophies of Martin Heidegger and Jean-Paul Sartre." Tulane University. *Diss. Abs.*, Vol. 28/04-A, 1966, 1470.

Trager, John Duffy. "Freedom in Heidegger." University of Louisville. *Diss. Abs.*, Vol. 09/03, 1970, 156.

GROUND

Caputo, John David. "The way back into the ground: An interpretation of the path of Heidegger's thought." Bryn Mawr College. *Diss. Abs.*, Vol. 29/11-A, 1968, 4046.

GUILT

Brook, Roger. "Jung and the phenomenology of guilt." *Journal of Analytical Psychology*, Vol. 30, 1985, 165-184.

Chun, Jay Kyung. "The relation to education of guilt and conscience in the philosophy of Soren Kierkegaard and Martin Heidegger." Columbia University. *Diss. Abs.*, Vol. 46/08-A, 1985, 2225.

Doz, André. "L'ontologie fondementale et le problème de la culpabilité." *Revue da Métaphysique et de Morale*, Vol. 61, 1956, 166-194.

Gelven, Michael. "Guilt and human meaning." *Humanitas* (Pittsburgh), Vol. 9, 1972, 69-81.

Sasso, Javier. "La teoría de la culpabilidad en Heidegger." *Cuadernos Uruguayos de Filosofia*, Vol. 5, 1968, 83-119.

Schalow, Frank. "The hermeneutical design of Heidegger's analysis of guilt." *Southern Journal of Philosophy*, Vol. 23, 1985, 361-376.

Woocher, J. S. "From guilt feelings to reconciliation: Images of modern man." *Review of Existential Psychology and Psychiatry*, Vol. 15, 1977, 186-209.

HERMENEUTICS

Barratt, Barnaby B. "Critical notes on Packer's hermeneutic inquiry',. *American Psychologist*, Vol. 43, 1988, 131-133.

Day, Willard. "Hermeneutics and behaviorism." *American Psychologist*, Vol. 43, 1988, 129.

Packer, Martin J. "Hermeneutic inquiry: Response to criticisms." *American Psychologist*, Vol. 43, 1988, 133-136.

Russell, Robert L. "A critical interpretation of Packer's Hermeneutic inquiry in the study of human conduct'." *American Psychologist*, Vol. 43, 1988, 130-131.

HOLY

Harries, Karsten. "Heidegger's conception of the holy," *The Personalist*, Vol. 47, 1966, 169-184.

IMAGINATION

Lichtigfeld, A. "Imagination in Kant and Heidegger." *Filosofia* (Torino), Vol. 18, 1967, 807-836.

INTERSUBJECTIVITY

Dallmayr, Fred R. "Heidegger on intersubjectivity." *Human Studies*, Vol. 3, 1980, 221-246.

IRRATIONAL

Tint, H. "Heidegger and the irrational." *Proceedings of the Aristotelian Society*, Vol. 57, 1956-1957, 253-268.

LANGUAGE (see also Poetry)

Borgmann, Albert. "Language in Heidegger's philosophy." *The Journal of Existentialism*, Vol. 7, 1966-1967, 161-180.

Boufard, Albert Edmund. "Language and the ontological difference: Heidegger's quest for an experience with authentic language." Duquesne University. *Diss. Abs.*, Vol. 32/01-A, 1970, 482.

Budd, Matthew A. and Zimmerman, Michael E. "The potentiating clinician: Combining scientific and linguistic competence." *Advances*, Vol. 3, 1986, 40-55.

Conway, Jeremiah Patrick. "Why to poetry? A study of Martin Heidegger's philosophy of language." Yale University. *Diss. Abs.*, Vol. 40/01-A, 1978, 305.

Dean, Thomas Jackson. "The logic of language and persons: A methodological introduction to the interpretive metaphysics of Heidegger." Columbia University. *Diss. Abs.*, Vol. 30/04-A, 1968, 1597.

Graybeal, Jean McConnell. "Language and the feminine' in Nietzsche and Heidegger." Syracuse University. *Diss. Abs.*, Vol. 47/09-A, 1986, 3456.

Grugan, Arthur Anthony. "Thought and poetry: language as man's homecoming. . ." Duquesne University. *Diss. Abs.*, Vol. 33/08-A, 1972, 4473.

Hertz, Peter Donald. "Martin Heidegger: Language and the foundations of interpretation." Stanford University. *Diss. Abs.*, Vol. 28/07-A, 1967, 2685.

Lilly, Reginald Storrs. "The place of language: Art and nihilism in Nietzsche and Heidegger." Duquesne University. *Diss. Abs.*, Vol. 46/01-A, 1984, 171.

Owens, Wayne Dean. "The contribution of phenomenology to the philosophy of language: A study of the language phenomenon in Heidegger and

Merleau-Ponty." De Paul University, 1982. *Diss. Abs.*, Vol. 43/04-A, 1175.

Richardson, William J. "Heidegger and the origin of language." *International Philosophical Quarterly*, Vol. 2, 1962, 406-416.

Scott, Charles E. *The Language of Difference*. Humanities Press International, Inc., 1987, 260pp.

Steiner, Kenneth Mark. "Thinking being and language in the work of Martin Heidegger." State University of New York at Binghamton. *Diss. Abs.*, Vol. 37/06-A, 1977, 3702.

Stewart, John. "Speech and human being: A complement to semiotics." *Quarterly Journal of Speech*, Vol. 72, 1986, 55-73.

White, David Allen. "Heidegger and the language of poetry." University of Toronto (Canada). *Diss. Abs.*, Vol. 36/05-A, 1973, 2869.

Zeman, K. "The language of a symptom and symbol." *Ceskoslovenska Psychiatrie*, Vol. 73, 1977, 263-269.

LEARNING

McNally, Patricia Ann. "Language and learning: An interpretive study of the work of Martin Heidegger and an exploration of the implications of his thought for processes of learning." University of Massachusetts. *Diss. Abs.*, Vol. 41/03-A, 1980, 980.

LIFE

McGinley, John Willard. "The question of life in Heidegger's Being and Time'." Boston College. *Diss. Abs.*, Vol. 32/01-A, 1971, 490.

LITERATURE

Spanos, William V., editor. *Martin Heidegger & the Question of Literature: Toward a Postmodern Literary Hermeneutics*. Indiana University Press, 1980. 352pp.

LOVE

Peery, Rebekah Smith. "An interpretation of personal love founded on the phenomenological ontology of Martin Heidegger." Vanderbilt University. *Diss. Abs.*, Vol. 35/07-A, 1974, 4621.

MADNESS

Allen, Jeffner. "Madness and the Poet." *Review of Existential Psychology and Psychiatry*, Vol. 16 (1978-79), pp. 72-80.

Scott, Charles E. "Heidegger, madness, and well-being." *Southwestern Journal of Philosophy*, Vol. 4, 1973, 157-177.

MAN

Alderman, Harold. "Heidegger on being human." *Philosophy Today*, Vol. 15, 1971, 16-29.

Gray, J. Glenn. "The new image of man in M. Heidegger's philosophy," in *European Philosophy Today*, ed. by G. L. Kline. Chicago: Quadrangle Books, 1965, 31-59.

Luegenbiehl, Heinz Carl. "The essence of man: An approach to the philosophy of Martin Heidegger." Purdue University. *Diss. Abs.*, Vol. 38/02-A, 1976, 847.

Renaut, Alain. "Qu'est-ce que l'homme?" *Man and World*, Vol. 9, 1976, 3-44.

Silverman, Hugh J. "Man and the self as identity of difference." *Philosophy Today*, Vol. 19, 1975, 131-136.

MEANING

Bridges, Thomas William. "The concept of meaning in Heidegger's Sein und Zeit'." Columbia University. *Diss. Abs.*, Vol. 35/10-A, 1972, 6757.

Gelven, Michael. "Martin Heidegger's understanding of ultimate meaning and reality." *Ultim. Real Mean.*, Vol. 3, 1980, 114-134.

Stack, George J. "Heidegger's concept of meaning." *Philosophy Today*, Vol. 17, 1973, 255-266.

METHOD

Gans, Steven Lawrence. "An analysis of the philosophical methodology of Martin Heidegger." Pennsylvania State University. *Diss. Abs.*, Vol. 29/03-A, 1967, 929.

MOOD

Ballard, Bruce William. "The role of mood in Heidegger's ontology." University of Texas at Austin. *Diss. Abs.*, 1986, Vol. 47/12-A, 4409.

Gendlin, Eugene T. "*Befindlichkeit*: Heidegger and the philosophy of psychology." *Review of Existential Psychology & Psychiatry*, Vol. 16, 1978-79, 43-71.

Pressler, Charles Alan. "Portraits of the life-world: Hegel, Heidegger, and the ontology of emotions." University of Notre Dame. *Diss. Abs.*, Vol. 46/03-A, 1985, 814.

Smith, Joseph H. "The Heideggerian and psychoanlytic concepts of mood." *Human Inquiries*, Vol. 10, 1970, 101-111.

Smith, Quentin. "On Heidegger's theory of moods." *Modern Schoolman*, Vol. 58, 1981, 211-235.

NIHILISM

Petrick, Eileen Bagus. "Heidegger on nihilism and the finitude of philosophy. . ." Pennsylvania State University. *Diss. Abs.*, Vol. 35/01-A, 1973, 520.

PAIN

Clark, Orville. "Pain and being: An essay in Heideggerian ontology." *The Southwestern Journal of Philosophy*, Vol. 4, 1973, 179-190.

PHENOMENOLOGY

Boelen, Bernard. "M. Heidegger as a phenomenologist," in *Phenomenological Perspectives*, historical and systematic essays in honor of Herbert Spiegelberg. Ed. by Philip J. Bossert (Phanomenologica, 62). The Hague: Martinus Nijhoff, 1975, 93-114.

Kersten, Fred. "Heidegger and transcendental phenomenology." *The Southern Journal of Philosophy*, Vol. 11, 1973, 202-215.

Seeburger, Francis F. "Heidegger and the phenomenological reduction." *Philosophy and Phenomenological Research*, Vol. 36, 1975, 212-221.

Spiegelberg, Herbert. See above HUSSERL.

Watson, James R. "Heidegger's hermenutic phenomenology." *Philosophy Today*, Vol. 15, 1971, 30-43.

POETRY

Deck, Barbara Ann. "The healing power of poetry: From Heidegger's Poesis' to illustrations from representative nineteenth-century thinkers." Brandeis University. *Diss. Abs.*, Vol. 38/05-A, 1977, 2843.

Gray, J. Glenn. "Poets and thinkers: Their kindred roles in the philosophy of M. Heidegger," in *Phenomenology and Existentialism*, ed. by Lee & Mandelbaum. Baltimore: Johns Hopkins University Press, 1967, 93-111.

Halliburton, David. *Poetic Thinking: An Approach to Heidegger*. University of Chicago Press, 1982.

Hoeller, Keith. "Is Heidegger really a poet?" *Philosophical Topics*, Vol. 12, 1981, 121-138.

Hoeller, Keith. "Thinking and poetizing in Heidegger's turning." Pennsylvania State University, 1982. *Diss. Abs.*, Vol. 43/01-A, 184.

White, David A. *Heidegger & the Language of Poetry*. University of Nebraska Press, 1978, 245pp.

PRIMITIVE

Henry, J. The term primitive' in Kierkegaard and Heidegger." *Neue Züricher Zeitung*, No. 2898, 1-2 of 27.9.1959. [Fernausgabe, No. 264, 26.9.1959].

PSYCHIATRY, PSYCHOLOGY

Binswanger, Ludwig. "M. Heidegger und die Psychiatrie." *Neue Züricher Zeitung*, No. 2898, 1-2 of 27.9.1959

Brinkmann, D. "Existentialismus und Tiefenpsychologie," in *Actas del primer Congreso nacional de Filosofia*, 2, Mendoza 1949, 1346-1360.

Campo. M. "Psicologia, logica e ontologia nel primo Heidegger." *Rivista di Filosofiea Neo-Scolastica*, Vol. 31, 1939, 474-491.

Hoeller, Keith, editor. *Heidegger & Psychology*. Seattle: Review of Existential Psychology & Psychiatry, 1988. 200pp.

Kung, H. See DASEIN.

Meinertz, J. *Moderne Seinsphilosophie in ihrer Bedeutung für die Psycholgie. Heidelberg, 1948.*

Meinertz, J. *Philosophie, Teifenpsychologie, Existenz.* Tiefenpsychologische Keime und Probleme in der Philosophie des Idealismus und in der Existenzphilosophie. München-Basel, 1958.

Tymieniecka, Anna-Teresa. "Cosmos, nature and man and the foundations of psychology," in *Heidegger and the Path of Thinking*, ed. with an introd. by John Sallis, Pittsburgh, Pa; Duquesne University Press, 1970, pp. 191-220.

PSYCHOLOGISM

Stewart, Roderick Milford. "Psychologism, Sinn and Urteil in the early writings of Heidegger." Syracuse University. *Diss. Abs.*, Vol. 39/02-A, 1977, 924.

PSYCHOTHERAPY

Chessick, Richard D. "Heidegger for psychotherapists." *American Journal of Psychotherapy*, Vol. 40, 1986, 83-95.

Lukacher, Ned. *Primal Scenes: Literature, Philosophy, Psychoanalysis.* Cornell University Press, 1988, 344pp.

Westerman, Michael A. "Meaning and psychotherapy: A hermeneutic recon-
ceptualization of insight-oriented, behavioral, and strategic approaches."
International Journal of Eclectic Psychotherapy, Vol. 5, 1986, 47-68.

REASON

Boss, Medard. "Is psychotherapy rational or rationalistic?" *Review of Existential Psychology & Psychiatry*, Vol. XIX, 1984-85, 115-128.

RELIGION

Bhadra, Mrinal K. "The existentialist basis of the psychology of religion."
Samiksa, Vol. 29, 1975, 95-109.

Cushman, Marlene Lila. "Heidegger and the limits of theology." Pennsylvania
State University. *Diss. Abs.*, Vol. 47/04-A, 1986, 1354.

Gall, Robert Stephen. "Beyond theism and atheism: Heidegger's significance
for religious thinking." Temple University. *Diss. Abs.*, Vol. 45/01-A, 1984,
210.

Guagliardo, Vincent Anthony. "The future of an origin: Being and God in the
philosophy of Martin Heidegger." Graduate Theological Union. *Diss.
Abs.*, Vol. 42/06-A, 1981, 2714.

Mason, David R. "A study of time in the philosophies of Alfred North
Whitehead and Martin Heidegger with implications for a doctrine of
providence. . ." University of Chicago. *Diss. Abs.*, Vol. X, 1973, 1973.

McBride, Christopher E. "The later Heidegger: On the theistic implications of
his thought. . ." University of St. Michael's College (Canada). *Diss. Abs.*,
Vol. X, 1979.

McGrath, Michael J. "Heidegger and theology: A resolution to the problem."
Claremont Graduate School. *Diss. Abs.*, Vol. 45/04-A, 1984, 1143.

Oshima, Sueo. "Theology and history in Karl Barth: A study of the theology of
Karl Barth in reference to the philosophy of Martin Heidegger." University
of Chicago. *Diss. Abs.*, Vol. X, 1970, 1970.

Patricca, Nicholas A. "God and the questioning of being: An analytical
comparison of the thinking of Martin Heidegger and Paul Tillich. . ."
University of Chicago. *Diss. Abs.*, Vol. X1973, 1972.

Scott, Charles Edward. "Martin Heidegger's concept of man's presence to
himself: toward a reconsideration of religious awareness." Yale University.
Diss. Abs., Vol. 26/04, 1965, 2269.

Staten, John Cummings. "Toward an understanding of the reality God': Man as
conscience' in recent theological thought—a constructive study based on

the work of Gerhard Ebeling and Martin Heidegger." University of Chicago. *Diss. Abs.*, Vol. X1976, 1975.

Thomas, J. Mark. "Toward a theonomous technology: An inquiry into the social ethics of technology in Parsons, Marcuse and Heidegger based on Paul Tillich's theology of culture." University of Chicago. *Diss. Abs.*, Vol. 10, 1983.

REVERENCE

Fiand, Barbara. "The phenomenon of reverence with special reference to Heidegger's foundational thought." De Paul University, 1980. *Diss. Abs.*, Vol. 42/06-A, 2713.

SCHIZOPHRENIA

Borgna, Eugenio. "Schizophrenia as existential metamorphosis." *Rivista di Psichiatria*, Vol. 8, 1973, 135-154.

SCIENCE AND TECHNOLOGY

Alderman, Harold G. "Heidegger's critique of science." *The Personalist*, Vol. 50, 1969, 549-558.

Alvim, Fausto. "Notes on the relationship between subject and object in contemporary science." *Alter Jornal de Estudos Psicodinamicos*, Vol. 3, 1973, 7-15.

Borgmann, Albert and Mitcham, Carl. "The question of Heidegger and technology: A critical review of the literature." *Philosophy Today*, 1987, Vol. 31, pp. 99-194.

Clifford, Craig Edward. "On the essence and danger of technology: Plato on sophistic technique and Heidegger on modern technology." State University of New York at Buffalo. *Diss. Abs.*, Vol. 42/01-A, 1981, 246.

Emad, Parvis. "Technology as presence: Heidegger's view." *Listening*, Vol. 16, 1981, 133-144.

Hoeller, Keith. "Phenomenology, psychology, and science." *Review of Existential Psychology & Psychiatry*, Vol. XVI, 1978-79, 147-75. Also in Hoeller (Ed.), *Heidegger and Psychology*.

Hoeller, Keith. "Phenomenology, Psychology, and Science II." *Review of Existential Psychology & Psychiatry*, Vol. 18, 1982-83, 143-154. Also in Hoeller (Ed.) *Merleau-Ponty and Psychology*.

Hudson, Richard. "Heidegger at Marburg: The project of a scientific philosophy at the time of Sein und Zeit'." University of Ottawa (Canada). *Diss. Abs.*, Vol. X, 1984.

Kockelmans, Joseph J. "Heidegger on the essential difference and necessary relationship between philosophy and science," in *Phenomenology and the natural sciences*, ed. by J.J. Kockelmans and T. Kisiel. Evanston, Ill.: Northwestern University Press, 1970, 147-166.

Kolb, David A. "Heidegger on the limits of science." *J. Brit. Soc. Phenomenol.*, Vol. 14, 1983, 50-64.

Leuer, Drew. "Modes of totalization: Heidegger on modern technology and science." *Philosophy Today*, Vol. 29, 1985, 245-256.

Lovitt, William. "Techne and technology: Heidegger's perspective on what is happening today." *Philosophy Today*, Vol. 24, 1980, 62-72.

Richardson, William J. "Heidegger's critique of science." *The New Scholasticism*, Vol. 42, 1968, 511-536.

Rouse, Joseph T. "Heidegger's later philosophy of science." *Southern Journal of Philosophy*, Vol. 23, 1985, 75-92.

Rouse, Joseph T. "Kuhn, Heidegger, and scientific realism" *Man and World*, Vol. 14, 1981, 269-290.

Rubin, Charles Thomas. "Martin Heidegger's question concerning technology." Boston College, 1982. *Diss. Abs.*, Vol. 43/11-A, 3697.

Seigfried, Hans. "Heidegger's longest day: "Being and Time" and the sciences." *Philosophy Today*, Vol. 22, 1978, 319-331.

SELF

Bailiff, John Delaware. "Coming to be: An interpretation of the self in the thought of Martin Heidegger." Pennsylvania State University. *Diss. Abs.*, Vol. 27/09-A, 1966, 3075.

Ehman, Robert R. "Temporal self-identity." *The Southern Journal of Philosophy*, Vol. 12, 1974, 331-341.

Kunze, Robert W. "The origin of the self: A presentation of the philosophy of Levinas from the standpoint of his criticism of Heidegger." Pennsylvania State University. *Diss. Abs.*, Vol. 35/11-A, 1974, 7350.

Schrag, Calvin Orville. "The problem of existence: Kierkegaard's descriptive analysis of the self and Heidegger's phenomenological ontology of Dasein'." Harvard University, 1957. *Diss. Abs.*, Vol. X, 1957.

Toussaint, Bernard J. "The interpretation of the self' in the early Heidegger." De Paul University. *Diss. Abs.*, Vol. 33/01-A, 1971, 363.

Vogt, A. *Das Problem des Selbstseins bei Heidegger und Kierkegaard.* Emsdetten, 1936.

Zimmerman, Michael E. "The concept of self in Martin Heidegger's Being and Time'." Tulane University. *Diss. Abs.*, Vol. 35/04-A, 1974, 2344.

Zimmerman, Michael E. *Eclipse of the Self: The Development of Heidegger's Concept of Authenticity.* Ohio University Press, 1987.

Zimmerman, Michael E. "The unity of sameness of the self as depicted in *Being and Time.*" *Journal of the British Society for Phenomenology*, Vol. 6, 1975, 157-167.

Zimmerman, Michael E. "Heidegger's new concept of authentic selfhood." *Research in Phenomenology*, Vol. 5, 1975, 109-127.

SOCIAL PSYCHOLOGY

Malhotra, Valerie Ann. "A comparision of Mead's self' and Heidegger's Dasein': Toward a regrounding of social psychology." *Human Studies*, 1987, Vol. 10, 357-382.

SOCIAL WORLD

Weber, Renee Oppenheimer. "Individual and social being in Heidegger's 'Being and Time'." Columbia University. *Diss. Abs.*, Vol. 28/02-A, 1966, 735.

Theunissen, Michael. *The Other: Studies in the Social Ontology of Husserl, Heidegger, Sartre & Buber.* Trans. from the German. MIT Press, 1986.

SOUL

Pageler, John Charles. "The soul and time: First principles of modern metaphysical speculation as represented in the thought of Margin Heidegger." Claremont Graduate School. *Diss. Abs.*, Vol. 29/01-A, 1967, 292.

SPACIALITY

Borgna, Eugenio. "The metamorphosis of spaciality among schizophrenics." *Rivista di Psichiatria*, Vol. 9, 1974, 494-520.

SPEAKING

Johnson, Patricia Altenbernd. "A hermeneutic analysis of human speaking: An examination and extension of the work on language of Martin Heidegger, Paul Ricoeur, and Hans-Georg Gadamer." University of Toronto (Canada). *Diss. Abs.*, Vol. 40/12-A, 1979, 6310.

SPIRITUALITY

Zimmerman, Michael. "Heidegger and Heraclitus on spiritual practice." *Philosophy Today*, Vol. 27, 1983, 87-103.

HEIDEGGER BIBLIOGRAPHY

SUICIDE

Hoeller, Keith. "Phenomenological Foundations for the Study of Suicide." *Omega: The journal of death and dying*, Vol. 4, 1973, 195-208.

TECHNIQUE, TECHNOLOGY

Ahlers, R. "Is technology repressive?" *Tijdschrift voor Filosofie*, Vol. 32, 1970, 651-700.

Alderman, Harold. "Heidegger: Technology as phenomenon." *The Personalist*, Vol. 51, 1970, 535-545.

Betros, Charles L. "Heidegger's critique of technology." Fordham University. *Diss. Abs.*, Vol. 47/04-A, 1986, 1353.

Loscerbo, J. *Being in Technology: A Study of the Philosophy of Martin Heidegger*. Martinus Nijhoff, Netherlands. Kluwer Academic Publishers, 1981, 200 pp.

Moser, S. "Toward a metaphysics of technology." *Philosophy Today*, Vol. 15, 1971, 129-156.

THINKING

Bartky, S. L. "Originative thinking in the later philosophy of Heidegger." *Philosophy and Phenomenological Research*, Vol. 30, 1970, 368-381.

Fay, Thomas A. "Heidegger: Thinking as *noein*." *The Modern Schoolman*, Vol. 51, 1973-1974, 17-28.

Nicholson, Graeme. "Heidegger on thinking." *Journal of the History of Philosophy*, Vol. 13, 1975, 491-503.

TIME

Blaisdell, Chuck. "Heidegger's structure of time and temporality. A new repudiation of the classical conception." *Dialogue* (PST), Vol. 18, 1976, 44-53.

Caputo, John D. "Time and being in Heidegger." *The Modern Schoolman*, Vol. 50, 1972-1973, 325-349.

Faulconer, James E. and Williams, Richard N. "More on temporality in human action." *American Psychologist*, Vol. 42, 1987, 197-199.

Faulconer, James E. and Williams, Richard N. "Temporality in human action: An alternative to positivism and historicism." *American Psychologist*, Vol. 40, 1985, 1179-1188.

Heine, Steven. "Existential and ontological dimensions of time in Heidegger and Dogen." Temple University. *Diss. Abs.*, Vol. 41/05-A, 1980, 2166.

Keyes, C. D. "Time, ambiguity, miracle: A theological investigation based, in part, on the methods of M. Heidegger's Being and Time'." University of Trinity College (Canada), 1967. *Diss. Abs.*, Vol. C1977.

Krell, David F. *Intimations of Mortality: Time, Truth, & Finitude in Heidegger's Thinking of Being.* Pennsylvania State University Press, 1986.

Millikan, James Dean. "Heidegger, time, and self-transcendence. ". . Yale University. *Diss. Abs.*, Vol. 27/08-A, 1966, 2561.

Schwartz, Adria E. "Being-in-time: A phenomenological exploration of the existential past." *Review of Existential Psychology and Psychiatry*, Vol. 15, 1977, 150-162.

Sheehan, Thomas J. "Heidegger: From beingness to the time-being." *Listening*, Vol. 8, 1973, 17-31.

White, Carol Jean. "Time and temporality in the existential thought of Kierkegaard and Heidegger." University of California, Berkeley. *Diss. Abs.*, Vol. 38/02-A, 1976, 853.

Wild, John. "The new empiricism and human time." *Review of Metaphysics*, Vol. 7, 1953-1954, 537-557.

TOOL

Schmitt, Richard. "Heidegger's analysis of tool'." *The Monist*, Vol. 49, 1965, 70-86.

TRANSCENDENCE

Langan, Thomas D. "Transcendence in the philosophy of Heidegger." *The New Scholasticsm*, Vol. 32, 1958, 45-60.

TRANSFERENCE

Phillips, James. "Transference and encounter: The therapeutic relationship in psychoanalytic and existential psychotherapy." *Review of Existential Psychology & Psychiatry*, Vol. XVII, 1980-81, 135-152.

TRUTH

Argyros, Alexander. "The question of truth in Sartre, Heidegger, and Derrida." Cornell University. *Diss. Abs.*, Vol. 38/12-A, 1977, 7362.

Cohn, P. H. "Are philosophers difficult? Apropos of Heidegger's theory of truth." *Texas Quarterly*, Vol. 17, 1974, 73-95.

Farber, Marvin. "Heidegger on the essence of truth." *Philosophy and Phenomenological Research*, Vol. 18, 1957-1958, 523-532.

Meny, James Frederick. "On finitude and truth: The livability of the philosophy of Martin Heidegger." University of Toronto (Canada). *Diss. Abs.*, Vol. 38/09-A, 1975, 5528.

Turner, Jeffrey Scott. "The concepts of truth in science and morality with occasional reference to Heidegger and Kierkegaard (Kuhn, Nietzsche, emotivism)." Yale University. *Diss Abs.*, Vol. 49/02-A, 1987, 0271.

UNCONSCIOUS

Bartels, Martin. See FREUD.

Richardson, William J. "The place of the unconscious in Heidegger." *Review of Existential Psychology and Psychiatry*, Vol. 5, 1965, 265-290.

VALUES

Emad, Parvis. *Heidegger & the Phenomenology of Values*. Forward by Biemel, Walter. Torey Press, 1981, 179pp.

Haight, David F. "The ground of knowledge and value or, the philosopher." *ReVISION*, Vol. 4, 1981, 55-67.

VIOLENCE

Huvos, Christopher. "Violence & human existence: The existential theories of Medard Boss." *Review of Existential Psychology & Psychiatry*, Vol. XIX, 1984-85, 267-282.

VISION

Levin, David Michael. "The opening of vision: seeing through the veil of tears." *Review of Existential Psychology & Psychiatry*, Vol. 16, 1978-79, 113-146.

WILL

Birmingham, Peg Elizabeth. "*Entschlossenheit*: Martin Heidegger and the question of will." Duquesne University. *Diss. Abs.*, Vol. 47/05-A, 1986, 1747.

Boelen, Bernard J. "Heidegger's approach to will, decision and responsibility." *Review of Existential Psychology and Psychiatry*, Vol. 1, 1961, 197-204.

Van Kaam, Adrian. "Clinical implications of Heidegger's concepts of will, decision and responsibility." *Review of Existential Psychology and Psychiatry*, Vol. 1, 1961, 205-216.

WORLD

Sabatino, Charles Joseph. "World as a context of meaning: Heidegger's gift. . ." University of Chicago, 1974. *Diss. Abs.*, Vol. X, 1974.

Sallis, John Cleveland. "The concept of world: A study in the phenomenological ontology of Martin Heidegger." Tulane University. *Diss. Abs.*, Vol. 25/07, 1964, 4193.

Sobel, Jerry Edward. "Heidegger's conception of the world." Harvard University, 1974. *Diss. Abs.*, Vol. X, 1974.

V. BIBLIOGRAPHIES

Hoeller, Keith. "Heidegger Bibliography of English Translations." In Shahan, Robert and Mohanty, J.N. (Eds.). *Thinking About Being: Aspects of Heidegger's Thought*. Norman: University of Oklahoma Press, 1984, pp. 221-230.

Sass, Hans-Martin. *Martin Heidegger: Bibliography and Glossary*. Bowling Green: Philosophy Documentation Center, 1982, 513 pp.

CONTRIBUTORS

JEFFNER ALLEN is Associate Professor of Philosophy, State University of New York (Binghamton). She is the author of numerous articles in phenomenological philosophy and psychology, including "A Husserlian Phenomenology of the Child," *Journal of Phenomenological Psychology,* "Husserl Bibliography of English Translations," *The Monist,* and "The Role of Imagination in Phenomenological Psychology," *Review of Existential Psychology & Psychiatry.* She is the Co-Editor (with Iris Young) of *The Thinking Muse: Feminist Philosophy and Continental Thought* (forthcoming).

MEDARD BOSS is Director of the Daseinsanalysis Institute for Psychotherapy and Psychosomatics in Zürich and Professor of Psychotherapy at the University of Zürich. He has worked closely with Martin Heidegger in applying Heidegger's philosophy to his own theory and practice of Daseinsanalysis. He is the author of the *Meaning and Content of Sexual Perversions* (Grune and Stratton), *Psychoanalysis and Daseinsanalysis* (Basic Books), and *I Dreamt Last Night* (Halsted). His most recent book is *Existential Foundations of Medicine and Psychology* (Aronson).

EUGENE GENDLIN is Professor of Psychology, University of Chicago. He is the former Editor of *Psychotherapy: Theory, Research, and Practice.* In 1970 he was chosen the Distinguished Professional Psychologist of the Year by the American Psychological Association. He is the author of numerous articles on psychotherapy, including "Experiential Psychotherapy," in *Current Psychotherapies,* ed. R. Corsini (Peacock), and "A Theory of Personality Change," in *Creative Developments in Psychotherapy,* ed. A. Mahrer (Case Western). He is also the author of *Experiencing and the Creation of Meaning* (Free Press). His most recent book is *Let Your Body Interpret Your Dreams* (Chiron).

KEITH HOELLER is the Editor of the *Review of Existential Psychology & Psychiatry* and Lecturer, Department of Medical History and Ethics, University of Washington. He is the author of "Phenomenological Foundations for the Study of Suicide," *Omega: The Journal of Death and Dying,* "Is Heidegger Really a Poet?" *Philosophical Studies,* and "Attention: Traditional Vs. Phenomenological Approaches," *Review of Existential Psychology & Psychiatry.* He has recently completed *Heidegger and Poetry* (forthcoming).

JOSEPH J. KOCKELMANS is Professor of Philosophy, Pennsylvania State University. He is the Co-Editor of *Man and World* and the author and editor of many books on recent Continental philosophy, including *Phenomenology* (Anchor), *Edmund Husserl's Phenomenological Psychology* (Duquesne University Press), and *Martin Heidegger (Duquesne University Press).* His most recent book is *On the Truth of Being* (Indiana University Press).

FRANÇOIS H. LAPOINTE is Professor of Psychology and Humanities at Tuskegee Institute. He is the author of *Sartre and His Critics, Gabriel Marcel and His Critics, Merleau-Ponty and His Critics,* as well as over 70 essays published in the *American Psychologist, Journal of Phenomenological Psychology, Man and World, Philosophy Today, Journal of the History of the Behavioral Sciences, Modern Schoolman, Studi Internazionali di Filosofia, Dialogos, Review of Existential Psychology & Psychiatry,* and the *Journal of the British Society for Phenomenology.*

DAVID MICHAEL LEVIN is Professor of Philosophy, Northwestern University. He is the author of *Reason and Evidence in Husserl's Phenomenology* (Northwestern University Press), as well as numerous essays, including "The Embodiment of Compassion: How We Are Visibly Moved," *Soundings,* and "Self-Knowledge and the Talking Cure," *Review of Existential Psychology & Psychiatry.* His most recent book is *The Opening of Vision* (Routledge).

WILLIAM J. RICHARDSON is Professor of Philosophy, Boston College, and Psychoanalyst with the Austen Riggs Center, Stockbridge, MA. He is the author of *Heidegger: Through Phenomenology to Thought* (Nijhoff), as well as several articles on Heidegger, including "Heidegger's Critique of Science," *New Scholasticism,* and "Heidegger and the Unconscious," *Review of Existential Psychology & Psychiatry.* His most recent work, with John P. Muller, is *Lacan and Language* (International Universities Press).

CHARLES E. SCOTT is Professor of Philosophy, Vanderbilt University. He is Co-Editor, with Edward G. Ballard, of *Martin Heidegger in Europe and America,* (Nijhoff), and editor of a special Medard Boss issue of *Soundings.* He is also the author of several articles on Heidegger, including "Heidegger and Consciousness," *Southern Journal of Philosophy,* and "Heidegger, Madness, and Well-Being," *Southwestern Journal of Philosophy.* His most recent book is *The Language of Difference* (Humanities).